Ex Líbrís
GIFT

CREDIT DEPARTMENT MANAGEMENT

Margaret A. Hoffman
Gerald C. Fischer

Robert Morris Associates

The National Association of Bank Loan and Credit Officers
1616 Philadelphia National Bank Building
Philadelphia, Pennsylvania 19107

Library of Congress Catalog Card Number: 80-65026

International Standard Book Number: 0-936742-00-3

Library of Congress Cataloging in Publication Data

Hoffman, Margaret A.
Credit department management.

Bibliography: p.
Includes index.
1. Bank loans. 2. Credit management. I. Fischer, Gerald C., joint author. II. Title.
HG1641.H56 332.1'753'068 80-65026

Contents

List of Exhibits

Introduction

Effective performance of the commercial credit department function is vital to every bank whether it is one of the nation's largest with a worldwide clientele or a small institution with customers almost exclusively from its local community. The organization of the credit function in one bank may not resemble that in another, however, for banks differ not only in size but in structure—branch, unit, holding company affiliate—in customer and loan composition, and in numerous other characteristics. As a result, the same function that is assigned as one of many duties to a single person in one bank may be performed by a full department in another.

But while the organization may differ, the basic principles related to the credit function are essentially the same for all banks. Therefore, throughout this book much of the discussion is devoted to general principles applicable to even the smallest bank. And where the emphasis is on implementation, the text considers the problems faced by banks with no credit departments as well as by those with well-established departments.

In this book, "credit functions" is used to describe those duties frequently performed by a bank's commercial credit department. Those functions are identified as credit files, statement spreading, credit analysis, loan quality control, commercial credit information exchange, and training.

Objectives

The primary objective of this book is to provide material which can be used by small- and medium-size banks in strengthening their performance of the commercial credit function. For banks that do not have a formal credit department and particularly for those considering the formation of one, the book offers several types of helpful information. It includes an analysis of the essential elements of the credit function, a discussion of key operational and training areas, and some thoughts on types of functional or departmental organization which can be used to carry out the required tasks.

In addition, the book should serve as a ready reference tool for banks of any size, including those with sizable credit departments. In a bank with an existing credit department, the utility of the book could stem from its value as an aid in analyzing the logic and completeness of the existing organization and in planning future expansion in this area. And in all banks, with the possible exception of the industry giants, it can serve as a source of ideas and benchmarks for bankers in their efforts to achieve optimum performance of the credit function in their banks. Every bank has its own unique characteristics and no one can pretend to have discovered *the* best form of organization for all banks. Nevertheless, by having knowledge of these yardsticks and by having access to materials drawn from top experts in the credit field, the task of achieving this optimum performance should be less difficult.

Finally, since the basic principles underlying the performance of the credit function are essentially the same regardless of the size of a bank, much of this book may be used in bank training programs. The fundamentals discussed in the text should be excellent background for the beginner who is trying to secure a general understanding of the activities in this vital area as well as a source of practical information for the more experienced person. Thus, this book can provide the basic principles and perspective so essential to the trainee. These important guidelines are easily lost in the highly complex operations of the large organization and too often omitted even in the training activities of relatively small institutions.

Approach

The book is aimed at the credit professional. It is not a theoretical text, not a general managerial overview of the credit function. For lack of a better term, it might best be described as a "how to" book for the credit department organizer or manager—a source of information directly applicable to the job situation. The reader will have to interpret the statements made in light of the prevailing conditions in his or her bank. Given this caveat, the authors have prepared the text with the goal of achieving maximum direct on-the-job application in every section of the book. While the emphasis throughout the book is on basic principles, these principles are related to specific functions, tools, and forms of organization; they are not simply presented in the text as broad generalizations.

Although this is a how to book, it does not pretend to be a skills manual for those performing the various duties in the credit area. Consider, for example, the topic "spreading financial statements." The book describes the most basic considerations regarding the goals of this activity, who performs it, its special characteristics, and its potential problems. The text reviews such things as fundamental operations techniques to ensure prompt receipt of current data, and it supplies examples of spread sheets. But it does not attempt to teach statement spreading techniques. Instead, the book discusses in detail the various elements of the credit function without giving instruction in the technical skills needed to perform them.

The topics in the book are standard ones for those in the credit area. Nevertheless, since the credit functions are performed in rather different ways, numerous decisions had to be made regarding when a particular question would be addressed, or, for that matter, if it would be considered at all. For example, automation is given limited coverage and the effect of branch banking receives only minor attention.

In the case of automation, addressing the possible impact that its extensive use might have on the organization and operation of a credit department proved impractical because the differences among banks are so great. And in the case of branch banking, we found the ultimate impact that structure had on the credit function was determined by bank size, proximity of other offices to the credit department, and the sophistication of the available communication facilities, among other things. These variables made it impractical to generalize about the impact bank structure would be likely to have on the credit department.

Summary of the Chapters

Chapter 1 of the book, "Management, Organization, and Staffing," provides the framework for developing or improving a commercial credit department. This chapter emphasizes the importance of establishing realistic objectives that reflect the goals of the bank and also identifies those functions that could be performed within a credit department.

The balance of the book is divided into six chapters that discuss various credit department functions in detail. All chapters provide many illustrative exhibits that with some modification could be adapted for use in a particular bank. References to names of companies and individuals and their business operations that appear in certain exhibits are fictional. Any resemblance to the names or operations of real companies or individuals is unintentional and purely coincidental.

Chapter 2 is concerned with credit files, from the arrangement of a single credit folder to the bulk storage of documents on microfilm. The control of credit files, including storage and retrieval, is also explored.

Chapter 3 describes the statement spreading function, both manual and computerized. In this chapter, practical suggestions are made for organizing and managing the function so that financial statements are processed in a thorough and timely fashion by trained personnel.

Chapter 4 provides an overview of the credit analysis function and its place in the banking organization. It discusses many aspects of credit analysis including its purposes, organization of the function, follow-up and control systems, staffing, and sources of information for use in analytical work.

Chapter 5 presents the many loan quality control functions, including loan review, that could be performed by credit department staff. Key aspects of loan quality control, such as documentation and collateral control and loan profitability analysis, are discussed. The exhibits include sample loan rating systems and sample formats for use in loan quality control.

Chapter 6 explores the exchange of commercial credit information. It stresses the importance of developing a professional staff and establishing internal policies and procedures for conducting this important function.

Chapter 7 describes the role the credit department can play in training lending and credit personnel. A systematic approach to developing a training program is presented, and suggestions for gathering and selecting training resources are provided. Exhibits include a hypothetical curriculum and evaluation forms.

Bibliography

A lengthy bibliography is included, and the entries are listed by category for ease of reference. Nevertheless, because of the vast number of outstanding publications available in the commercial banking field, no doubt some resources have been inadvertently overlooked. While Robert Morris Associates (RMA) does not endorse or vouch for the quality of the texts and articles listed, they should provide a starting point for further research and additional readings.

Contributors

Many people contributed their time and expertise in the development of this book. The project originated with the Southeastern Chapter of RMA, and much of the early work on the book was done by its Credit Department Organization and Operations Committee. During this important phase of the project, the committee was led by Wilford R. Pruett, now with the Federal National Bank and Trust Company, Shawnee, Okla. Others who contributed in this developmental phase of the project include:

Jack R. Crigger, American National Bank & Trust Co., Chattanooga
James A. Formby, National City Bank of Rome, Ga.
James E. Gallagher, Philadelphia National Bank
Preston T. Holmes, United Virginia Bankshares, Inc., Richmond
W. Thomas Maloan, now with Bankers' Educational Services, Knoxville
John C. Moreau, Rapides Bank and Trust Co., Alexandria, La.
Edward M. Penick, Jr., Twin City Bank, North Little Rock, Ark.
Alford C. Sinclair, Atlantic National Bank, Jacksonville, Fla.

As the project progressed, valuable assistance was provided by many well-known bankers. Individuals who contributed significantly to the contents of the book and helped revise the text include:

Glenn R. Heinemeyer, Chase Manhattan Bank, New York City
John T. Henderson, First National Bank of Boston
Joan P. Hofmann, Crocker National Bank, San Francisco
Ronald L. Kirkpatrick, Peoples Trust Bank, Fort Wayne
Jay M. McDonald, Citizens & Southern, Atlanta
T. Lincoln Morison, Jr., First National Bank of Boston
Edgar M. Morsman, Jr., United States National Bank, Omaha
Jerome L. Roderick, Robert Morris Associates, Philadelphia
S. George Scarfo, American Express Co., Phoenix (formerly with New England Merchants National Bank, Boston)
David T. Snowden, retired (formerly with Mellon Bank, Pittsburgh)

The authors were assisted by many other bankers who reviewed the text and provided comments and information essential to the manuscript. While the names of all these contributors are too numerous to list, special thanks are extended to:

Ray Castle, First National Bank, Perryton, Tex.
Rodney P. Cornwall, Seattle-First National Bank
Joseph L. Kish, Jr., Fenvessey Associates, New York City
Robert I. McCulley, Security Pacific National Bank, Los Angeles
Michael A. Micek, United States National Bank, Omaha
James L. Nicholson, Jr., Central Carolina Bank, Durham, N.C.

Larry J. Orman, First National Bank, Perryton, Tex.
Norman I. Pickles, consultant (formerly with The Northern Trust Company, Chicago)
Curtis S. Reis, Bankers Trust Company, New York City
John Sweeney, First Pennsylvania Bank, N.A., Philadelphia
Susan S. Wilkinson, Bendix Corp., Dayton (formerly with Winters National Bank and Trust Co., Dayton)
Judith A. Wilson, First Pennsylvania Bank, N.A., Philadelphia

The authors also wish to thank the RMA Credit Division Council for its support and contributions during the preparation of this book. Naturally, however, while many people have made significant contributions to this book, the responsibility for any shortcomings must rest with the undersigned.

Margaret A. Hoffman
Robert Morris Associates

Gerald C. Fischer
Temple University

1

Management, Organization, and Staffing

There are over 14,500 commercial banks in this country, and each is to some degree unique. Each has its own market objectives, problems, assets, liabilities, personnel, customers, and a host of other factors which set it apart from even its closest competitor. Given this variation among banks, each credit department is also unique and reflects the bank's structural characteristics and the functions and personnel assigned to, or assumed by, the department. Therefore, it is difficult to generalize about credit department management, organization, and staffing because there appear to be almost as many differences as similarities among credit departments.

One way to approach the structure and organization of a credit department is to think in terms of zero-based budgeting. In many ways, it is much easier to start something from ground zero than it is to take something already up and running and try to improve it. Therefore, this chapter approaches the subject from the viewpoint of the individual faced with the challenge of setting up a new credit department. It doesn't really matter if, in reality, a credit department already is established. The creative manager, instead of asking where to begin, will use the same information to evaluate where the department is now and where it should be.

Three Basic Considerations

This chapter does not attempt to provide a standardized organization for a credit department, which through adding or deleting certain modules could be applied to any bank. Nor is it designed to replace individual managerial ability, initiative, judgment, or imagination. It does offer, however, a sound approach to managing, organizing, and staffing the credit department to perform specific functions and to accomplish defined objectives. This chapter looks at these goals and objectives, and it develops a basic analytical framework for the manager to help ensure the goals and objectives are consciously selected, defined, and accomplished.

Goals and Objectives of the Bank

First, the manager must consider both long-term and short-term objectives of the bank. While these goals may not always be well articulated, the credit department manager should try to recognize and understand them. These goals might include a desire to increase total footings or simply to expand total deposits or total loans outstanding. Of course, with today's emphasis on the bottom line, improved profitability would be very important on any list. Related to profitability would be questions of what constitutes an acceptable risk or risk level or what the pricing policy should be.

Thus, as these few illustrations suggest, there are many different, sometimes unwritten, aspects of a bank's goals. The credit department manager should recognize and understand them if the credit department is to make its maximum contribution to the success of the bank and if it in turn is to receive maximum support from management.

The Loan Policy

Given the objectives of the bank, the credit department manager and staff should become familiar with the bank's loan policy. This policy should be in writing and should present the bank's lending philosophy, standards, and special requirements. Any facet of the loan policy that is directly related to the credit department should be noted by the manager. In fact, any significant aspect of the loan policy should be pointed out to the staff so the department may maximize its contribution to the bank. The loan policy should also provide a good picture of the operating structure and responsibilities of the lending function and enable the manager to understand better the existing loan approval process.

Bank Personnel

In addition to considering the goals of the bank and its loan policy, the credit department manager should try to assess objectively the quality of existing bank personnel. Are most personnel experienced in banking? Will extensive training be required to improve the skills of credit department and other staff? Should new specialists be recruited to upgrade the department's functions rapidly? In addition, the manager must consider the quantity of existing personnel. Is the bank generally understaffed, or could some individuals assume additional responsibilities? What are the possibilities of hiring additional personnel?

These are basic considerations to keep in mind even before thought is given to the structure of the credit department.

Organizational Structure

The next step is to decide where the credit department will fit into the organizational structure of the bank, to whom it will report, and who will appraise the department's performance and evaluate the individual managing it. There are many possibilities, and all of them must be considered, keeping in mind the bank's size and the specific functions to be performed by the credit department.

A review of the organizational structure of a number of banks reveals no set pattern in who evaluates the credit department and to whom that department reports. For example, the credit department might report to the senior loan officer, the president, or even the board of directors.

While there are no established rules in this regard, one point of view holds that it is crucial for the person who will evaluate the overall performance of the department and its manager to be the same individual to whom the department ultimately reports. For most banks, small- and even large-size ones, that person would be the senior loan officer, the same individual who is responsible for the total loan operations of the bank. Exhibit 1.1 illustrates the organizational structure of a bank in which the credit department reports to the senior loan officer. While it can be argued that the credit department should report to the board or to the president, it is difficult to envision either entity performing the complementary role of evaluator, except in very small banks.

In considering the question of reporting, there is one organizational structure which does not seem advisable. It is not a good idea for the credit department to report to a line commercial loan officer. Both the credit department and the commercial loan division should be on the same organizational level, usually reporting to the senior loan officer. Certainly, considering employee morale and overall coordination with bank policy, this method of reporting is more satisfactory.

Exhibit 1.1 — Organizational Structure

This organizational chart shows one way of positioning the credit department within the overall bank structure. Here the credit department reports to the senior loan officer as do the commercial lending, retail lending, and mortgage lending divisions. This basic chart is applicable regardless of the size of the bank or the credit department.

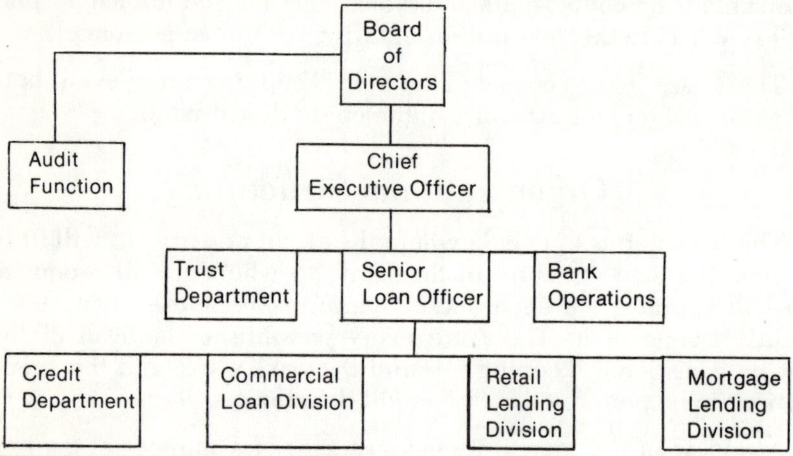

Staff and Line Functions

The credit department is a staff function. As such, individuals in the department will be expected to do work for and be responsible to many different line personnel and functions. In other words, the credit department may be doing work for the commercial loan department, the correspondent banking department, the installment loan department, or any number of areas of the bank. Thus, the credit department is placed in a position of potential conflict because someone is setting goals for and is evaluating a staff department that is performing work for line departments.

The point here is that even under the most logical and commonly used organizational arrangements, conflict may arise between staff and line functions. The positive approach to alleviating the problem is to ensure that the objectives of the credit department are well thought out, clearly defined, and communicated to all the line users of credit department services. All the people who are requesting services from the credit department should understand its functions, priorities, and goals. Thus, potential conflict will be markedly reduced. More will be said about reducing possible friction later in this chapter. For now, it is sufficient to establish the importance of communicating objectives to bank management, credit department staff, and line personnel.

Once these goals are established and accepted by senior management and communicated to the credit department staff and lending personnel, the credit manager should formally and periodically review these goals. There is no reason why this review should not be annual, perhaps roughly coincident with the bank's budgeting process. This review should consider the current objectives of the department to see if they are being achieved, if they remain valid, and if they are being communicated to and understood by the line users. The review process is critical in working with a nonprofit center as is almost universally the case with credit departments. These centers must normally be justified in qualitative terms with little or no revenue data to compare with costs.

Establishing Objectives—An Overview

The initial determination of what the credit department ought to accomplish should be a joint function of senior management, the senior loan officer, and the credit department manager. These parties should be able to present, clarify, and coordinate the objectives of the bank, of the loan function, and of the credit department. Given this information, the credit department manager will then have to decide how the department staff is to be organized.

At this point, the manager should set forth the objectives of the credit department. The following is a checklist of functions that a credit department could perform and that bank management might want to consider:

1. Analyzing new loan requests
2. Performing loan review
3. Handling commercial credit inquiries and investigations
4. Training
5. Monitoring substandard loans
6. Reporting current activity
7. Managing credit files
8. Monitoring compliance with laws and regulations
9. Conducting research

Some credit departments may perform only a few of these tasks; others will offer a much broader range of services. The text which follows describes each of the nine functions. They are not presented in any special order, and many are discussed in greater detail and from different viewpoints in subsequent chapters.

New Loan Requests

One question that should be addressed is how much the credit department should assist the loan officer in approving or working up new loan requests. In this case, the primary objective might be to identify poor credit risks before they are placed on the books by providing information and support services to the loan officer who is considering the credit. This is a proper function of a credit department, and the manager should seek to establish good communication between the analyst and the loan officer.

A close working relationship developed between lending and credit analysis personnel can minimize conflicts arising from misunderstanding of the facts or a misreading of the data. For example, frequently the analyst never has an opportunity to meet the customer, see the plant, or discuss financial data with the accountant responsible for their preparation. If communication is good and the loan officer and the analyst take time to discuss the credit fully, differences of opinion can be avoided.

While the above procedure has definite advantages, banks do differ. The credit department manager and senior management must decide, based on a given bank's operations and personnel, the degree to which an analyst should be involved in the review of new credits. In many cases, staff quality, available time, volume of loan requests, and training and development goals strongly influence this decision.

Some banks may determine that analysts should only analyze financial statements and other "hard data." And perhaps other personnel will be assigned to assist loan officers directly in making site visits and conducting research. No single system is best for all banks; therefore, it is important that all the alternatives be considered before a direction is chosen. If the manager is to establish a department that is responsible for full analysis of new credits, its role and objectives must be well defined, and its work must be credible and professional. This point and others are examined more carefully in Chapter 4 on credit analysis.

Loan Review

There is a question of whether loan review should be segregated from the credit department function. Those who believe loan review should be a separate function are, in effect, stating that loan review and evaluating a bank's loan portfolio should be totally independent of any credit processing function. The segregation of loan review may be the ideal arrangement, and in larger organizations bank management often can afford to separate loan review from the credit department. In smaller banks, however, it is often included as a credit department function.

From the standpoint of the credit department manager, separating the loan review function would mean the department could not perform one of its possible major roles. Also, without loan review, many unique training opportunities in the department would be eliminated. Therefore, the decision to divorce loan review from the credit department should be made only after careful evaluation of the pros and cons of such a move.

If it is decided to perform loan review in the credit department, the scope of that function must be clearly defined. Loan review can encompass some or all of the following: evaluating credit quality, checking compliance with the bank's loan policy, assessing the loan against profitability guidelines, verifying the existence and adequacy of collateral, reviewing documentation, verifying that loans comply with state and federal laws and regulations, and determining whether the loans comply with the terms and covenants in related loan agreements.

There are, of course, many other factors to be considered before establishing a loan review function, and greater attention is paid to the subject in Chapter 5. Nevertheless, these brief comments may be useful to those charged with the responsibility of determining whether or to what degree loan review functions should be assigned to the credit department.

If both loan review and the analytical support services already discussed are performed in the credit department, a possible conflict of interest could arise if the same analyst who performs loan reviews also works on credit proposals for the loan officer. Surely the potential problems in this circumstance are obvious, and proper management can help foster the necessary objectivity.

Commercial Credit Inquiries and Investigations

The handling of inquiries and investigations is an important function which is sometimes slighted in credit training and in the development of the credit department. This is surprising in a way, because most people who analyze loan losses often cite the lack of thorough credit checkings at the inception of the loan relationship as a major contributing factor. Chapter 6 examines this function in considerable detail.

Training and Development

The manager might consider establishing a training and development program for credit department personnel and for trainees and staff in other areas of the bank. The establishment and scope of this function will be directly related to the needs of the bank and its personnel. The training and development function is presented in Chapter 7.

Substandard Loans

Still another function that might be included under credit department objectives is establishing and maintaining a watch list or list of loans rated as substandard risks. If the department is grading loans as to risk, it might take the lower classification of the loans and call that the watch list. This list should be issued periodically, perhaps monthly or quarterly. It should report the steps which were taken to upgrade loan quality since bank management should be informed on a continuing basis of what is being done to improve that portion of the portfolio.

If a bank is large or has significant loan problems, it may very well have a separate workout function that handles both problem loan administration and reporting. Nevertheless, if loan quality is such that there are few problems, the credit department itself might be responsible for reporting on substandard or workout loans, regardless of who actually administers the loans. Issuing a watch list is a valuable service that a credit department may provide. However, the value of this function being performed by the credit department will vary depending on bank size, structure, mode of operation, extent of loan problems, and other factors.

Monitoring Current Activity

Another responsibility that might be included in the credit department is monitoring current activity, such as accounts receivable aging schedules. In other words, if the bank has agreed to advance to a borrower 80% of current receivables, someone must ensure that the bank is doing just that. The department might also maintain certain break-even points on various borrowers and monitor sales figures to determine if the break-even point is being reached. In addition, it might monitor balances maintained in checking accounts and perform any number of similar tasks.

The credit department might also consider publishing a monthly or quarterly document enumerating those items which are, in effect, past due. Similar to a past due note list, this report could include "past due" financial statements of principals and guarantors and inventory and receivables agings, among other things. Naturally, the need for such service by the credit department will vary depending on the size of the bank, its organization, and available electronic data processing capabilities. In many banks, some, or all, of these monitoring functions might logically be handled by other departments. The point is that someone should be monitoring excessive technical exceptions, and in many banks, the credit department is ideally suited to perform this task.

Credit Files

Yet another goal of the department could be maintaining and controlling credit files. This is not an easy task because these files should always present a true picture of the customer's relationship with the bank. This function is discussed at great length in Chapter 2.

Compliance with Laws and Regulations

A credit department function which has developed fairly recently is loan compliance. The Fair Credit Reporting Act, the Equal Credit Opportunity Act (Regulation B), the Truth in Lending Act (Regulation Z), and many other laws and regulations have placed additional requirements on the lending and credit functions. As a result, in many banks, the credit department manager also serves as the bank's loan compliance officer. If the manager assumes that role, he or she should stay informed of all new laws, regulations, amendments, and related opinion letters or interpretative materials affecting lending or credit.

Overseeing loan compliance is a staff role, and each loan department might wish to designate its own internal compliance specialists to periodically spot-check their department's compliance procedures. Their findings, in turn, would be passed on to the compliance officer.

If the credit department manager also serves as the compliance officer, he or she would be expected to conduct training sessions and would be responsible for explaining the proper use of any new forms and for clarifying new operating procedures. In many banks, it might be unrealistic to expect the credit department manager to have sufficient time to perform this function properly. Nevertheless, it is not unusual for this responsibility to be assigned to the credit department. For that reason, compliance functions are more fully discussed in Chapter 5.

Research

The credit department might also conduct research into local industry trends. If, for example, the bank has significant exposure in lending to the coal industry, the credit department could analyze that industry and evaluate how this exposure might affect the loan portfolio. Some banks may choose to establish a separate research department while others might place the research responsibilities in the credit area. But if no specific research function exists, the manager might begin by periodically looking at the largest industry concentrations in the portfolio and evaluating the health of these industries.

Creative Management

Nine different tasks have been listed for consideration by the credit department manager and senior management as possible credit department duties. Other potential credit department services will be identified in later chapters. The creative manager probably can identify numerous other objectives that would be valuable to a particular bank.

This is an area where a strong credit department manager can take the initiative and present ideas to top management. A good manager should not complacently wait for instructions but should be part of the management process.

One way to consider these objectives, in starting a new credit department or in periodically evaluating an existing one, is for executive management and the senior loan officer to discuss all realistic objectives with the credit department manager. The manager, in turn, should give priority to the objectives, determine what the credit department can do to implement them, and report to top management with a specific plan.

Before talking about how the department can be organized and staffed, the objectives have to be established. The nine possible objectives of a credit department noted here are far from exhaustive. However, we believe they include all the more common responsibilities, as well as a few others which merit consideration. Although we realize every bank is different, the tasks likely to be faced in any credit department are sufficiently similar to make the checklist a good place to begin one's evaluation.

Operational and Analytical Functions

In studying the organization of a credit department, it is logical to separate the department into two distinct areas: the operational portion and the analytical portion. The operational portion would include credit inquiries and investigations, maintenance of credit files, secretarial duties, and preparation of recurring reports. The analytical side would include loan review, analysis of new credits, training, research, statement spreading, and related activities. This separation of functions is presented graphically in Exhibit 1.2.

It is a basic principle of management that work should be accomplished at the lowest step on the organizational ladder where it is possible and logical to do so. If other staff is available, for example, an analyst should not be filing loan memoranda nor typing credit correspondence. If this is taking place, it suggests management procedures need some review.

In an organization of sufficient size, the credit department manager might consider strictly separating the operational and analytical functions, including separating them physically. In other words, those performing analytical functions should be in an environment which is conducive to analytical work. For this activity, people should have a quiet atmosphere and ready access to any needed computational equipment or reference tools. If operational and analytical functions are combined, which happens far too frequently, higher paid analytical personnel may be performing operational duties that should be handled by less technical personnel.

Exhibit 1.2 — Analytical and Operational Functions

This chart shows how a credit department might be organized to reflect the separation of analytical and operational functions. In a small credit department, one person, possibly the manager, might perform all the analytical functions while another individual would perform all the operational functions. In a moderate-size department, the analytical functions might be divided among several individuals, and the operational functions would become highly specialized. It is desirable, however, to physically separate the analytical and operational functions. The chart emphasizes the importance of organizing the department by function, rather than by specific jobs titles and numbers of people.

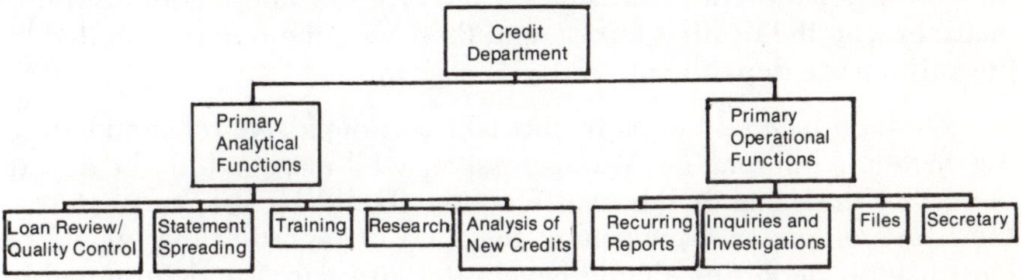

Recurring Reports

Preparing recurring reports, an operational function, merits special attention given its significance and because this area often does not receive the attention it deserves. If the credit department is to prepare such information, it is essential that all reports created on loan activity be periodically assessed. Credit departments, as well as other departments, often go on for years submitting time-honored compilations of data to management, the board, loan committees, and others without any critical evaluation of the need for the information provided. Many credit departments would despair if they knew of the cursory treatment given to much of the material they prepare.

The reporting process should be reviewed periodically. Careful thought should be given to timing and frequency of reports as well as to eliminating only marginally useful compilations of data. One way to eliminate unnecessary reports is for the credit department manager to distribute a questionnaire to each recipient of a recurring report. This survey could be conducted on an annual basis and might include such questions as:

- Does the recipient wish to continue receiving the report?
- Is the format useful in the performance of a specific function?
- Can the recipient provide any suggestions for improvement, additions, or deletions?

The manager should also discuss the reports with senior management to determine if all necessary statistics are provided in an appropriate manner. It is useful for the credit department manager to observe occasionally a meeting of any group for whom reports are prepared. In this way, he or she can see how this information is or is not used. This can lead to changes in the reports which make them more valuable or less time-consuming to prepare.

Whether the reporting function is a major responsibility of the credit department again depends on numerous factors, including the size of the bank and its operations. Ideally, part of this reporting can be computerized or compiled outside the credit department. In such cases, the credit department could suggest the types of information useful to management, the desired format, and then have the report compiled by the appropriate department.

Frequently, credit departments take a very passive role and merely put together information. An aggressive, well-managed credit department that understands the loan function should be able to suggest to the board or senior management the kind of reporting that would be most useful. Reporting should have a definite purpose, determined by the bank's goals and policies. Reports could cover such areas as loan concentrations, technical exceptions, risk ratings, loans not in compliance with policy, and substandard loans. When applicable, the reports should indicate the disposition of the loans in question. Trend analyses and, in some cases, liquidity analyses may also be prepared. In summary, reports should be distributed to the appropriate people and should be presented in the most useful format.

Staffing

The credit department manager will probably recognize the desirability of separating the analytical and operational functions and be aware of their individual objectives. However, the realities presented by his or her own bank may cause a considerably different structure to evolve. Much will depend, of course, on the number and qualifications of staff members available to the department. One would like to think that once goals are established, adequate staffing will be provided. But as anyone knows who has actually tried to obtain additional staff, translating personnel goals into actually acquiring more people is often difficult.

For example, if the objective is to review all loans in the portfolio during a one-year period, the manager must determine how many loan reviews will accomplish the goal. The manager should have a good idea of how much time a qualified individual will take to complete the loan review desired. This estimate will help establish how many qualified individuals would be required to perform the given task. Whether the staff is provided, the objective modified, or some other course of action chosen naturally remains to be seen.

In addition to estimating the staff size required, personnel qualifications must be considered. If it is determined that some analytical tasks will include loan review, industry research, and analysis of new loan requests, then the manager has to decide what staff qualifications and experience will be needed. For convenience, qualifications might be divided into four areas:

- Academic skills
- Technical skills
- Overall experience
- Knowledge of the particular bank

Academic (Externally Acquired) Skills

By "academic skills," we mean those skills needed to perform the credit function and acquired primarily from sources outside the bank. These sources would include formal educational institutions and banking industry workshops and schools. Some specific analytical skills are intermediate or managerial accounting, business law, and written and oral communications. Shorthand and typing are examples of operational skills that might also be included within the academic skills category.

The manager should enumerate the minimum academic skills needed to accomplish given tasks and then determine how that skill level can best be achieved. It is important that people think not just in terms of degrees, such as a bachelor's or master's degree in business administration. Rather, managers should look at those academic skills needed to perform the designated duties in the particular bank. For this purpose, a few courses in selected areas may suffice, unless a broad academic background is desired to fill expected future bank needs.

Technical Skills

The second group of personnel qualifications may be broadly designated as technical skills. These skills are generally and most logically taught within the bank. Doubtless, there will be some overlap with outside sources; for example, statement spreading could be taught either in-house or outside. However, such skills as executing loan documentation using specific forms and credit information exchange generally require considerable knowledge of a bank's internal operations and, at times, information drawn from bank files to illustrate methodology or key points.

Overall Experience

A third qualification for credit department personnel might be defined as overall banking experience. This relates to knowledge and skills gained through participation in credit department and other bank activities. For an analyst, it is likely to involve experience with specific types of credit extensions such as short-term loans with cash flow projections, term loans with projected changes in financial position, Small Business Administration guaranteed loans, loans to various types of industries such as contractors or insurance companies, and possibly workouts and liquidations.

For someone involved in operational functions, previous experience in a banking environment might enhance filing, typing, and shorthand skills, especially since employees would be familiar with banking terminology. Experience is an important factor, for it is the only way that credit department personnel develop a full knowledge of the problems likely to arise in the course of a bank's lending and credit operations.

Specific Knowledge of the Bank

A fourth qualification for credit department work relates to knowledge of the bank itself and the environment in which it operates. The desired background includes exposure to various operational functions such as bookkeeping and proof and transit because employees who understand such procedures are better able to comprehend overall bank operations. In-depth knowledge of bank policies, services, marketing goals and plans, competitive environment, customer base, and similar factors is highly desirable. This type of knowledge is likely to be acquired only by bank employees.

Budgeting

The credit department manager will often be responsible for establishing the department's budget. In the credit department, costs are primarily attributable to salaries; therefore, it is essential to have a sound salary administration program. This system should provide written job descriptions outlining the major accountabilities and necessary skills of each position. Examples of written job descriptions are presented as Exhibits 1.3 and 1.4.

The manager must consider how the department's salary ranges relate to other salary levels within the bank, particularly those of the commercial loan department. In some banks, for example, the salary difference between experienced credit managers and even junior loan officers is significant. If such a gap exists, bank management may be inadvertently encouraging a high turnover of credit department employees. On the other hand, some banks expect credit department personnel to transfer to line functions. Nevertheless, if a sizable salary increase is awarded at the time of transfer, it implies that highly skilled credit department employees are in fact underpaid.

Before drawing up a budget, the manager should review the entire credit department organization and staffing process. When establishing the number of analysts and trainees required, consideration must be given to employee turnover. Experienced analysts, who have demonstrated they are qualified candidates for lending positions, may pressure management for early transfers to loan divisions. Also, unexpected vacancies do occur. A valuable credit department employee might be transferred to fill a key position at the request of senior management. The credit manager should be alert to these possibilities and through proper planning avoid serious disruption of analysis work flow due to an early transfer or loss of an employee. Such planning is especially difficult in a small-to-medium-size bank where the loss of one employee is equivalent to losing one-half or one-third the entire department. In this case, special consideration might be given to developing well-rounded employees who can at least provide temporary coverage.

Exhibit 1.3 — Sample Job Description: Senior Analyst

Date Written: / /
Position: Senior Analyst
Department: Credit
Salary Range: $ - $
Supervisor's Title: Credit Department Manager

Position Summary:
Performs credit analysis on accounts handled by the commercial loan department, including new and existing credits. Assists in training other credit personnel.

Reporting Relationship:
Reports directly to the credit department manager, along with the junior analysts and the operational staff. Assists the manager in evaluating the development of those involved in the training program.

Primary Skills/Experience Required:

1. Accounting — intermediate to managerial level.
2. Business law — familiarity with the basics of loan documentation and banking laws and regulations.
3. Written and oral communications skills.
4. Credit analysis — including ability to analyze financial statements and prepare projections.
5. Ability to conduct research.

Exhibit 1.3 continued

Major Accountabilities:

1. Contribute to the loan decision-making process by providing in-depth, high-quality credit analysis.
2. Contribute to sound portfolio management by preparing loan reviews on existing credits.
3. Monitor compliance with various laws and regulations affecting credit grantors; monitor compliance with policies established by the bank.
4. Contribute to the development of other credit personnel by assisting the manager in the training function.

Specific Responsibilities and Duties:

1. Spread and make interpretive analyses of financial statements and prepare appropriate statement memoranda for use in loan decision-making. Work closely with loan officers in evaluating new credits.
2. Review commercial loans granted to ensure proper documentation is obtained, executed, and on file.
3. Review existing commercial loan portfolio and prepare written reports in accordance with bank's loan review schedule.
4. Review in-bank reports, such as past due lists, demand deposit account reports, etc., for information concerning borrowing customers. If a problem account is recognized, senior analyst, on own initiative, calls for the loan file, reviews credit, and informs superior of any deterioration in credit quality of the particular loan.
5. Assist in training and evaluating other credit personnel as requested by supervisor. Experienced analyst will be expected to assume the role of an instructor or administrator in conducting training sessions or seminars. The analyst also attends in-house and outside seminars.
6. Assist lending personnel in financial forecasting through use of computer-based forecasting models.
7. Monitor accounts receivable and inventory loans, reporting findings to supervisor and respective loan officer. This may involve independent verification on the part of the credit department.
8. Identify poorly organized credit files and those lacking sufficient credit information; refer these files to operational staff for improvement.
9. Identify and inform superior of any violations of federal or state banking laws and regulations, Comptroller of the Currency guidelines for national banks, and policies regarding credit quality established by bank's board of directors.
10. Participate in bank's business development program to promote and cross-sell bank services and develop new customer relationships. Identify new or additional services that a customer could use.
11. Assume other responsibilities and routine or special duties associated with the function of bank's credit department as may be delegated by supervisor.
12. Conduct and develop research projects useful to the lending function.

Exhibit 1.4 — Sample Job Description: Credit File Clerk

Title: Credit File Clerk
Department: Commercial Credit
Supervisor: Credit Department Manager
Salary Range: $ - $
Date Written: / /

General Description of Responsibilities:

1. Maintains "A-Z" business credit files. Receives and files all documents such as work sheets, financial statements, agency reports, clippings, correspondence, and credit reviews in appropriate sections of credit files.
2. Assists in maintaining credit file system. Prepares and files new credit folders when needed, making sure files are cross-referenced when appropriate.
3. Reports to supervisor any unauthorized or questionable request for a file or access to the files.
4. Assists in researching and responding to internal requests for information regarding bank customers. This includes information from or requests for a credit file.
5. Ensures that all credit files are accounted for properly. This includes following established procedures for removal of files from the department and for prompt retrieval of overdue folders.
6. Assists in pulling files in time for all loan committee meetings.
7. Orders searches, agency reports, and other reports in accordance with requests from loan officers and the supervisor.
8. Date stamps, sorts, and delivers all incoming credit department mail.
9. Maintains files of periodicals received by credit department.
10. Maintains research files, by subject and by industry.
11. Files paid-out loans.
12. Provides backup and assistance to credit department secretary, particularly in typing credit correspondence.

Education:

High school graduate. Filing experience preferred but not required. Good spelling ability.

Manual Skills:

Typing — 45 wpm manual, 55 wpm electric. On-the-job training will be provided.

Knowledge:

1. **Procedures and methods:** fundamental knowledge of filing system in use and requirements for maintaining credit files. Must be able to identify information requested and know where it can be found. Must know how to locate information maintained in other departments' records.
2. **Practices and policies:** must be aware of bank's policies and practices regarding authorized recipients of credit information. Must have a basic understanding of bank's policies regarding confidential nature of information in credit files. Should have a basic understanding of the Fair Credit Reporting Act.

Exhibit 1.4 continued

3. **Other:** ability to detect improper filing or maintenance of materials within a file and make appropriate corrections.

Personal Contacts:
Principally with bank personnel of every organizational level, frequently by telephone.

Accuracy:
High degree of accuracy required in all aspects of the job. Credit files must be maintained in proper order and be readily available.

Independent Action:
Will operate principally within established procedures and policies. Should require a minimum of supervision.

Supervisory Responsibilities: None

Effort and Conditions:
Mostly standing, walking, and researching within credit files section. Will be required to go to other departments on occasion. Conditions are pleasant, with an electric typewriter, good lighting, and sufficient filing space. Photocopying equipment is located on the same floor.

After this review of department organization and staffing, job descriptions that fully identify required skills and state proposed salary ranges should be prepared. The manager must then study each objective in terms of the salary costs required to achieve it. The dollar amount computed will be primarily salary costs plus fringe benefits. All other itemized costs, including occupancy expense, cost of equipment, contracts for agency reports, searches, telephone bills, and the like, must be added to the figure. Then, the grand total and all supporting schedules should be reviewed with management. As an aid to developing and presenting the budget, the manager might wish to use a budget planning form similar to the one presented as Exhibit 1.5.

If management is unwilling or unable to meet the expense projected and the basic computational procedures are accepted, it should be made clear to management that some initial objectives must be modified. At this point, reviewing objectives and setting priorities must begin again, and, ultimately, a revised budget will have to be developed. For example, it may not be possible to review all of the portfolio, thus only a portion may be reviewed. Such give-and-take should go on during the budgetary process, not through the manager's unilateral actions during the budget period. Invariably, there are minor, and sometimes major, emergencies which will alter the manager's operational plan. But these difficulties should not be increased by agreeing to a budget and a set of objectives which knowingly leave the department understaffed before the budget period even begins.

Exhibit 1.5 — Budget Planning Form

Sheet # ________ Cost Center Name: Commercial Credit Department Period Covered to

(Budget Expenses Only on this Sheet: Use Separate Sheets for Income/Cost Reimbursements)

Account Description	Account Number	January	February	March	April	May	June
Officer Salaries							
Employee Salary Expense							
Fringe Benefits							
Medical Exam							
Occupancy Expense							
Department Office Machines							
Department Furniture & Fixtures							
Equipment Maintenance							
Repairs & Maintenance, Furniture & Fixtures							
Printing & Supplies Expense							
Telephone & Telegraph							
Postage							
Agency Contracts							
Searches—UCC, Title, etc.							
Association Membership							
Conferences, Business Meetings, etc.							
Seminars, Workshops, etc.							
Training Program Materials							
Marketing Expense							
Computer Time-Sharing							
Subtotals:							

(Attach additional sheets as needed) Total Amount

Naturally, in preparing budgets departmental income should be recognized. Some credit departments have direct income from fees for investigations, reimbursement of such expenses as telephone calls, or computer terminal fees for performing analytical work. In most credit departments, the direct income figure would be generally so small that it would be insignificant compared with total expenses.

However, the credit department's loan reviews, profitability analyses, and investigations are some activities that have an impact on bank loan losses. These functions—which can reduce losses—are difficult to measure in terms of income. Moreover, there are numerous intangibles involved in considering a credit department budget. For example, some customers might maintain accounts primarily because of the high-quality work the credit department does. Typically, the department engages in training and development activities which are critical to the bank in general and the lending divisions in particular.

Because of these intangibles, it is difficult to develop precise measures of the costs-benefits trade-off from credit department operations. Thus, the department's budget must not only reflect direct income and expense but should consider the impact, both tangible and intangible, that the department has on the entire bank.

Effective Management

Bank management tends to focus attention on two areas: those that produce or are likely to produce major problems and those that generate the bulk of the profit. Since the credit department would rarely fit in either category, it tends to be somewhat out of the mainstream. As a result, to maximize its contribution to the bank's loan activities, the credit department needs the support of someone in senior management who understands and appreciates its role.

Usually, the credit department can best attain its goals by communicating through the senior loan officer who best understands the department's functions and thinks positively about them. It is also helpful, because of the credit department's relatively low profile, if the manager is able to play an active and aggressive role in the bank. In this way, he or she may ultimately achieve many of the department's objectives. At the same time, the manager may make significant contributions to developing loan policies and introducing new services which draw on the department's special knowledge and capabilities.

Getting Started

A smaller bank may have only one or two individuals, or even part-time personnel, responsible for credit department functions. Surprisingly, it may require better organization to achieve these goals in this environment than it would in a much larger operation where many full-time personnel are assigned to these functions. It is usually easier to manage a specialized organization, where individuals focus on a limited number of objectives. The point is that careful planning regarding the performance of credit department functions may be even more important in a small bank than it is in a large one.

Priorities must be established, goals set, and appropriate full- or part-time staff selected and trained. In any event, it will take time to build up a viable credit department in a moderate-size bank or credit function capability in a smaller institution. Therefore, when the officer charged with the responsibility begins to plan a new organization or the development of an existing credit department, the task should not be treated lightly. He or she should set forth the main objectives of the department, plan the kind of organization needed to accomplish these goals, and then select the persons to perform the tasks.

Even during preliminary planning, the manager should prepare a statement of objectives and an organizational plan. A basic outline will help the credit manager clarify the department's goals and structure. It also will be invaluable for use in discussions with senior management. An example of such an outline is presented as Exhibit 1.6. As the plan evolves and objectives become more explicit, the detail included in the statement will probably increase. Different sets of objectives, within given time frames, could be prepared to clarify and project short-term, intermediate, and long-term goals for the department and its staff.

There is probably no way to arrive at the ideal credit department function overnight, and a professionally staffed credit department may be several years in the making. The only logical way to start is by building a good team of people. This is a slow process. Frequently, in the small-to-medium-size bank it entails selecting and training one person at a time and having that person make a commitment to the bank's objectives.

Exhibit 1.6 — Objectives and Organization of the Credit Department (a hypothetical outline)

I. Objectives

A. To prepare a written review of the following types of commercial loans at least annually; all loans exceeding $50,000; term loans exceeding $25,000; all floor-planning arrangements, interim construction loans, and commercial real estate loans, regardless of amount outstanding. All accounts receivable and inventory loans will be reviewed at least semiannually. Such reviews will cover the following points relating to the credit under consideration:

1. Credit quality — review will include financial statement analysis and will rate loan on a scale of 1 to 5
2. Compliance with loan policy as approved by board of directors
3. Adherence to profitability guidelines
4. Proper documentation
5. Valuation of collateral

B. When requested by a commercial loan officer, credit department will assist in analysis of a potential borrower before credit is granted.

C. Department will handle all commercial credit inquiries and investigations.

D. Department will establish a minimum inventory of skills for its personnel and conduct or provide training to ensure these skills are being developed.

E. Department will maintain a "watch list" of loans representing excessive credit risks and will report to management on a monthly basis concerning progress in the area of principal and interest reductions and additional security obtained.

F. Department will monitor the following current activities: receipt and analysis of accounts receivable aging schedules, percent advanced on receivable and inventory loans, break-even points, and receipt of current financial statements.

G. Department will conduct research as directed by the senior loan officer into such areas as industry trends.

H. Department will ensure credit files are properly maintained.

II. Organization

A. Department will report to the senior loan officer who will also appraise performance of the department and its manager. All requests for services of the department will be directed to its manager.

B. Manager will be responsible for accomplishing objectives as stated above. In addition, he or she will prepare the annual budget for the department and ad-

Exhibit 1.6 continued

minister salaries and performance appraisals. Manager will select and terminate subordinates when necessary and be responsible for their training and development.

C. In addition to the manager, department will contain one senior analyst, one junior analyst, one secretary, and one clerk.

III. Qualifications of Staff (salary ranges and complete job descriptions will be developed for each position)

A. Manager and senior credit analyst will have the following qualifications:

1. Academic skills
    - a. accounting to the intermediate and managerial level
    - b. corporate finance
    - c. economics
    - d. money and banking
    - e. business law
    - f. written and oral communication skills
2. Technical skills
    - a. financial statement analysis including ability to prepare projections and perform cash flow analysis
    - b. laws and regulations, e.g., UCC, Federal Reserve regulations and Comptroller of the Currency requirements
    - c. documentation
    - d. credit information exchange
3. Knowledge of the bank
    - a. operations
    - b. marketing
    - c. trust
    - d. legal and regulatory environment
    - e. loan policy
4. Experience
    - a. manager and the senior analyst should have previous experience in both the banking industry and in financial statement analysis; credit department experience is desirable
    - b. manager should have demonstrated the ability to supervise subordinates; organizational expertise is an important qualification

B. Junior analyst should have acquired or be in the process of acquiring the academic skills outlined in A(1). Technical skills and knowledge of the bank can be developed while in the credit department. Banking experience is desirable but not required.

C. Secretary should type at least 55 words per minute on an electric typewriter and should possess stenographic skills. Accuracy is essential. Previous secretarial experience is desirable.

D. Clerk should be accurate and be able to maintain an orderly filing system. This employee will be trained to record and respond to requests for credit information; therefore, telephone contact with the public will be important.

Environment

Surely, the manager seeks to establish a strong credit department that can capably carry out its assigned responsibilities. He or she tries to obtain the best possible personnel, equipment, and services. But the special importance of the work atmosphere is sometimes overlooked. In performing a staff function, it is easy to lose sight of one's contribution, and it is important to consider the prestige factor. The manager should pay particular attention to such things as the department's physical location—especially its proximity to related line functions—proper working space, noise levels, lighting, suitable equipment, and even such considerations as carpeting and appropriately decorated walls.

The environment can have a positive or negative impact on departmental operations. If trainees are brought into a confusing, cluttered atmosphere with resulting low employee morale, their training experiences are likely to be adversely affected. If credit files are stacked on the floor due to lack of proper filing space, not only will departmental prestige be lost but efficiency will suffer. And an analyst cannot be expected to perform competently if the phones are constantly ringing with credit inquiries. Through some basic planning and recognition of the vital role the credit department can and should play in a bank, these and other unfortunate situations can be avoided. It is certainly a major responsibility of the credit department manager to get this message across to top management.

Common Complaints

Certain complaints from credit department personnel are so common that the credit department manager should attempt to resolve them as quickly as possible. Frequently voiced complaints, including several already noted, relate to:

1. Poor working conditions that do not provide an atmosphere conducive to analytical duties
2. A very routine work load
3. Constant interruptions
4. Poor training
5. Lack of thought given to salary administration
6. Lack of employee recognition (often leading to rapid turnover of employees)

There is a good chance that any banker reading this book will find similar complaints in his or her bank's credit department, which is one reason why good communications through periodic review are essential to a smoothly operating organization.

Review and Appraisal

The manager needs to establish a dialogue with credit department staff. A good way to accomplish this, at least in part, is through performance appraisal. Responsible for this appraisal and salary administration, the manager should establish a job description and a salary range for each position in the department. It is possible that all analysts will have one salary range and one job description. But in some banks each individual in the department has a different set of objectives and salary possibilities. Whatever the arrangement, it is essential that each individual's performance be evaluated periodically in accordance with the objectives set forth in the job description. Both the employee being evaluated and the manager should discuss as objectively as possible how goals are being met. Any factors that may interfere with achieving objectives should be noted, whether they involve lack of a specific skill or certain conditions existing within the department or the bank.

The manager must then arrive at an overall evaluation of an individual's performance. Frequently, a 1-5 rating system is used which corresponds to the following evaluation categories: provisional, adequate, competent, commendable, or superior. This evaluation should relate to how a salary increase (or absence of one) is determined and should affect frequency of future review. More important, it should be a guide for the manager and the employee in pinpointing weak areas and outlining methods for improvement. This two-way exchange should bring out positive as well as negative findings, determine why problems exist, and develop a plan for overcoming specific areas of difficulty.

Summary

In reviewing the existing credit department function or in establishing a new department, the manager must consider the goals of the bank, loan policy, and bank personnel. The credit department manager, together with bank management, must provide for an organization structure that is conducive to the proper performance of staff functions and establish objectives that are realistic and clearly defined.

The manager, regardless of bank size, is responsible for accomplishing these objectives, for developing staff, and for allocating personnel time and talents in a logical manner. Ideally, the manager should be creative, so that sound ideas for new services are generated by the credit department and presented to bank management. Attaining identified goals is essential, for only in this way can the credit department receive the recognition and support it needs in order to develop.

2

Credit Files

For all practical purposes, bank credit departments and structured credit files did not develop until after World War I. Previously, what composite knowledge there was about customers, including the bank's experience with them, was retained almost informally or exclusively in the minds of the bankers handling the credits. As the customer base became larger, this procedure was no longer adequate. Loan officers began preparing memoranda and accumulating data, but this information was usually not available for general use nor was the material centralized.

As the economy grew, business organizations became more complex in structure and larger in size. And many banks began expanding the geographical areas they served. As a result, banks were faced with a more diversified clientele. Therefore, they needed a more systematic approach to retaining credit information so it would be readily available to lending and credit personnel. The credit folder was developed to meet these needs. Although it has been modernized over the years, the credit folder continues to serve the credit and loan function in present-day banking much as it did four or five decades ago.

Importance of Files

Comprehensive and well-structured credit files are an absolute necessity in maintaining the continuity and history of the relationship between a bank and its borrowing customers and prospective customers. Well-documented credit files are invaluable to lending, credit, loan review, management, legal, and audit personnel. Good files may assist in keeping loan losses to a minimum and provide information useful in the exchange of credit information.

For example, good files should permit a prompt reply to credit inquiries, since authorized employees can readily study the file's contents and obtain the history of a bank's experience with a given customer. The files also provide information to satisfy various regulatory agencies, including bank examiners. Obviously, it is important that credit files be accessible and yet secure; they should also be as complete and accurate as possible.

Credit files are important to a bank's customers as well as to the bank. Customers have a right to expect that their past credit relationships are a matter of record and that a bank has sufficient information on file to assist them in establishing credit with others. Furthermore, if credit files are properly maintained, customers can be served by anyone in the bank rather than by only a single employee. This eliminates, or at least minimizes, delays or inconvenience caused by account officer vacations, illnesses, or other unforeseen events.

While complete files must be maintained on all borrowing customers, sufficient information regarding nonborrowing customers is also important so the bank may properly service these accounts and reply to credit inquiries. For business development and other purposes, it is often useful to establish the identities and principal activities of nonborrowing customers. Such information should be kept in addition to filing records of credit inquiries and investigations on these nonborrowing accounts. This information may be valuable in nurturing a future credit relationship or in marketing other banking services.

The Credit Folder

It is important to develop files that are consistent with a bank's needs, both present and future. This involves some seemingly mundane yet significant decisions about cost and long-run utility of the folders, the organization and arrangement of the folders, and the filing of information.

Selecting the Folder

When selecting binders or portfolios for the construction of credit folders, for example, an important consideration is the type of material used. Coupled with this are the elements of size, numbers, and costs. For light-activity accounts, the most commonly used folders are made of manila stock. A portfolio-type folder, with pockets on the inside cover, might also be suitable.

As the contents of the file and its usage increase, a more durable folder is required. Pressboard folders are used for high-activity accounts and major borrowing relationships. These folders have distinct advantages because they are durable and available in a variety of colors. The latter feature is important for a color-coded filing system. Folders made of synthetic material such as vinyl are also popular. For a new system, remember that 8½-by-14-inch folders are often preferred to letter-size since legal-size and large financial documents may be filed in them without damage.

While the decisions involved in selecting filing materials may seem routine, nonetheless they are important. The choice of types and sizes of folders can affect not only the utility of the credit files but long-run expense outlays. It may be advisable, therefore, to test several types of folders and make cost comparisons before reaching a final decision. If, for example, the credit department frequently mails folders, testing should include repeated mailings and inspections of the folders for durability under these circumstances. Clerical staff responsible for maintaining credit files might experiment with folders containing different types and numbers of divisions, internal filing surfaces, pockets, prongs, or other fasteners. Personnel can help the manager evaluate the folders as to ease of filing and locating data. Again, decisions about folders may seem trivial, but this is a shortsighted view. Good credit folders will repay the modest initial cost invested in them many times over.

Organizing the Folder

The organization of a credit folder should contribute to ease of filing and access to information. To cite an obvious but often overlooked fact: As the quantity of material increases, placing all filing under one fastener creates difficulties. The constant movement of paper on and off prongs, hooks, or other types of fasteners may damage the material; eventually sheets will become loose or lost.

Therefore, many banks use folders with two or more additional pressboard center flaps which increase filing surfaces. The most active types of data are given top positions; less important data are filed at the lower position. Heavy or bulky items are usually relegated to the last position of the folder or to a separate statement or document file. If forms of varying sizes are fastened by prongs or other devices, the smaller forms should be placed on top. If this is not done, smaller forms may be overlooked as the referencer thumbs through the material. Whenever possible, however, all bank forms should be the same size.

Here is another obvious fact frequently ignored: Active credit files should contain only pertinent information applicable to servicing, developing, and evaluating the banking relationship in a professional manner. Other data should be maintained in backup files which, while separate, are readily accessible. If backup files are maintained, every file should be clearly identified so that users immediately know how many files are maintained on a customer. If, for example, one customer's complete credit file comprises three separate folders, then the first folder should indicate "folder 1 of 3." Cross-references to other credit folders, such as those of affiliated companies, principals, or guarantors, should also be highly visible and easily understood.

Credit Folder Arrangements

Many banks use six basic divisional guides within the pressboard credit folder. These categories may include:

1. Information sheets and credit approvals
2. Spread sheets and financial statements
3. Memoranda and correspondence with the customer
4. Commercial credit inquiries and investigations
5. Agency reports, searches, and news clippings
6. Collateral records

Additional filing guides may be added when needed. These may include such categories as commitment letters, loan reviews, telexes, affiliations, appraisals, and various agreements.

One illustration of a typical credit folder with six divisions is presented as Exhibit 2.1. Assuming that the credit folder has no internal pressboard divisions, the left-hand side of the folder might contain spread sheets, recent financial statements, profitability analyses, and the loan history summary.

The right-hand side of the credit folder would contain the divisional guides including a flyleaf as shown in Exhibit 2.2. The flyleaf is a general information sheet that usually lists name and address of the business and provides a summary of bank services used. It is helpful in handling inquiries, reviewing and servicing an account, promoting new business, and assisting in an officer call program.

The first divisional guide, "credit approvals," could contain loan presentation sheets which have been submitted to various loan committees

Exhibit 2.1 — Typical Credit Folder

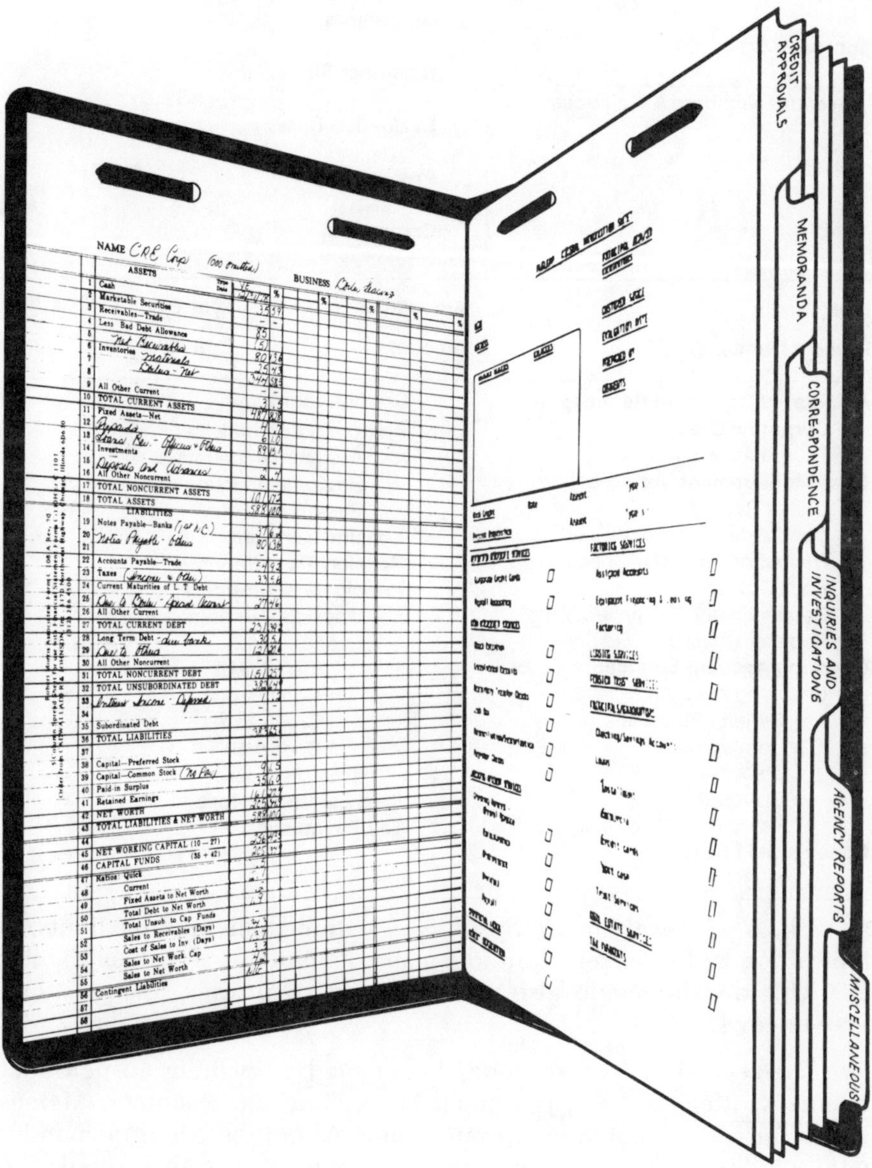

Six divisional guides (right) are used in this typical credit folder to separate and accommodate various pieces of information. A spread sheet is visible on the left side. Other documents on this side of the folder might be recent financial statements, profitability analyses, a loan history summary, and the like.

Exhibit 2.2 — Flyleaf: General Information Sheet

Name:

Address:

Account Numbers & Balances:

Principal and/or Guarantors:

Customer Since:

Evaluation Date:

Prepared by:

Comments:

High Credit:	Amount:	Type(s):
Present Outstanding:	Amount:	Type(s):

Automated Corporate Services
- Corporate Credit Cards ☐
- Payroll Accounting ☐

Cash Management Services
- Check Retention ☐
- Consolidated Deposits ☐
- Depository Transfer Checks ☐
- Lock Box ☐
- Reconciliation/Summarization ☐
- Register Checks ☐

Checking Account Services
- Checking Account —
  - General Purpose ☐
  - Concentration ☐
  - Disbursement ☐
  - Dividend ☐
  - Payroll ☐

Commercial Loans ☐

Credit Information ☐

Factoring Services
- Assigned Accounts ☐
- Equipment Financing & Leasing ☐
- Factoring ☐

Leasing Services ☐

Pension Trust Services ☐

Principals/Guarantors
- Checking/Savings Accounts ☐
- Loans ☐
  - Installment ☐
  - Commercial ☐
  - Credit cards ☐
  - Spot cash ☐
- Trust Services ☐

Real Estate Services ☐

Tax Payments ☐

as well as approvals made by officers within their lending limits. A typical format for presentation to a loan committee is shown as Exhibit 2.3. This division could also include credit summaries, analyses, and loan reviews.

The second divisional guide, "memoranda," includes all pertinent memos written by bank personnel concerning the customer. Memos should provide detailed background information: the conditions under which a loan was made, any special circumstances that should be known, information about repayment plans, reports of site visits, summaries of relevant conversations, and so on. These items may also be accumulated on comment sheets.

Officers should be encouraged to document the initial and ongoing

Exhibit 2.3 — Credit Memo for Loan Committee

(Date) **(Officer)**

To: Officer's Loan Committee

Subject:

Request:

Collateral/Guarantors:

Purpose:

Sources of Repayment (Primary and Alternative):

Repayment Schedule:

Rate (Profitability Analysis attached):

History and Nature of Business:

Comments and Summary:

Attachments (Specify):

Approved: ____________

Date: ____________

borrowing relationships through memos or comments if the credit folder is to perform its function and if bank management is to be kept informed. An example of a comment sheet is presented as Exhibit 2.4.

"Correspondence," the third division, contains all correspondence to and from the customer filed chronologically.

The fourth division, "inquiries and investigations," may contain credit correspondence and records of telephone credit inquiries, as well as reports of investigations. The credit correspondence in this section is frequently preceded by telephone inquiry record sheets. These list date of inquiry; name, address, and telephone number of the inquirer; purpose of the inquiry; amount involved; information provided by the bank in response to the inquiry; respondent's name or initials; and date of response. (A sample credit inquiry form for internal use is presented in Chapter 6.)

If credit inquiries on a borrowing customer are frequent, many banks find it useful to maintain credit inquiry log sheets. These sheets make it easy to ascertain the volume and nature of the inquiries made on a particular account. They would be filed at the front of the divisional guide. An example of a summary sheet is shown as Exhibit 2.5.

Exhibit 2.4 — Comment Sheet

Customer Name: ABC Services, Inc.

Loan Number: 543/752/1

Date	Officer Initials	Comments
2/3/X8	MAS	Site visit conducted today with senior credit analyst. Inspected South Ave. premises. Facilities in good condition with the exception of the warehouse used to house most of the paper products inventory. Warehouse conditions were poor — including generally sloppy appearance and evidence of water seepage. Since the inventory on which we have a lien is stored here, it is cause for concern. Discussed this and other matters related to the 12/31/X7 financial report with the treasurer (J. Bard) and the office manager (C. Schwartz). Cash flow seems to have deteriorated in the last quarter. Recommend that our audit personnel follow-up and perform complete review of A/Rs, A/Ps and inventory control as soon as possible.
2/6/X8	MAS	Audit team selected — report due by 3/7/X8.
3/6/X8	MAS	Received telephone call from treasurer at 10:30 a.m. requesting an increase in the line from $250,000 to $300,000. Will await audit report prior to review of line. Requested 1/31/X8 receivables aging prepared by company. The company is running late on preparing this document.

Exhibit 2.5 — Summary Sheet: Credit Inquiry Record

Name of Customer:

Date	Inquirer	Purpose & Amount of Inquiry	Answered By

"Agency reports," the fifth division, contains reports of the type issued by Dun & Bradstreet, National Credit Information Services (NACIS), Standard & Poor's, and others. This section could logically be expanded to include searches and other items obtained from the public records, such as notices of liens, suits, and judgments.

"Miscellaneous," the last division, contains all items not elsewhere classified and includes newspaper clippings, articles, appraisals, and other items of interest.

If this, or a similar system is used, all but the most recent financial statements would probably be maintained in a separate folder to reduce the bulk of the most actively used records. Similarly, copies of loan agreements, blueprints, and other bulky documents would be housed in numerically identified backup folders or portfolios.

If it is not necessary to use divisional guides in some folders, the data filed should be maintained in the same order as the material in those files with divisional guides. This uniformity facilitates filing and retrieval of information. Larger credit folders with more filing surfaces may be used if the volume of material warrants it. These folders may contain as many as six or more "built-in" pressboard divisions.

Filing Noncustomer Information

In addition to maintaining records on bank customers, credit departments that conduct investigations on behalf of their customers must also file noncustomer credit information. It is not logical to file this information in the credit folder of the bank customer who requested the investigation since retrieval would be virtually impossible. This is important because another customer may well request that an investigation be made on the same subject or the records of these investigations may be required in the future.

A filing system which has proved useful in noncustomer information uses color coding. Often, five different colored folders are used. The specific number used would be determined by the bank's retention policy. If it is assumed that the colors selected are red, blue, green, yellow, and gray, then all investigations conducted in the current year would be filed alphabetically, by subject name, in the red folders. In the following year, blue folders would be used. The remaining colors would be used in succeeding years. Should an existing subject's name be investigated again in a subsequent year, the previously compiled data would be pulled and refiled in the colored folder applicable to the current year.

After five years have elapsed, all the red folders would be extracted from the files and removed from the active filing area. Thereafter, red folders would be used for the next year's investigations. This system separates those names that are noncustomers, provides an efficient record retention-destruction system, and permits rapid relocation of such records.

Storage Facilities

Careful attention should be given to selecting proper, effective storage facilities for credit folders. Factors to be considered include availability of existing equipment, such as filing cabinets, physical space requirements and limitations, type of equipment available, costs, and security needs. Some other considerations in file storage involve available floor and wall space, number of files to be housed, weight-bearing capacity of the floor, location of the filing area, and whether fireproof facilities are required.

Before purchasing new equipment, a review of existing file storage facilities in the bank may reveal unused equipment. This equipment may be compatible with present and future credit department needs. Standardization of file storage facilities throughout a bank tends to produce cost-saving benefits. Additional storage space, whether on the bank's premises or located elsewhere, should also be identified and selected. It is unrealistic to think it will not be necessary to transfer historical records from the credit area at some time.

Many types of facilities are available for storing credit folders. A common and widely used type of filing equipment is the upright multidrawer metal filing cabinet. This kind of cabinet is available in a variety of colors and sizes and may be purchased with fire-resistant features.

A variation of the upright cabinet file is one commonly referred to as the lateral file. Lateral files look like drawer files; however, they may be opened from the side and have shelves that pull out. Since lateral files can also be used as credenzas or room dividers, they are frequently the most practical when space is critical. Lateral files occupy approximately 15% more floor space than do upright drawer files; however, they provide about 40% more filing capacity. The use of lateral files can result in a substantial reduction of cost-per-linear-inch of records stored. Furthermore, they displace significantly less space when open than do drawer files.

Filing cabinets are available with locks, and consideration should be given to the type of lock selected. It may be preferable to equip all credit department cabinets with the same locks so that one key can open all files. Security needs may make it advisable, however, to have different locks or combination lock systems.

Many banks use modular open-shelf equipment to save floor space. Space savings—and cost savings—could be considerable, depending on number of shelves and units required. Additional benefits of modular shelving are their flexibility and suitability for color-coding systems. They also provide easier access to files, longer folder life, and larger capacity. A factor sometimes overlooked is the significance of shelving height. This is important because as height increases efficiency may decrease and available lighting frequently becomes a problem.

Security requirements should also be researched before investing in modular equipment. Modular shelving can be equipped with individual doors or closet-like sliding doors, which make the shelving more secure and attractive. However, these doors can nullify many of the aforementioned advantages. To overcome this problem, some banks seal off the entire credit file area to provide appropriate protection.

Large credit departments may wish to evaluate mechanized filing systems. These are revolving structures which use floor-to-ceiling space and make it relatively easy to access credit folders. However, mechanical failure is a possibility and should be considered. Mobile tub files are available to provide repeated relocation of credit files. Clearly, there are many decisions relating to storage which must be made, and the significance of these decisions in terms of operating costs and efficiency should not be underestimated.

Filing Systems

Unfortunately, in some banks, credit department files seem to take on the character of Topsy—they just grow without plan or design. This can cause serious problems because credit files are not the only files found in many credit departments. Credit departments are often responsible for maintaining prospect files and files on credits declined by officers or loan committees. Other files may include charged-off loans, special sections for recurring reports related to the credit function, various correspondence, and collateral records and documents. Therefore, it must be decided exactly what files are to be maintained in the credit area before an efficient filing system can be implemented.

Selecting the System

Once the manager has determined the types of files to be housed in the credit area, a uniform and appropriate filing system must be developed. Procedures for controlling how credit folders are filed vary from bank to bank. Some banks have elaborate, written procedures manuals, others use basic outlines, and too many have no set rules.

In essence, four basic filing systems are used: alphabetical, numerical, geographical, and decimal. Since few banks file their primary credit folders on a geographical or decimal basis, the credit manager will probably have to decide between an alphabetical or numerical system.

Alphabetical Systems

Alphabetical systems offer unlimited expansion capabilities. Access to alphabetically filed folders does not require a cross-index or list of folder names. Many reference books and secretarial manuals contain detailed filing instructions, and some basic rules that may be sufficient for small credit departments are presented here.

Individual names. Individual names are alphabetized by surnames. They are followed by given names or initials, then middle names or initials.

Name	File
R. John Drew	Drew, R. John
John C. Smith	Smith, John C.
John C. Smith, III	Smith, John C., III

Names of businesses. When the name of a business is composed of names of individuals, the same order that applies to filing for individual names is used.

Name	File
John C. Smith and Daughters	Smith, John C., and Daughters
J. R. Drew, Inc.	Drew, J. R., Inc.

When a business organization name does not include the name of an individual, the name is filed in its natural order.

Name	File
Chemicals for the Home	Chemicals for the Home
The Farm Products Corp.	Farm Products Corp., The

When a business' name begins with a word(s) that denotes the type of institution (such as Hotel America, Bank of New Jersey, or University of Florida), the word that describes the type of business is filed after the distinctive word.

Name	File
Hotel America	America, Hotel
Bank of New Jersey	New Jersey, Bank of
University of Florida	Florida, University of

Government offices. Names of government offices should be filed under the name of the governing body, followed by the name of the department, agency, bureau, or institution.

Federal	State
U.S. Government	Pennsylvania (State of)
Treasury (Dept. of)	Education (Dept. of)
Mint (Bureau of the)	Magnet Schools Program

County	City
Burlington (County of)	Nashville, Tennessee
County Clerk (Office of the)	Recreation (Dept. of)

Other rules of alphabetizing. Files are alphabetized according to the first word in the name as indexed. When two or more names are of unequal length but contain the same words and letters at the beginning of the name, the shorter name is filed first. For example, Smith, P. precedes Smith, Pat and Smith, Pat L. National Bank precedes National Bank and Trust Company. When letters are used as words, they are filed as if they were words. For example, A A Dry Cleaners precedes A B C Stationery and Acme Cleaners. Abbreviations such as Geo., Jos. and Chas. should not be used in filing but should be spelled out to avoid confusion.

Articles, prepositions, and conjunctions should be disregarded in determining alphabetical sequence. When a name contains a number, it should be alphabetized as if the number were spelled in full. It is a good idea to spell the numerical name on the file label. For example, 222 Evanston House would be labeled and filed as Two Twenty-Two Evanston House. There are many additional filing rules that have been developed to cover special situations. Regardless of which set of rules are adopted by the bank, they should be followed consistently.

Numerical Systems

These are indirect filing systems since they must be used with cross-indexes. Numbers are placed on the file folders, and the folders arranged numerically. An index card must be prepared for each folder, and the index cards are arranged in alphabetical order. Numerical systems result in more rapid and accurate refiling and permit unlimited expansion. The major problem is the necessity of making, maintaining, and referencing a cross-index.

Numerical systems are often desirable or necessary when the bank uses computerized systems. For example, some banks have developed central information file (CIF) systems which use computerized information processing. These systems can centralize customer information and, in some cases, can consolidate accounting functions. The CIF method creates an integrated system that will eliminate or reduce duplication of data within a bank. At the same time, it provides a centralized record of all the accounts that a customer maintains with the bank.

While each system is unique, all such efforts require centralizing separate bank department records. Usually, this means that each bank customer is assigned a single number for reference purposes.

Master Index

Regardless of what filing system is used, all information stored in the credit department could be indexed to aid in retrieval. A master indexing system, comparable to a card catalog in a library, can use 3-x-5 cards for this purpose. All the names on which the department has information should be included in this index. Relevant facts about the name can be included, such as address, whether it is an account or a prospect, whether the file is stored at a warehouse or in the immediate area, and whether the name has its own file or is cross-referenced to another affiliated file. Such a system is not only useful for those who wish to review a file but it is also invaluable if the credit department is attempting to locate customer information requested by subpoena or other process of law. One point which merits special emphasis: Even if a master index is not maintained for active folders, it is essential that some record be kept on all folders that have been permanently transferred from the credit area or destroyed.

Control Procedures

In addition to determining how files should be arranged, it is advantageous to set up procedures governing how memos, letters, financial statements, and other relevant data will flow through the bank and be filed properly. Personnel in charge of the filing area are normally faced with two basic problems.

First, some bankers tend to keep one or more copies of everything they write. The two most frequent explanations for this procedure are that "it's always handy" and "you cannot be sure of getting material back once it has been sent to files." This attitude can produce serious problems for the bank if left unchecked because of the cost in added paper, space, equipment, and labor. This is especially true since often *all* the copies eventually wind up in the credit file area, adding to the volume of work.

Second, there are some people who send virtually nothing to the credit file—equally undesirable. Generally speaking, these individuals are not convinced they can locate the material promptly once it leaves their immediate area. If loan officers and others routinely do not forward material to the filing section, there is no way credit files will contain all the necessary information. Therefore, bank employees must be instructed to send pertinent materials to the credit files promptly. This procedure is vital because a lack of information significantly hinders the best use of the file as well as effective servicing of the customer. Furthermore, inadequate documentation may create serious problems when it must be demonstrated that regulatory and other requirements were followed.

The Flow of Data

Care should be taken to keep personal or extraneous information out of the credit files. And account officers should be reminded that the contents of a credit file may be subpoenaed. Written comments of a speculative or highly personal nature could be interpreted as having a nonfactual or extraneous bearing on the decision-making process, especially in the event of litigation. Account officers and credit personnel should be alerted to the possible dangers of having documents of this type in existence, and policies should be adopted to preclude the entry of such comments into the credit folder.

In addition to establishing procedures to ensure that materials actually reach the credit filing area, some thought should be given to receiving filing instructions from the originator of the materials. He or she can determine whether material should go to the files at all. In some instances, the originator may specify which filing group is appropriate, such as credit files, general files, document files, etc. Some think that the account officer has a better understanding of what the material contains and should designate the section in which it should be filed.

One tool used to direct materials to the files is a "routing slip." This is merely a preprinted slip of paper which provides a block for designating the file unit or divisional guide in which material is to be placed. A similar system makes use of a rubber stamp. Each document is stamped and the proper filing section circled. In either case, the sender's name is given.

Another method of filing is to designate specific staff members responsible for reading, sorting, and filing all material generated inside and outside the bank. It is possible for this responsibility to be shared by the analysts and the filing staff. For example, analysts could review all correspondence and reports relating to customers under their surveillance and then act on or route the material appropriately. It is sometimes suggested that analysts receive all materials from loan officers and other sources before they are filed. In this way, the analysts can be more aware of developments that affect a loan and in a better position to act promptly on requests relating to the credit. Analysts could also classify the information, indicating the appropriate section of the credit folder to be used, and they could forward the material to the file clerk.

Still another alternative is to assign all sorting and filing responsibilities to the file clerks. After receiving information from loan officers and other sources, these persons would classify the information, verify titles, do cross-referencing, and refer originals or duplicates to other bank personnel. Handling the filing in this manner may produce greater uniformity in classifying information and be less costly than having executives doing this work. It may also result in reducing the amount of unimportant material being circulated, and permit better interaction with the various filing units. When using such a system, only a limited number of people need training in correct filing procedures. Obviously, this approach lacks some benefits of the systems already described; therefore, the pluses and minuses of the alternatives have to be weighed.

Several other devices can speed up the sorting process for filing. Most banks use multicopy forms, and it has been found helpful for all credit file copies to be the same color. Forms could also have one carbon copy imprinted with "credit file" at the top or bottom of the page. Another common practice is to have types of correspondence and memoranda prepared on different colored paper. Many banks buy or print special stock labeled "memo" to speed filing. It is also easy and inexpensive for the writer to indicate what the document is at the top of the typewritten paper. Any of these devices will assist those who must make filing decisions.

Delivery and Retrieval

Credit folders may be delivered and retrieved in numerous ways. In larger banks, common methods include dumbwaiters that deliver folders directly to the lending area, use of scheduled messengers or runners, interdepartment mail, and secretaries or clerical personnel who deliver the folders. In a relatively small bank, lending and other personnel may go to the credit area when they need files.

Control of the delivery and retrieval of credit folders should be delegated to specific people. Whether the unit serves a small group or many groups, specific individuals should have sole responsibility for the folders. This precludes direct access to the credit files by anyone else. Too often a folder borrowed for only a few minutes becomes the one lost because no record of its removal exists.

There are a variety of charge-out systems in use. One type, appropriate when folders remain in proximity to the file unit, uses a "blotter record" as presented in Exhibit 2.6. This is a daily log sheet on which the file clerk records the date, the title of the folder taken out, and to whom it was delivered. As folders are returned, this information is crossed out and date of return entered. If files are to be returned to the credit area each night, this is an easy way to determine the status of all charged-out items for the day. The "blotter" charge-out system has a built-in means of determining which folders are outstanding. But it is not practical for large, heavy-volume credit file operations because names become difficult to locate as the list grows. The log system does provide an excellent audit trail and, even in medium-size banks, can be effective when coupled with charge-out cards.

When credit folders are sent to various locations and will be out of the filing area for several days, tighter controls become necessary. Charge-out cards fill this need. They have lines on the back and front providing spaces for date, title of file, name of requesting party, and area to which the folder was sent. "Out" cards with plastic windows that accommodate charge-out slips are often used. Depending on internal procedures, charge-out slips (Exhibit 2.7) may be filled out by either the individual requesting a file or the file clerk. "Out" cards also make it less time-consuming to refile credit folders because they mark the positions on the shelves or in the drawers from which the material was taken. If forms are designed to be used in requisitioning material from the credit area, they may also function as charge-out slips or be used to keep records of folders that were requested. Banks that require a faster delivery time sometimes permit telephone requests for files.

The longer credit folders are out of the filing area, the more difficult it becomes to locate them. Active files tend to pass from one person or department to another, and responsibility for keeping track of them must be designated. Bank personnel who have credit folders must be trained to notify the filing area whenever a folder is transferred to another person or department. Recharge notifications may be written on special forms, or they may be made over the telephone depending on bank policy.

Any experienced hand in the credit area will surely agree that "past due" credit folders must be retrieved as promptly as possible. One simple technique that a number of banks employ is to use window charge-out cards with two or three different tab colors. By rotating the colors over a period of time, the aging of charged-out folders can be easily accomplished.

For example, green tabs may be used in January and blue tabs used in February. Midway through February, file clerks could go to the green charge-out windows and list missing folders and the names of those responsible for them. The file clerk would then put the date and his or her initials on the charge-out slips and replace them with a different colored window that indicates a past due folder. People on the list should then be called or sent an overdue notice. Some credit departments have reduced, if not eliminated, the past due credit folder problem. They list the folders that are seriously overdue and note the individuals responsible on a recurring report circulated to management.

But regardless of the care with which circulation of files is monitored, credit department personnel will sometimes find they must replace a destroyed or lost credit folder. Therefore, banks should develop procedures for reconstructing file materials. This task may involve gathering information from the loan officer, audit or loan operations, records management, transfer files, and such other areas as applicable.

Exhibit 2.6 — Credit Department Log Sheet

Date Charged-Out	Credit Folder Title	Charged-Out To:	Re-Charged To:	Date of Re-Charge	Date Returned

Exhibit 2.7 — Sample Charge-Out Slip

Date: ____________________

Name of File: ____________________

Person Requesting File: ____________________

Department: ____________________

Extension: ____________________

Special Instructions:

Signature: ____________________

Branch Systems

Special consideration must be given to the proper use and control of credit folders in a branch situation. The selection of an appropriate system for a branch bank should only be made after evaluating a bank's policies, personnel, and organizational structure. Factors affecting location and management of credit folders in a branch environment include total loan volume, number of branches, proximity of branches to the main office, and loan activity at various branches. The need for prompt accessibility to the credit folders by credit information exchange personnel, analysts, loan review staff, and various loan committees should also be considered.

Although modifications may be more suitable in specific situations, there are three basic options to review:

- Full centralization
- Branch files
- Dual records

Fully Centralized Credit Files

All credit folders could be stored in the main, or centralized, credit department. Maintaining all files in one location is especially desirable when commercial credit information is exchanged by a centralized credit function. Up-to-date customer information must be readily available in order to initiate or respond to credit inquiries. This system also makes it relatively easy to account for all folders.

Furthermore, it may improve security, helps ensure uniform filing procedures are consistently applied, and permits files to be readily accessible for loan review and inspection by various loan committees or bank examiners. A centralized system may not be practical if many branches are active in the commercial loan function. In such cases, the value of centralization will depend in large part on the proximity of the branches to the central files and the ability to deliver and retrieve credit folders promptly.

Branch Credit Files

Another credit file option is for each branch to maintain credit files for the loans it administers. This system has the obvious advantage of assisting branch personnel in handling customers' requests promptly, since all current information is readily available. If branches perform the credit information exchange function, loan review, or analysis, this type of system might be suitable for the bank.

To encourage uniformity, each branch should be instructed in standardized filing procedures. This is particularly important because branch systems can present problems in file control and maintenance.

Some banks overcome such difficulties by requiring regular inspection of all branch credit folders by credit department personnel. This can be accomplished by visits to the branch or in connection with loan reviews or analyses performed at the main office. If this system is used, the main office must be kept informed of titles of all credit folders maintained at the branches. This may be done either by a computerized report of loans or by a manually maintained card index. Someone at the bank must have a complete list of all credit folder titles and branch locations in order to determine the branch responsible for administering a customer's account.

Dual Record-Keeping

Various systems can be developed for the maintenance and accessibility of credit files both at the main office and at branches. For example, a credit files unit could be centralized with skeleton-type files maintained at branches. Such a system does involve duplication of work, but it may be worth the effort in some banks. Unless carefully controlled by a centralized filing and routing staff, however, a combined system may mean that each of the folders contains only partial information, or put another way, no one credit folder is complete.

If the dual record approach is adopted, it is essential to prepare and distribute guidelines on what materials (such as financial statements, correspondence, and agency reports) will be duplicated as a standard practice and forwarded to the office involved. Such a dual system can be made more manageable if microfilm is used by a bank. This topic is discussed later in the chapter.

Retention, Transfer, and Purging

Banks are becoming increasingly aware of the need for comprehensive retention and destruction schedules. Banks tend to use four basic standards for setting such schedules for all records:

- Statutory record-keeping requirements that are binding on the banks
- Need for certain documents as evidence in possible claims against the bank or losses
- Tax accounting and audit considerations
- Requests for statistical and historical information

Clearly, the advice of counsel should be obtained in reaching any decisions regarding record retention. The following comments are supplements to legal advice—they are not substitutes for it.

Regarding statutory requirements, various Federal Reserve regulations contain record-keeping provisions. For example, Regulations B and Z establish several standards that must be considered in formulating record-keeping practices in the credit department. Banks should consult the *Guide to Record Retention Requirements* which is available from the Superintendent of Documents in Washington, D.C. In addition, state banking departments should be contacted since states also have laws that affect record retention.

Requests for information, the fourth category, have been found to be the most arbitrary. They are usually based on individual or group preferences as opposed to legal requirements. For example, certain individuals may prefer that all financial statements received from a customer be retained in the active credit folder indefinitely, even if their statements cover a 10-year period. Therefore, as the need for filing space becomes critical, "category four" should be given close review since the tendency in most banks is to be ultraconservative in setting retention limits.

It is important to establish a records management group within the bank. This group should be responsible for establishing filing, retention, and destruction procedures and policies for all records and reports. Even in a relatively small bank, such a unit is useful for it helps ensure retention uniformity, aids in eliminating unnecessary duplication of records, places responsibility on designated parties, and coordinates legal opinions with bank policy. As noted earlier, the importance of seeking legal counsel on the matter of record retention and destruction cannot be overestimated. And if a bank has in-house counsel, the attorney could be part of the records management group.

Classifying material according to its importance to bank operations is essential. Certain hard copy records, computer tapes, or microfilmed data may be given "vital record" status. This designation would require vault storage or retention of material in vital record centers that are not on the premises. This information may be retained in two or more locations, with a working copy kept in the credit area. A publication that may provide assistance in this area is entitled *Emergency Preparedness and Security Measures*. Published by the Bank Administration Institute, it describes detailed operational procedures for the protection and classification of essential records throughout the bank.

Individual departments with filing operations, such as the credit department, should develop procedures manuals or at least provide checklists that give maintenance instructions. This material should provide specific rules covering length of time information is to be retained and locations where it is to be kept. This is significant not only in day-to-day operations but when the bank must show reasonable adherence to retention and destruction procedures. These situations can include legal proceedings and subpoenas that require various bank records going back several years. If guidelines are followed, most doubt about whether the records are available should be eliminated.

Banks that take a systematic approach to record-keeping usually require periodic re-evaluation of all retention, destruction, and storage policies. This is necessary to keep up with the changing demands in usage, space, the law, and technology. Similarly, the transfer and purging of outdated material in credit folders should be done on a continual basis. This kind of maintenance by file or lending personnel, depending upon individual bank policy, tends to enhance the credit file function and better allocate work schedules.

Unfortunately, many banks tend to view file maintenance as a low priority function. They perform it on an annual basis only or when a file becomes too cumbersome and difficult to use effectively. This task can be simplified at least somewhat if bank personnel use a stamp that says "retain" on materials that are not to be removed from active credit files. For such items, retention schedules would be disregarded.

When materials in the credit folders are being prepared for storage, transfer files should be clearly marked to indicate contents and anticipated destruction date. A record should be kept in the central credit area to indicate that a file has been transferred and its new location. This is easily accomplished by making a notation on the master indexing system or by using 3-x-5 cards filed alphabetically.

Security

The safekeeping of credit folders and the information they contain can be a challenge. Credit folders should be secure from unauthorized internal and external parties. Security must be considered in terms of site selection, access to the filing area, types of equipment, delivery, and retrieval controls.

In addition, the added protection that comes from a well-defined and publicized directive or policy statement from the chief executive officer cannot be overemphasized. This statement should formally define the bank's position in regard to individuals or groups that are permitted access to information. It should also indicate what data can be released to outsiders, under what conditions, and by whom. All personnel should understand that violations of procedures affecting security will not be tolerated. Finally, a periodic review and testing of security measures should be conducted regularly as a matter of policy.

Microfilm

The microfilm process involves the photographic reproduction of printed materials in a miniaturized format that cannot be read by the naked eye. Originally, microfilm was intended to store "dead" records. Although this use of microfilm is still popular, advanced technology has led to an increase in microfilm storage and retrieval of active as well as semiactive records.

The manager should take a careful look at the possible uses of microfilm in the credit department and then consider the pros and cons of the types of equipment and systems available. It is advisable to consult with many sources and suppliers before instituting any system. Some institutions choose an outside consultant to assess their needs for microfilm and recommend appropriate systems. Nevertheless, the credit department manager should become familiar with the practical applications of microfilm processes. He or she should do so before proposing recommendations to management.

Basic Types of Microforms

Microfilm is made, used, and stored in many forms. Each format, or microform, has a variety of applications, and it is important that the most appropriate and cost-efficient form be selected to meet short-term and long-term needs of the credit department and the bank. A few of the more commonly used forms are identified below.

Reels and Cartridges

Microfilm that can be stored on reels or in cartridges is available in 16mm and 35mm sizes. This type of microfilm is best suited for storing and retrieving large numbers of records that can be filed sequentially in alphabetical, numerical, or chronological order. Microfilm used on reels or in cartridges is low cost and provides a high degree of assurance that filed documents will not be lost or misfiled. But this form is not suitable when frequent updating is required. Microfilm on reels must be handled carefully, because the reels require threading and may be marked by fingerprints or suffer other damage in handling. The 16mm microfilm is often used for correspondence, checks, and similar documents. The 35mm size is used for such large documents as drawings, plans, newspapers, and maps.

Cassettes

In addition to using reels and cartridges, long strips of microfilm can be stored on cassettes. Cassettes afford good protection for the film and contain two cores, one to feed and one to take up the film. Rewinding is eliminated with the use of cassettes, and a frame may be held in viewing position for later reference.

Jackets

Made of acetate or other types of plastic, microfilm jackets are an economical means of storing records that must be periodically updated and duplicated. These jackets consist of two clear acetate sheets with 16mm or 35mm channels used to store short strips of microfilm. It is relatively easy to change or update the material housed in the jacket: New records are merely inserted and any obsolete film removed, transferred, or discarded. Each jacket can be visibly titled so that the contents are clearly identified. Film in jackets should be handled carefully to ensure no microfilm strips are lost when material inside the jacket is being changed.

Microfiche

A microfiche, or fiche, contains multiple microimages arranged in grid pattern. Available in different sizes and styles, microfiche offers reduction ranges from 18 to 48 times. Therefore, one fiche can contain either a few or several hundred images. An advantage of using fiche is that it can be visibly identified to assist in storing and retrieving the microfilmed images. Recently, updatable fiche has been developed so that the original filmed records can be changed, deleted from, or added to after the first filming is complete. This feature may be of special value to those interested in maintaining records of active credit folders on microfilm.

Ultrafiche

Ultrafiche is similar to microfiche but permits storing thousands of images per fiche. Images are reduced more than 90 times, thus many records can be housed in a limited amount of space.

Microfilm Processes

Source Document Microfilming

In this type of microfilming, the microfilm images are prepared by photographing actual paper records. Various types of cameras can be used in filming. The rotary-type camera is often used in banks since it is designed to film business records, forms, and correspondence. The camera automatically photographs the documents as they pass in front of the lens. The planetary camera is designed for the precision filming of bound books and documents, engineering drawings, and records too large for a rotary camera. Step-and-repeat-type microfiche cameras film *and* process film rapidly. This system is completely dry and is designed to film 8½-x-11-inch or 11-x-17-inch documents.

Some banks may decide to have source document microfilming done on the premises by qualified staff, while others may choose an outside firm. The decision in a given bank will depend upon the volume of work, availability of personnel, access to and quality of service from outside processors, and other factors.

Computer Output Microfilm (COM)

COM is a microfilm process that does not require paper records. Microfilm images are prepared by equipment that interacts with computers. For example, the images can be prepared from data stored on magnetic disks or tape, or the images can be transmitted directly from a computer's central processor. The microfilm images are produced by "writing" directly on the microfilm or by photographing the data as they are projected on the face of a cathode ray tube. COM permits direct filming of any data that can be processed on a computer without the necessity of creating a paper record. If a bank has computerized record-keeping or processing, the manager might want to investigate a compatible COM system.

Some Advantages of Microfilm

A great deal of space can be saved if records are stored on microfilm. Microfilm can provide a 98% reduction in record storage space. Duplicate microfilm files can be prepared inexpensively and retained at other locations. This is useful when all credit files are maintained in a central area, but bank branches need copies of selected records on their premises.

Microfilm can also be an asset when decentralized filing is used. For example, each branch or department responsible for maintaining credit files could be supplied with microfilm equipment that provides filming, storage, viewing, and reproduction capabilities with little loss of space.

Duplicate files can also provide record protection. The danger of loss is reduced since records on microfilm can be easily stored in various locations to guard against their destruction by fire, flood, or some other disasters.

Furthermore, with microfilm records, data never have to leave the files, and all records are always accounted for. Records stored on microfilm are also protected from misfiling, loss, or alteration because they are maintained in a fixed sequence. Microfilm can be mailed at low cost, and paper copies of original documents can be produced in seconds from microfilmed images.

Other Considerations

The decision to use microfilm should be carefully considered, since the time and costs involved in systems evaluation, purchase of equipment and supplies, and conversion can be significant. Equipment selection alone requires a considerable amount of investigation because the types and brands of cameras, viewers, readers, reader-printers, storage facilities, and other products are numerous and possess different capabilities.

Moreover, employees will have to be trained to use new equipment properly, and some employees may be reluctant to use microfilm readers. Many employees prefer the more traditional credit folder; however, as they become more accustomed to using microfilm, some of this resistance will be overcome. Also, new technology has reduced equipment size and complexity and produced a better definition of the image.

It is essential that all federal and state laws affecting the legality of microfilmed records be considered. Bank counsel or the records management group should be consulted before any microfilm system is instituted or any original paper records are destroyed. Information in credit files is frequently required as evidence in legal procedures. Thus, care should be taken to ensure that no legally required original records are destroyed and that microfilmed images meet acceptable standards for quality of the image, accuracy of indexing, and security protection. Almost every federal and state court or agency accepts microfilm as *prima facie* evidence in lieu of the original paper record, providing certain indexing and quality control standards are met.

As noted regarding record retention, banks should consult the *Guide to Record Retention Requirements* and should also contact local state banking departments. In addition, it would be advisable to contact the audit or compliance divisions of the appropriate regulatory agencies to determine if they have any special requirements relating to microfilm and the destruction of original records.

Some Applications of Microfilm

Some banks will find microfilm most practical and economical when used exclusively for storing "dead" records, such as credit files that have been completely inactive for a specific time. Other banks have developed a system to film bulky documents that consume large amounts of space in credit files. For example, financial statements, loan agreements, research studies, plans, and the like could be placed on fiche and then filed in a holder which is stapled inside the credit folder or stored in a separate file.

As mentioned, some banks with centralized credit file areas and many branches may give the branches duplicate credit files or selected documents through the use of microfilmed records. The long-range goal of some banks is to maintain all active records on microfilm and to be able to locate and retrieve these data in many different categories and formats. The development of computer output microfilm has greatly increased flexibility along these lines, both in input and possible types of output on microfilm. Microfilm can also be used as a security system for storing and safeguarding duplicates of important records.

The rapidly increasing costs of floor space, labor, and equipment associated with conventional hard copy record storage makes the capital investment in microfilm equipment seem more attractive. Both cost reduction and the need to get information to users quickly and in an acceptable form contribute to the increasing popularity of microfilm.

While microfilm may not be desirable or practical in many banks, credit department managers could at least investigate the process and assess its usefulness. Many managers will probably find that microfilm, which they have viewed for years as impractical for their banks, is now, or soon will be, well within their means.

Summary

Comprehensive and well-maintained credit files are vital to a bank's efficient and effective operation. Bank personnel rely upon them to serve customers' needs properly and promptly, to keep losses to a minimum, and to effectively exchange accurate credit information. Bank customers need to have their past credit relationships documented so that credit may be extended again by the bank or established with others.

The importance of developing logical and efficient systems and policies for handling the volume of important and sensitive material contained in credit files cannot be overestimated. The combination of well-defined policies, procedures, and properly trained personnel will contribute to effective bank operations and enhance the bank's professional reputation in the community and with supervisory authorities.

3

Spreading of Financial Statements

Although financial statements are only one of many factors considered in making loan decisions, they are a critical element in assessing creditworthiness of a present or prospective borrower. Statements are important both in the initial extension of credit and in monitoring existing credits. That is why banks routinely require financial statements to be submitted periodically throughout the life of a loan. Most bank credit files are constructed to highlight financial information, and this regular flow of interim and annual financial data from a borrower is essential for an effective follow-up system.

As a result, financial statements are processed by a bank on an ongoing basis. This material may be received by loan officers as well as the credit department. Therefore, suitable procedures should be established for receipt, control, and internal distribution of statements. This is necessary to help ensure they will be thoroughly and promptly analyzed. In addition, bank personnel other than those who normally receive financial statements directly from customers will need to review them; therefore, such information should be accumulated in a central location where all authorized parties will have access to it.

Availability, of course, is just one consideration. It is equally important that financial data be organized and presented so that a company's current financial condition and trends over a period of time can be evaluated. As discussed in Chapter 2, the credit files provide the accessibility, but it is the spreading function which facilitates the interpretation of financial information.

The actual spreading of the statement expedites the review and analysis by transferring financial data to a standard spread sheet. This function is essential to financial analysis: Statement spreading highlights the most important financial details and presents the numbers in a manner that permits year-to-year comparisons and trend analysis. When done properly, the spreading function encompasses more than just the transfer of data to a standard form. It includes a complete review of each report and the identification of unusual patterns or developments which can then be brought to the attention of appropriate parties.

Responsibility for the Statement Spreading Function

Because of the unique structure of each bank, no single system can be recommended for the spreading function. Every bank must analyze its own resources and needs and determine the best method of handling such recurring activities as spreading financial statements. Of course, work volume and personnel availability and skill levels undoubtedly will be primary considerations in selecting an appropriate system.

The Loan Officer

Many banks delegate the responsibility for statement spreading to the loan officer administering the account. The rationale is that the loan officer is responsible for making, following up, and collecting a loan and is therefore the one most immediately concerned with the financial information. He or she should be the one who can and must interpret and react to its implications most quickly. Financial reports are frequently sent or delivered directly to the loan officer by the borrower, and analysis can be done immediately on their receipt. As the individual who is most familiar with the borrower's financial condition, the loan officer is presumably the best person to determine what information is significant.

The loan officer should recognize changes in accounting policies that affect the form rather than the substance of the financial information. In addition, the officer should notice any trends which could spell trouble or indicate a revision of a borrowing arrangement is required. The officer may also know of circumstances affecting the financial statements that would not be apparent to others. Thus, the loan officer would seem an appropriate person to be responsible for statement spreading.

The Credit Department

While there are sound reasons for assigning the spreading function to the account officer, there are several equally strong arguments which support statement spreading by the credit department. Credit department personnel are not usually concerned with handling direct customer relationships on a day-to-day basis. Some bankers argue that this gives them an independence and a certain objectivity to view a loan from a somewhat different perspective. Moreover, some critics of loan officer statement spreading suggest that the credit department staff is less likely to be influenced by natural biases that may result from a close association with the borrower.

There are additional reasons for using credit department personnel to spread a statement. Since the credit area is responsible for maintaining files, responding to inquiries, and, in many cases, training and research, it needs to have access to the financial statements of customers. In fact, timely processing of financial data is a prerequisite to the satisfactory performance of many credit department duties. Similarly, this procedure is in line with the previous recommendation that financial reports be centrally located, assuming the credit department is convenient to those who wish to use the statements.

Unlike many loan officers, credit department personnel will, over time, see reports from most if not all of the bank's present and prospective customers. This should give the statement spreader a broad base of experience and enhance his or her ability to spot unusual trends or events. Like the account officer, seasoned credit department personnel will become knowledgeable about a company's affairs, nature and extent of the bank's financial involvement, the firm's accounting procedures, and other considerations which contribute to effective statement spreading. As the credit department grows, increasingly sophisticated analytical techniques can be employed, industry statistics can be compiled, and data relating to geographical factors and other external influences collected and analyzed.

Another argument used to support statement spreading by the credit department is that loan officers are often responsible for many existing relationships, as well as generating new business. The time pressures produced by serving many customers and prospects may lead the loan officer to postpone spreading a statement or even to ignore it entirely. The latter can occur, especially if the borrowing relationship has always been satisfactory, because the loan officer may not have enough uninterrupted time necessary for statement spreading.

Failure to review financial statements in a timely fashion can lead to critical delays in recognizing changes in a borrower's financial condition. This wastes valuable reaction time, and it can result in reduced alternatives available to correct a problem. Delay in the review of a financial report also impedes the loan quality control function and efforts of auditors, examiners, and management to ensure that the assets of the bank are in, and remain in, satisfactory condition.

By assigning responsibility for statement spreading to a staff area, many of these problems can be overcome. Whoever is responsible for the function should be able to devote all or part of his or her time to statement spreading. Where such division of labor is possible, the function can be performed intelligently and effectively by competent, trained credit department staff. It can also result in more efficient organization of functions and better allocation of employee time. Therefore, routine statement spreading is not the best use of a loan officer's time, except in rare circumstances.

Dividing the Responsibility

In some banks with small credit departments and many loan officers, dividing the responsibility for statement spreading between the lending and credit department functions may be necessary. If such a division is made, specific policies should be adopted to organize work flow. One possibility is to allocate the work by volume—that is, simply divide the number of statements received by the number of available personnel and distribute statements accordingly. Another is for loan officers to spread all statements related to their active accounts, while the credit department spreads statements received from new business prospects. Or a third option is for the credit area to spread statements involving specific types and sizes of loans while the loan officers are responsible for the others. The alternatives should be carefully considered. A well-devised statement spreading system can keep the bank better informed on the condition of its borrowing customers and thereby reduce problems in a bank's loan portfolio as well as provide other benefits.

Managing the Work Flow

At certain times of the year, the inflow of financial reports will peak. Normally, this time falls between late March and early May when December 31 annual and March 31 quarterly statements arrive at the bank. Then, a backlog of work will almost certainly develop; therefore, the spreader must understand the priorities in handling financial reports. Priorities should be determined by size, complexity, and timing of existing or contemplated borrowing arrangements. Knowledge of the bank's relationship with a customer, gained by reviewing the credit file and reading the loan officer's special instructions, is critical in determining these priorities. Nevertheless, to avoid delays, it may still be necessary to assign temporary personnel to the department. Of course, the staffing problem can be somewhat alleviated if other bank personnel are trained as part-time spreaders.

Organizing the Spreading Function

It is recognized that many banks will not have staff to perform the spreading function on a full-time basis. Nevertheless, the following discussion assumes at least one full-time spreader is available. This approach should provide constructive ideas for organizing the function even if it is performed only on a part-time basis.

Receipt of the Statement

Present or prospective borrowers will forward financial statements directly to the loan officer handling the relationship or to the credit department, depending on bank policy. Sometimes, statements are received by both the loan officer and the credit department, especially if the credit department requests financial statements from customers on a recurring basis.

On receipt of a financial statement, the loan officer should review the report briefly and forward it to the credit department with any special spreading instructions. If the credit department receives the statement first, it may be desirable to record its receipt, then forward it to the loan officer for a brief review prior to spreading.

If a statement is received by any other bank employee, that individual should forward the report to the loan officer responsible or to the credit department, whoever is specified by bank policy. In some banks, whoever first receives the financial statement is directed to follow three basic operational procedures. These procedures, listed below, apply to loan officers, credit department staff, mail room personnel, and all other bank employees.

1. Financial statements are date stamped on receipt, as a standard operating practice.
2. If the statement is presented in a bound folder, the contents are not removed from the binding or cover. The reason is that in litigation the bank can demonstrate that the contents of a financial statement are intact, and they have not been altered from the original presentation made by the customer.
3. If a statement is mailed to the bank, rather than presented personally by a customer, the postmarked envelope is retained with the statement. This, too, is useful evidence if a fraudulent

statement is discovered by the bank and the question of attempting to defraud by using the U.S. mails is raised.

These procedures are costly in time and in filing space, and they may not be suitable for all banks. Each bank should seek advice from its legal counsel in choosing procedures that are cost-effective and legally advantageous.

Processing the Statement

The person who receives financial reports for spreading should note on the report and in an independent log, the date of receipt and the initials or name of the loan officer responsible for the credit. The log system should also reflect the date of the financials involved; the type of statement received, such as an annual report, interim report, pro forma statement, aging of receivables or inventory, or a cash flow projection; and whether the statement was prepared by management or an outside auditor. If an auditor is involved, the firm or practitioner's name could be recorded and an indication made of whether the preparer is a certified public accountant. It might also be useful to note whether the financial report is a fully audited statement, a compilation only, or a review.

Depending on the purposes of the log, it might also include a brief description of the auditor's opinion and the company's Standard Industrial Classification (SIC number). This log, a mechanism to control the whereabouts and processing of the statements, could be used to identify companies for industry comparisons, industry concentrations, or study by geographic area. The log will also assist in identifying those accounting firms which share relationships with the bank, and it will ultimately establish a means of assessing the quality of their efforts. An example of a log sheet is presented as Exhibit 3.1.

Monitoring Financial Statements

Depending on bank size, the number of statements received, and the degree of functional specialization, the same log or a separate monitoring device could be used as a tickler to determine which financial statements have been received by the bank and which customers need to submit statements.

For example, a card log might be maintained for all borrowing customers and guarantors. Each card in the system could be color-coded and filed according to the month when this statement should be received. Such a log system makes it easy to know which statements have and have not been received. And it facilitates identifying those past-due financial statements that should be obtained. In some banks, this type of tickler system is computerized.

Either the loan officers or the credit department might be responsible for requesting financial statements from bank customers. Many banks use form letters to request statements, with different forms used to request annual, interim, or personal financial information. To save time and expense, photocopies are frequently made of the first letter so that it may be stamped "second request" and used again if the statement is not received promptly.

A procedure should establish when letters are sent, how many letters are sent to any given customer, when telephone calls are placed, and when stronger action is required if there is no response. Internal follow-up might be handled through a separate list of required statements prepared for each officer with information copies forwarded to bank management.

Once the statement has been accounted for in all related recording or logging systems, then the financial statement, together with any instructions or comments, should be forwarded with the appropriate credit folder to the person responsible for statement spreading.

Exhibit 3.1 — Sample Log Sheet

Name: ______________________ Loan # ______________
Address: ____________________ Officer: ______________
Type of Business: ______________
SIC Number: ______________

Statement Type—Annual/Interim (Cash Forecast/Pro Forma)	Statement Date	Date Received	Date Spread	Spread By	Date Sent to Officer	CPA/Firm Other	Opinion Expressed	Comments

The Statement Spreading Process

Assessing the Information

Once the statement is logged in and the credit folder has been pulled, the spreader should review any special instructions and comments from the loan officer to make sure they are understood. The financial report should then be read thoroughly. Among other things, the spreader should assess quality and acceptability of both audited and unaudited statements, study the footnotes, and identify any accounting changes that might affect the presentation. If the statement is audited, particular attention should be paid to the auditor's report and the opinion expressed.

In addition, the spreader should review spreads of prior years to ensure he or she understands previous summaries and recognizes superficial changes in accounting descriptions. For example, major reclassifications or format changes may even warrant respreading previous financials. There is always a temptation to open immediately to the numbers and spread them, but that urge should be resisted. If not, important information might be missed.

Selecting the Format

Before actually beginning to spread the statements, the spreader should consider the type of statement on hand and the appropriate spread sheet format for its presentation. Several general types of financial statements are received by a bank including annual reports, interim reports, agings of accounts receivable or inventory, cash budgets indicating anticipated sources and uses of funds, pro forma income and expense statements based on assumptions of future developments, and personal financial statements. In all probability, every financial statement received will not be spread, but these general types are received often enough that developing formats and procedures for spreading them should be considered.

Various types of spread sheets are available with different numbers of columns. An example of a five-column spread sheet is presented as Exhibit 3.2. This type of spread sheet is often used for interim and annual reports. Formats can also be designed to present the financial statements of a particular industry. For example, a format prepared for spreading statements of finance companies is presented as Exhibit 3.3.

If a bank is involved with several different borrowing customers in the same line of business whose statements follow a pattern unique to that industry, the bank might select an expert on its staff to prepare a standardized format. In the case of an unusual company that does not conform to a standard spread sheet presentation, the spreader may find it advisable to prepare a special format.

Another possibility is a spread sheet format that allows comparison of a bank's customer with common size financial data compiled for the same industry. For example, the RMA *Annual Statement Studies* contains composite financial data on over 300 lines of business engaged in manufacturing, wholesaling, retailing, services, and contracting. Financial statement data on each industry are shown in common size form and are accompanied by widely used ratios. The publication also contains the comparative spread sheet that is presented as Exhibit 3.4. If a bank's customer is to be compared with any such composite data or with another customer, such a format could be useful.

Exhibit 3.2 — Five Column Spread Sheet

NAME BUSINESS

	ASSETS Type Date		%		%		%		%		%
1	Cash										
2	Marketable Securities										
3	Receivables—Trade										
4	Less: Bad Debt Allowance										
5											
6	Inventories										
7											
8											
9	All Other Current										
10	TOTAL CURRENT ASSETS										
11	Fixed Assets—Net										
12											
13											
14	Investments										
15											
16	All Other Noncurrent										
17	TOTAL NONCURRENT ASSETS										
18	TOTAL ASSETS										
	LIABILITIES										
19	Notes Payable—Banks										
20											
21											
22	Accounts Payable—Trade										
23	Taxes										
24	Current Maturities of L. T. Debt										
25											
26	All Other Current										
27	TOTAL CURRENT DEBT										
28	Long Term Debt										
29											
30	All Other Noncurrent										
31	TOTAL NONCURRENT DEBT										
32	TOTAL UNSUBORDINATED DEBT										
33											
34											
35	Subordinated Debt										
36	TOTAL LIABILITIES										
37											
38	Capital—Preferred Stock										
39	Capital—Common Stock										
40	Paid-in Surplus										
41	Retained Earnings										
42	NET WORTH										
43	TOTAL LIABILITIES & NET WORTH										
44											
45	NET WORKING CAPITAL (10 — 27)										
46	CAPITAL FUNDS (35 + 42)										
47	Ratios: Quick										
48	Current										
49	Fixed Assets to Net Worth										
50	Total Debt to Net Worth										
51	Total Unsub. to Cap. Funds										
52	Sales to Receivables (Days)										
53	Cost of Sales to Inv. (Days)										
54	Sales to Net Work. Cap.										
55	Sales to Net Worth										
56	Contingent Liabilities										
57											
58											

Robert Morris Associates—Form C-108 A Rev. 70
5 Column Spread Sheet for use with Financial Statement Forms C-110H or C-110T
Order from CADWALLADER & JOHNSON, Inc., 5170 Northwest Highway, Chicago, Illinois 60630
(312) 286-4500

Exhibit 3.3 — Spread Sheet for Finance Companies

NAME

	ASSETS (Thousands Only)		%		%		%		%		%
1	Cash										
2	Auto Contracts—Retail										
3	Auto Contracts—Wholesale										
4	Small Loans										
5	Industrial and Equipment Notes										
6	Open Accounts and Notes										
7											
8											
9	*Less—Reserve For Bad Debts*										
10	*Dealers' Reserve, Hold Back*										
11	*Reserve For Unearned Discount*										
12	TOTAL RECEIVABLES (Net)										
13	Repossessions										
14	Marketable Securities										
15											
16	TOTAL CURRENT ASSETS										
17											
18	Receivables—Miscellaneous										
19	Due From Officers and Employees										
20	Due From Affiliations—Subsidiaries										
21	Investments—Affiliations—Subsidiaries										
22	Investments—Other										
23	Fixed Assets (Net)										
24	Deferred Charges and Prepaid Expenses										
25											
26	TOTAL ASSETS										
27	LIABILITIES										
28	Notes Payable—Banks & Open Market										
29	Funded Debt Considered Current										
30	Notes Payable—Other										
31											
32	Due to Affiliations—Subsidiaries										
33	Due to Officers—Employees										
34	Accounts Payable and Accruals										
35	Reserve For Taxes										
36											
37	TOTAL CURRENT LIABILITIES										
38											
39	Funded Debt Deferred										
40											
41	TOTAL LIAB. AFFECTING LIQ. CAP.										
42	Subordinated Debt										
43											
44	Capital Stock—Preferred										
45	Capital Stock—Common										
46	Earned Surplus										
47	Capital Surplus										
48	TOTAL CAPITAL FUNDS										
49	TOTAL LIAB. & CAPITAL FUNDS										
50	Contingent Liabilities										
51	Net Liquid Capital (Line 16 Minus 41)										
52	Ratio Tot. Liab. to Liq. Cap. (Line 41 to 51)										
53	Volume										
54	Net Profit										
55	Dividends										
56	Surplus Adjustments (Net)										
57	Total Bank Lines										
58	Notes Pay.—Open Market (Inc. Line 28)										
59	See Memo Dated										

Exhibit 3.4 — A Comparison of RMA Statement Studies Data with Customer in Similar Industry

Name | Location | Robert Morris Code

	Date		Date		Date	
	RMA	Customer	RMA	Customer	RMA	Customer
ASSETS						
Cash & Equivalents						
Accts. & Notes Rec. - Trade (net)						
Inventory						
All Other Current						
Total Current						
Fixed Assets (net)						
Intangibles (net)						
All Other Non-Current						
Total Assets	100.0%	100.0%	100.0%	100.0%	100.0%	100.0%
LIABILITIES						
Notes Payable-Short Term						
Cur. Mat.-L/T/D						
Accts. & Notes Payable - Trade						
Accrued Expenses						
All Other Current						
Total Current						
Long Term Debt						
All Other Non-Current						
Net Worth						
Total Liabilities & Net Worth	100.0%	100.0%	100.0%	100.0%	100.0%	100.0%
INCOME DATA						
Net Sales	100.0%	100.0%	100.0%	100.0%	100.0%	100.0%
Cost Of Sales						
Gross Profit						
Operating Expenses						
Operating Profit						
All Other Expenses (net)						
Profit Before Taxes						
RATIOS						
Current						
Quick						
Sales/Receivables						
Cost of Sales/Inventory						
Sales/Working Capital						
EBIT/Interest						
Cash Flow/Cur. Mat. L/T/D						
Fixed/Worth						
Debt/Worth						
% Profit Before Taxes/Tangible Net Wortn						
% Profit Before Taxes/Total Assets						
Sales/Net Fixed Assets						
Sales/Total Assets						
% Depr., Dep., Amort./Sales						
% Lease & Rental Exp/Sales						
% Officers' Comp/Sales						
Net Sales ($)						
Total Assets ($)						

The spreading process may also include presentation of accounts receivable and inventory aging schedules. These schedules are frequently provided by borrowing customers or by the bank's audit personnel. They are especially important when receivables or inventory are used as collateral for a loan or when a receivables financing arrangement specifies that the money advanced by the bank is calculated as a percentage of acceptable receivables. A basic spread sheet like that shown as Exhibit 3.5 may be used for presenting several aging schedules as a unit. Of course, additional information or different aging periods could be added depending on the bank's requirements.

Some borrowers will provide pro forma financial statements, cash budgets, or other types of projections. These estimates are often useful planning tools, but the actual results may vary widely. Therefore, personnel will often be requested to spread such projections so that they may be compared with actual results. If, for example, an analyst or loan officer knew that a certain customer's projections consistently overestimated gross sales by a certain percentage, the figures used by the bank could be adjusted accordingly. But if previously submitted estimates compared favorably with actual results, the analyst and the loan officer would be more comfortable with a current loan proposal supported by projections. An example of a projection form is presented as Exhibit 3.6. Such a form could be used by the customer or by the spreader.

Exhibit 3.5—Aging of Accounts Receivable

Customer Name:

Account Number:

Loan Officer:

Spreader:

	As of ______		As of ______		As of ______		As of ______	
Current	$______	%____	$______	%____	$______	%____	$______	%____
Over 30 days	______	____	______	____	______	____	______	____
Over 60 days	______	____	______	____	______	____	______	____
Over 90 days	______	____	______	____	______	____	______	____
	$______	%____	$______	%____	$______	%____	$______	%____

Exhibit 3.6 — Projection of Financial Statements

PROJECTION OF
FINANCIAL STATEMENTS

SUBMITTED BY____

			ACTUAL	PROJECTIONS ☞				
SPREAD IN HUNDREDS ☐		DATE						
SPREAD IN THOUSANDS ☐		PERIOD						
	1	NET SALES						1
P	2	Less: Materials Used						2
R	3	Direct Labor						3
O	4	Other Manufacturing Expense						4
F	5							5
I	6	COST OF GOODS SOLD						6
T	7	GROSS PROFIT						7
	8	Less: Sales Expense						8
and	9	General and Administrative Expense						9
	10							10
L	11	OPERATING PROFIT						11
O	12	Less: Other Expense or *Income* (Net)						12
S	13	Income Tax Provision						13
S	14							14
	15	NET PROFIT						15
	16	CASH BALANCE (Opening)						16
C	17	Plus RECEIPTS: Receivable Collections						17
A	18							18
S	19							19
H	20	Bank Loan Proceeds						20
	21	Total						21
P	22	Less: DISBURSEMENTS: Trade Payables						22
R	23	Direct Labor						23
O	24	Other M'fg Expense						24
J	25	Sales, Gen'l and Adm. Exp.						25
E	26	Fixed Asset Additions						26
C	27	Income Taxes						27
T	28							28
I	29	Dividends or Withdrawals						29
O	30							30
N	31	Bank Loan Repayment						31
	32	Total						32
	33	CASH BALANCE (Closing)						33
	34	ASSETS: Cash						34
	35	Marketable Securities						35
	36	Receivables (Net)						36
	37	Inventory (Net)						37
	38							38
	39	CURRENT ASSETS						39
B	40	Fixed Assets (Net)						40
A	41							41
L	42							42
A	43							43
N	44	Deferred Charges						44
C	45	TOTAL ASSETS						45
E	46	LIABILITIES: Notes Payable—Banks						46
	47	Trade Payables						47
S	48	Income Tax						48
H	49							49
E	50							50
E	51	Accruals						51
T	52	CURRENT LIABILITIES						52
	53							53
	54							54
	55							55
	56	CAPITAL STOCK } Net Worth for						56
	57	SURPLUS } Partnership or Individual						57
	58	TOTAL LIABILITIES AND NET WORTH						58
	59	WORKING CAPITAL						59

As a rule, any given spread sheet should be limited to a specific type of report. For example, interim unaudited figures should not be combined with year-end data, and actual historical data should not be combined with projections. While analytical work may in fact combine such data for comparative purposes, the basic spread sheets maintained in the credit folders should not be used for such comparisons. Rather, the basic spread sheets should include only one type of data so that additional information may be added in a logical and consistent manner.

There are many options in determining the content of a spread sheet. For a major seasonal borrower, for example, comparisons might be facilitated if the same quarter of different fiscal years were presented on one spread sheet. If all quarterly reports and the annual statements were spread in this manner, then four spread sheets would be maintained for the customer. In other cases, all interim reports might be spread on one sheet, with the annual audited reports on a different sheet. This procedure might be preferred if interim operations were fairly steady or if interim reports were not received regularly throughout the year.

Naturally, the treatment of a given firm may be unique. Special instructions are sometimes received from the loan officer or the supervisor which indicate that only selected items should be spread or that a special format or unusual comparison of data is required. Thus, the format of spread sheets is not necessarily the same for all customers. But even for the exceptions, the basic rules of logic and consistency apply.

Preparing the Spread Sheet

Thought should be given to how the permanent entry is to be made. Entries may be typed or written in ink or pencil. Pencil has the obvious shortcoming of being the least permanent and it deteriorates noticeably in a short time. However, if the permanent entry is typed, the work must be proofed by the spreader for accuracy of transcription and alignment.

Once these matters have been considered, the spreading process may begin. All components of the report, including the balance sheet, income statement, statement of changes in financial position, and reconciliation of net worth, are transferred to the spread sheet. The last two items, the statement of changes in financial position and the reconciliation of net worth, are required under generally accepted auditing standards to ensure a fair presentation of a company's financial position. They should always be spread since they contain disclosures that contribute to the spreader's understanding of changes in a firm's financial condition during the period under review. If they are not included, the financial report should be considered incomplete, and the spreader should request additional information.

Most banks, by policy or practice, do adjust certain balance sheet and income statement items to present the financial statements in a more conservative light. For example, spreaders may classify prepaid items as noncurrent assets, deduct from net worth the values assigned to intangible assets such as goodwill, or adjust the cost assigned to the inventory. Such modifications should be made consistently throughout the presentation, and unusual adjustments or restated presentations should be brought to the attention of the assigned loan officer. Departmental policies should cover the treatment of restated figures for certain specific companies or firms.

The spreader should retain custody of the file and the financial report until the spreading process is complete. If another person needs the file and the statement in the meantime, they may be released. It is suggested, however, that such activity be kept to a minimum and that a tickler file be maintained by the spreader to ensure prompt return of documents.

Final Routing

When possible, the spread sheet should be reviewed by another person, such as the credit department manager, supervisor, or senior analyst, before it is entered into the permanent credit file. Once the statements have been spread and the reviewing procedure completed, the spreader must then determine the correct routing of the file. In the absence of any special instructions or unusual circumstances, the file and the completed spread sheet should be sent to the appropriate loan officer for final review, initialing, and the completion of any analytical steps the officer may wish to take. The loan officer should then return the file to the central filing location to complete the cycle. Larger banks may have special analysis sections, and the spreader would probably forward the statement and the file to this section as an intermediate step.

If something unusual is noted in the financial statements, the spreader may wish to forward the file, the spread sheet, and a memo describing the problem to the supervisor, the head of the loan review function, or another appropriate person. One such problem might be a deterioration of the company's financial condition. In that case, the information might be forwarded immediately to the individual responsible for loan quality control or to the designated account officer. If statements are from a borrower whose relationship with the bank is governed by a loan agreement, information should also be forwarded to the person who monitors loan agreement compliance. Regardless of bank size, it is a good idea to provide the loan officer involved with all pertinent information.

Statement Retention Policies

Over time, a bank will receive many statements, and consideration must be given not only to those which should be spread but to those which should be retained in the credit file. Monthly statements are frequently received from companies whose financial situation may change rapidly or when the risk involved requires that the customer's activities be closely monitored. Monthly statements are generally prepared by management and are usually derived from assumptions which rarely reflect all the adjustments necessary for presentation in a company's annual report.

While monthly statements can be effective in monitoring a particular situation, it usually is not worthwhile to record all the monthlies in permanent spread sheet form. Such interim reports should be spread selectively. The monthlies that coincide with the close of fiscal quarters or peak borrowing periods are usually selected for spread sheet presentation. They are chosen because they provide important benchmarks for reference and can be meaningful for analysis, especially in highly seasonal situations. The progress of a company can then be observed during its fiscal year and compared with prior interim periods. Of course, annuals or year-end statements should always be spread, and the spread sheet should be permanently retained in the credit file.

As noted in the discussion of credit files in Chapter 2, the bank should establish its own record retention policy. Of course, this policy must reflect legal requirements and the bank's particular needs. No general rules can be presented here, but some knowledgeable credit personnel follow these principles: Credit files should be periodically purged of monthly statements other than quarterly or peak borrowing reports; files should contain only those quarterlies related to the current fiscal period; annual financial statements should be retained for the current and three preceding years. Such a schedule will keep the files from getting unnecessarily bulky, while retaining information sufficient for a detailed examination.

Banks may also maintain overflow files for active borrowers in which a full complement of monthlies and quarterlies for the preceding two or three years are kept plus annuals for two additional years. Many banks destroy outdated materials, send them to storage, or provide record retention on microfilm. But to repeat, the final decision on these questions must be consistent with the bank's retention and destruction policy, and this policy should be consulted before any records, including financial statements, are destroyed.

Staffing and Training

Staffing requirements relate directly to the objectives established for the spreading function. If the effort is to be completely mechanical in nature and procedures are well defined and articulated, the staff may be entirely clerical. If this is the case, all analytical, review, and similar activities must be performed elsewhere. As a result, training may be limited to ensuring that procedures are thoroughly understood.

To the extent that the spreading function incorporates other responsibilities, up to and including full analytical review, staffing and training requirements become increasingly rigorous. With expanded responsibilities, the spreading function will not only require highly trained permanent staff but it may also provide meaningful training for those whose involvement may be relatively short term.

High school graduates with good exposure to a business curriculum are the most obvious source of staff for less complex operations. For more complex departments, junior colleges, business schools, and local community colleges provide a considerable source of talent. Particular attention might be paid to those students pursuing degrees in evening programs. As employees, they may have more advanced skills than typical high school graduates and may also have more maturity and the potential for more rapid growth within the bank. In credit departments where the spreading activity is only one part of a comprehensive analytical activity, candidates having degrees through the master's level may be appropriate.

In any case, a good working knowledge of accounting and business is required. As the responsibilities of the function expand, so must the employee's level of expertise in these two important areas—business and accounting. This is not to say an individual must or should eventually possess the skills of a certified public accountant. However, financial statements are products of a complex accounting world in which procedures and practices often change. Financial statements are complex, even those from the smallest business enterprise with which the bank maintains a relationship; therefore, as analytical work related to statement spreading increases, the demands on those doing the work also grow.

The Future: Automated Statement Spreading

Many computer programs have been designed specifically for credit analysis purposes. In essence, an automated statement spreading system accepts data in the form of a profit and loss statement and a balance sheet. Based on these data, the computer will perform the ratio computations, prepare a sources and uses of funds statement, and provide other information as programmed. Typically, the data are entered manually from worksheets of the type presented as Exhibits 3.7 and 3.8. Once the first format sheet has been prepared for a customer's statements, input of new financial data is a relatively simple procedure. In addition to printing the final product, the computer can also print a worksheet with space to enter further data.

Exhibit 3.7 — Statement Spreading Worksheet

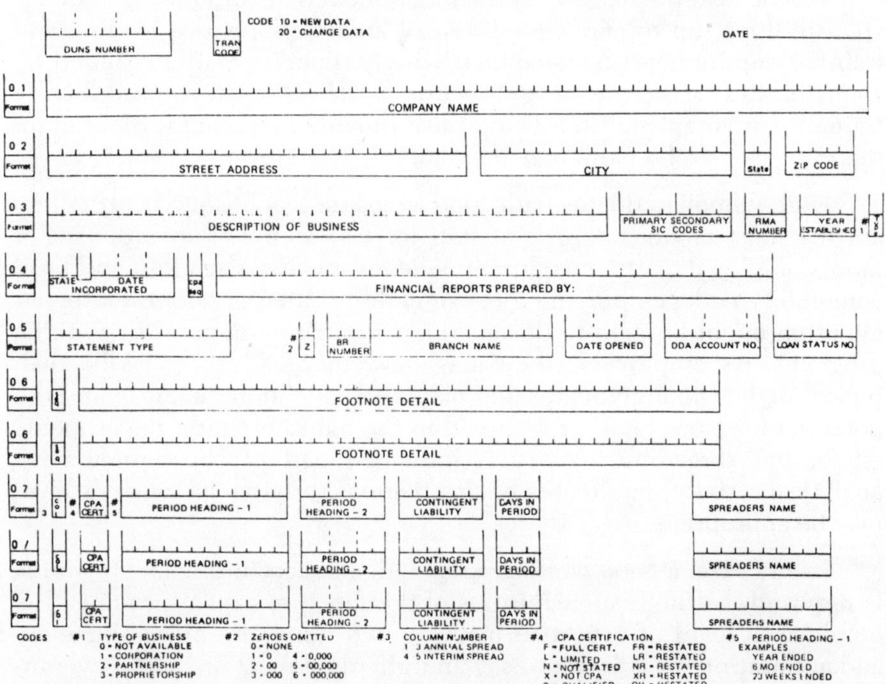
DUNS NUMBER
TRAN CODE
CODE 10 = NEW DATA
20 = CHANGE DATA
DATE

01 Format — COMPANY NAME

02 Format — STREET ADDRESS | CITY | State | ZIP CODE

03 Format — DESCRIPTION OF BUSINESS | PRIMARY SECONDARY SIC CODES | RMA NUMBER | YEAR ESTABLISHED | #1

04 Format — STATE | DATE INCORPORATED | cpa req | FINANCIAL REPORTS PREPARED BY:

05 Format — STATEMENT TYPE | #2 | BR NUMBER | BRANCH NAME | DATE OPENED | DDA ACCOUNT NO. | LOAN STATUS NO.

06 Format — FOOTNOTE DETAIL

06 Format — FOOTNOTE DETAIL

07 Format — #3 | #4 CPA CERT | #5 PERIOD HEADING – 1 | PERIOD HEADING – 2 | CONTINGENT LIABILITY | DAYS IN PERIOD | SPREADERS NAME

07 Format — CPA CERT | PERIOD HEADING – 1 | PERIOD HEADING – 2 | CONTINGENT LIABILITY | DAYS IN PERIOD | SPREADERS NAME

07 Format — CPA CERT | PERIOD HEADING – 1 | PERIOD HEADING – 2 | CONTINGENT LIABILITY | DAYS IN PERIOD | SPREADERS NAME

CODES

#1 TYPE OF BUSINESS
0 = NOT AVAILABLE
1 = CORPORATION
2 = PARTNERSHIP
3 = PROPRIETORSHIP

#2 ZEROES OMITTED
0 = NONE
1 = 0 4 = 0,000
2 = 00 5 = 00,000
3 = 000 6 = 000,000

#3 COLUMN NUMBER
1 3 ANNUAL SPREAD
4 5 INTERIM SPREAD

#4 CPA CERTIFICATION
F = FULL CERT. FR = RESTATED
L = LIMITED LR = RESTATED
N = NOT STATED NR = RESTATED
X = NOT CPA XR = RESTATED
Q = QUALIFIED QR = RESTATED

#5 PERIOD HEADING – 1
EXAMPLES
YEAR ENDED
6 MO. ENDED
23 WEEKS ENDED

Exhibit 3.8 — Balance Sheet

DUNS NUMBER | TRAN CODE | CO | DATE ______________

GP	SEQ		COLUMN 1	COLUMN 2	COLUMN 3
		CURRENT ASSETS			
0 1	1				
0 1	2				
0 1	3				
0 1	4				
0 1	5				
0 1	6				
0 1	7				
0 1	8				
0 1	9				
		FIXED ASSETS			
0 2	1				
0 2	2				
		OTHER ASSETS			
0 3	1				
0 3	2				
0 3	3				
0 3	4				
0 3	5				
0 3	6				
0 3	7				
		CURRENT LIABILITIES			
0 4	0				
0 4	1				
0 4	2				
0 4	3				
0 4	4				
0 4	5				
0 4	6				
0 4	7				
0 4	8				
0 4	9				
		LONG TERM DEBT			
0 5	1				
0 5	2				
0 5	3				
0 5	4				
0 5	5				
		OTHER LIABILITIES			
0 6	1				
0 6	2				
0 6	3				
0 6	4				
0 6	5				
		OWNERS EQUITY			
0 7	1				
0 7	2				
0 7	3				
0 7	4				
0 7	5				
0 7	6				
		TOTAL ASSETS	______	______	______

Among other things, computer programs can produce:

1. Balance sheet spreads
2. Income statement spreads
3. Statements of changes in working capital
4. Statements of sources and uses of funds
5. Ratio computations
6. Common size statements
7. Projections—including variable input cash flow projections
8. Conversions of foreign funds into U.S. dollars

Examples of the final product produced by one type of automated system are presented as Exhibits 3.9 and 3.10.

Some Essential Considerations

It is imperative that any bank which considers automated statement spreading and related analytical capabilities conduct a full cost analysis. The bank should investigate the advantages and disadvantages of such systems and be sure they are compatible with its particular operations. Some considerations are:

1. Automated statement spreading provides high production capability, enabling the bank to cope with peak seasons in a more efficient manner.
2. If a bank has its own automated function, the service can be sold.
3. If a bank does not spread a large volume of statements, automation may not be practical.
4. There is less margin for human error when using an automated system. On the one hand, the computer will refuse to accept certain programming errors. On the other, inaccurate data may be entered and less readily detected than might be the case with manual spreading.
5. Cross-training is needed because staff turnover or absences in any highly automated area will lead to breakdowns in the system and lack of continuity; a permanent trained staff is required.
6. The work flow of an automated function must be scheduled as carefully as that of a manually performed function. Time is still required to prepare the final product, and those requesting the service should recognize this fact. If a time-sharing arrangement is used, a strict schedule must be adhered to, both for computer use and for delivery of work to be processed. Also, personnel should be alert to the cost of time-sharing usage, and cost controls should be established.
7. Computerized functions offer speed, accuracy, and control and enhance record retention through off-premises tape storage.
8. Statements that are spread by computer have a professional

Exhibit 3.9 — Income Statement by Computer

NAME CRE CORPORATION DUNS #: 83-486-4000
BRANCH 616 DATE OPENED: JANUARY 1, 19X6 RMA: 794 SIC: 7300

ZEROS OMITTED: 000 ANNUAL	YEAR ENDED DEC 31, 'X6		YEAR ENDED DEC 31, 'X7		YEAR ENDED DEC 31, 'X8	
RENTALS	254	47.6	314	55.4	304	35.6
SALE OF EQUIPMENT	179	33.6	136	24.1	385	45.2
HAULING & SERVICE	98	18.4	94	16.6	65	7.6
INTERCOMPANY & OTHER	2	.4	22	3.9	98	11.6
NET SALES	533	100.0	566	100.0	852	100.0
OPENING INVENTORY	30	7.4	29	7.2	28	4.4
PURCHASES & FREIGHT	228	56.4	250	62.5	450	72.0
RENT	9	2.2	9	2.3	6	1.0
DIRECT LABOR	16	4.0	0	.0	23	3.7
FACTORY OVERHEAD	80	19.8	80	20.0	80	12.8
DEPRECIATION BOILERS	70	17.3	57	14.2	58	9.3
EQUIPMENT & BOILER RENT	0	.0	3	.8	5	.8
LESS: ENDING INVENTORY	(29)	(7.1)	(28)	(7.0)	(25)	(4.0)
COST OF GOODS SOLD	404	100.0	400	100.0	625	100.0
GROSS PROFIT	129	24.2	166	29.3	227	26.6
SALES SALARIES & COMM	23	4.4	27	4.8	35	4.1
TRAVEL & ENTERTAINMENT	5	.9	4	.7	4	.5
ADVERTISING	7	1.3	5	.9	7	.8
RENT	4	.8	4	.7	4	.5
JOB PROMOTION	2	.3	1	.2	0	.0
SUNDRY SELLING EXPENSES	9	1.7	11	1.9	15	1.7
TOTAL SELLING EXPENSES	50	9.4	52	9.2	65	7.6
OFFICERS SALARIES	17	3.2	20	3.5	26	3.1
SALARIES OTHER	10	1.9	15	2.7	8	.9
RENT	4	.7	4	.7	4	.5
PROFESSIONAL FEES	11	2.1	7	1.2	16	1.9
BAD DEBT EXPENSE	1	.2	3	.6	11	1.3
SUNDRY	18	3.4	15	2.6	20	2.3
TOTAL GENERAL & ADMIN. EXPENSES	61	11.5	64	11.3	85	10.0
NET OPERATING PROFIT	18	3.3	50	8.8	77	9.0
EARNED INTEREST	4	.7	6	.9	7	.7
SUNDRY	10	1.9	7	1.3	8	.9
OTHER INCOME	14	2.6	13	2.2	15	1.6
INTEREST PAID	36	6.7	31	5.4	32	3.6
RELOCATION EXPENSE	0	.0	0	.0	16	1.9
OTHER EXPENSES	36	6.7	31	5.4	48	5.5
PROFIT BEFORE TAXES	(4)	(.8)	32	5.6	44	5.1
INCOME TAXES	0	.0	2	.3	5	.6
NET PROFIT	(4)	(.8)	30	5.3	39	4.5
MEMO - DEPRECIATION INCLUDED ABOVE	70		57		58	
MEMO - OFFICERS' SALARIES INCLUDED ABOVE	17		20		26	
SURPLUS BEGINNING OF PERIOD	131		127		157	
ADD: PROFIT FOR PERIOD	(4)		30		39	
TOTAL	127		157		196	
TOTAL SURPLUS END OF PERIOD	127		157		196	

Exhibit 3.10 — Computer Generated Reports

F I N A N C I A L S T A T E M E N T R E V I E W 83-486-4000

FOR : CRE CORPORATION
LOCATION : 42 ALLENS ROAD TRENTON NJ 19100

BUSINESS : BOILER LEASING
SIC CODE : 7300

ESTABLISHED : 19X0
TYPE : CORPORATION
INCORPORATED : NJ MARCH 31, 19X8

D & B NUMBER : 83-486-4000
RMA NUMBER : 794

BRANCH : 616
DATE OPENED : JANUARY 1, 19X6
ACCT NUMBER : 782-469-3
STATUS NUMBER : 842-52

CPA PREPARED : WALTER & CO. (CPA)

FOOT NOTES : 1 BOILER REGARDED AS A SEMI-FIXED ASSET

SPREAD BY : 12/31/X6 COATES 12/31/X7 BAKER 12/31/X8 SHARP

* * * F I N A N C I A L R A T I O S * * *

CRE CORPORATION 83-486-4000

ANNUAL	DEC 31, 'X6	DEC 31, 'X7	DEC 31, 'X8
LIQUIDITY AND DEBT RATIOS			
CURRENT RATIO	1.533	1.587	2.108
QUICK RATIO	.311	.432	.497
NET WORTH/TOTAL DEBT	.426	.621	.536
TOTAL DEBT/NET WORTH	2.347	1.610	1.865
PROFITABILITY RATIOS			
NET PROFIT/NET PLANT	(.235)	5.000	9.750
NET PROFIT/NET WORTH	(.029)	.180	.190
COMMON DIVIDENDS/NET PROFIT	***	***	***
GROWTH RATIOS			
SALES GROWTH RATE		.061	.505
GROSS PROFIT GROWTH RATE		.286	.367
NET PROFIT GROWTH RATE		N/A	.300
TURNOVER RATIOS			
SALES PER DAY	1.5	1.6	2.4
COST OF SALES/INVENTORY/DAYS	25.8	25.2	14.4
COST OF SALES/PAYABLE/DAYS	12.5	7.2	31.1
PURCHASES/TRADE-DEBT/DAYS	22.1	11.5	43.2
SALES/WORKING CAPITAL/DAYS	76.4	77.0	108.2

appearance. This enhances their usefulness as an educational tool in discussions with the borrower.

9. Problems at the computer center can cause unexpected delays.
10. Lack of flexibility of the format is probably the major source of problems for a bank. For example, statements of manufacturers, retailers, wholesalers, and distributors, as well as many service-oriented companies, are readily spread by an auto-

Exhibit 3.10 continued

SOURCE AND USE OF FUNDS REPORT

CRE CORPORATION

SOURCE OF FUNDS			USE OF FUNDS		
FOR PERIOD: DEC 31, •X7 TO DEC 31, •X8			ZEROS OMITTED: 000		
NET PROFIT	$	39		$	
DEPRECIATION RESTORED		58			
			FIXED ASSET ADDITIONS		56
DECREASES - CURRENT ASSETS			INCREASES - CURRENT ASSETS		
INVENTORY MATERIALS		3	CASH		17
			RECEIVABLES TRADE		9
			BOILERS NET		134
			CSV LIFE INSURANCE		3
DECREASES - OTHER ASSETS			INCREASES - OTHER ASSETS		
PREPAID ASSETS		13	LOANS REC OFFICER&OTHERS		11
OTHER RECEIVABLES		4	DEPOSITS & ADVANCES		2
INCREASES-CURRENT LIABILITIES			DECREASES-CURRENT LIABILITIES		
N/P-FIRST NBT C/L		6	N/P-FIRST NBT T/L CURR		23
N/P-OTHERS CURR		23	N/P-FIRST NBT S		10
PAYABLES TRADE		46	N/P-BOILER CURR		27
INCOME TAXES PAY & ACCRD		6	DUE TO BOILER		11
OTHER TAXES & ACCRUALS		15			
INCREASES - LONG TERM DEBT			DECREASES - LONG TERM DEBT		
N/P-FIRST NBT -C/L		9	N/P-FIRST NBT T/L		17
N/P-OTHERS		98			
TOTAL SOURCES	$	320	TOTAL USES	$	320

mated statement spreading computer program. However, for a variety of reasons—volume, unique characteristics of each firm, special captions and ratios, etc.—finance companies, insurance companies, utilities, and some leasing and motor freight companies usually are hand spread. Furthermore, depending upon the bank's customer base, other types of statements also may be manually spread.

Approaches for the Smaller Bank

A bank could purchase its own full-size computer and develop specialized programs. While this approach gives the bank complete control over use of computer time and the development of various programs, the bank would be making a major investment in capital and personnel. In addition, in-house programming would require the time and expertise of a computer programmer. Some banks may wish to investigate recently developed, sophisticated mini-computers to determine if they could perform some automated statement spreading functions. Obviously, mini-computers do not require the capital investment needed for a full-size computer installation.

More realistic for most smaller banks, however, would be one of the many time-sharing programs that are available. These programs require little or no outlay of capital; all that is necessary is time-sharing availability and a computer program. Such programs have been developed by many data service companies and by some large banks. If time-sharing is used, the bank could buy an existing computer program or assist in the modification of one. A smaller bank might want to contact a correspondent bank to see if it provides such a service on a fee basis. In this case, the bank must consider whether:

1. It would have enough statements to make a contract attractive to the correspondent.
2. The correspondent would be able to spread the statements quickly enough for the smaller bank.
3. The formats that are used by the correspondent bank would be acceptable.

These three questions also apply to those banks considering a time-sharing arrangement with a data service company.

Organizing the Statement Automation Function

The following method of processing a statement through an automated statement spreading function was developed by a large bank. This bank spreads over 5,000 statements each year through a computer program on a time-sharing basis. While a small-to-medium-size bank probably would not handle such a large volume, the general procedures used by this bank may be helpful in planning the organization of a completely manual function.

In the bank in question, the entire statement spreading function, both manual and computerized, is divided into three groups:

- International — composed of five spreaders and a section head
- Regional — composed of four spreaders and a section head
- National — composed of five spreaders and a section head

For purposes of illustration, one financial statement is traced through the system. Its path is essentially as follows.

1. The loan officer receives a financial statement from a prospective borrowing customer. The officer then prepares instructions to the credit department as shown in Exhibit 3.11 to request that the statement be spread. Financial statements are attached and submitted in original form.
2. The instructions and the statements are delivered to the appropriate section head for action.
3. The section head logs in the statement for expense purposes and for departmental cost analysis. The log shows where the statement comes from, including department and name of the loan officer. It indicates the number of spreads to be prepared from the complete package of originals that is provided and

Exhibit 3.11 — Instructions to Main Office Credit Department

Date____________

Customer's Name ________________________________

Spread Statement(s) Dated________________________________

Return to Branch ________________________ by____________

Prepare Copies for:

☐ Regional Meeting on ____________________

☐ Loan Committee on____________________

☐ Directors' Loan Committee on ____________________

Loan Request: ________________________________

DATA FOR ANALYSIS:		AMOUNT	TYPE	RATE
Loans Owing Statement Date		$________	________	________
		$________	________	________
Net Average Balance (3 mo. avg.)	$________			
Profit (3 mo. avg.) (or loss)	$________			
Presently Owing		$________	________	________
		$________	________	________

Low $________ and Peak $________ during past 12 months

$________ $________

Other Remarks:

FROM ____________________ / ____________________
(Branch) (Individual)

also includes the expense code of the department requesting the spread, the Standard Industrial Classification code, and the date. This log also provides information for cost and billing.

4. The section head reviews the statement to see whether any unusual items need to be discussed with the loan officer before preparation of the spread. He or she also decides whether the statement should be spread by the computerized system or be prepared manually. The most appropriate spreader to handle the assignment is then selected.
5. Prior to actually entering the data, the spreader should check whether this spread was done before and if a format change is required. Previous formats are verified by an alphabetical and numerical list which contains hard copy printouts of previously spread financial statements.

6. Assuming automated spreading is selected, the spreader then makes the manual entries on the data submission sheet. This sheet is then forwarded to a clerk for direct entry into the computer tapes. In the afternoon (2:00 p.m.), the entries are transferred to a master tape which is delivered to the outside computer center. Tapes that are processed by 2:00 p.m. are returned to the bank by 9:00 the following morning. Poor input or operating difficulties can cause unexpected delays at this point.
7. After the spread sheets are returned, the data are manually proofed against the document of original entry before the sheets are distributed.

In conclusion, automated statement spreading can lead to a beneficial mix of personnel and technology, but careful evaluation is necessary before engaging in this activity.

Summary

A well-done spread sheet presentation is itself an effective analysis. The end product will permit a loan officer or other interested reviewer to determine quickly the present financial condition of a company and any unusual or significant trends. Assigning this activity to the credit department permits all authorized personnel to have easy access to the financial information, provides timely processing, and, perhaps most important, allows the financial statements to be scrutinized by objective specialists who have been exposed to reports from a wide range of bank customers.

4

The Commercial Credit Analysis Function

Credit analysis involves appraising the different kinds of information considered relevant in deciding on the creditworthiness of a customer. This activity includes not only the analysis of financial statements and reports of a given company but also numerous other factors which affect a company's past, present, and, most important, probable future performance. Credit analysis attempts to determine the risk involved in extending credit of a specific amount and for a certain period to a commercial borrower. In addition, credit analysis may also include examination of a borrower's position and operations considering the bank's funds situation and its lending policy.

Its Purpose

Meaningful credit analysis should present factual, relevant information so that other bank personnel can understand the reasoning used by an analyst to reach a conclusion based upon the available evidence. The analysis function must also determine whether the information submitted is adequate for decision-making purposes or if additional information or research is required. In most banks, the analysis function supports the work of the loan officers by assembling, organizing, and analyzing relevant data. This support assists those performing the lending function so that they can evaluate loan requests promptly and logically.

There are several byproducts of credit analysis. Since it brings together valuable information and presents it in a form which is useful both in making and evaluating loan decisions, it provides a mechanism for improving and organizing the decision-making process. Unless credit analysis is done entirely by the loan officer, other bank personnel become involved in the process. This involvement should strengthen the system of checks and balances within a bank. It may also provide constructive suggestions to improve the quality of a loan or help prevent oversights that can result from time pressures.

Written credit analysis may help to document the credit file and serve as a means for evaluating analysts, lending personnel, and other employees. And, finally, credit analysis is extremely valuable in training present and prospective loan officers and credit department staff; it can also assist the bank's marketing efforts by identifying bank services that a customer is using or might use.

This chapter provides an overview of the credit analysis function and its place in a banking organization. It discusses many aspects of credit analysis, including its scope and purposes, factors relating to the organization of the function, follow-up and control systems, selection of staff, and sources of information. Suggestions for an analytical report format, with exhibits, are also provided.

Organizing the Credit Analysis Function

It is difficult to outline an organization chart for the credit analysis function which would meet the specific needs of most banks. A small bank may find that an experienced credit department manager can perform the entire analytical function. Another bank may have one or more employees who spread statements and then forward them to the appropriate loan officer for analysis. In a large bank, several analysts may report to a senior analyst who in turn reports to the credit manager. In this case, some analysts may specialize in certain industries, such as utilities, insurance or finance companies, and may be supported by a research staff. Therefore, the following questions should be answered to organize this function efficiently.

1. Who should perform the work?
2. Which loans should be analyzed?
3. When should loans be analyzed?
4. How are analytical standards set?
5. What about existing credits?
6. Who is responsible?
7. Will recommendations and ratings be issued?
8. Are there related functions?

Performing the Work

First, a bank must determine who will do the work. In some banks, as already mentioned, loan officers are responsible for the credit analysis of their own loans. The staff contribution in those banks is fairly routine. It is usually limited to spreading financial statements for subsequent review by the loan officer. In many banks, and especially the larger ones, the analysis function is separated from the lending function primarily for reasons of efficiency. This separation is consistent with the management principle of accomplishing work at the most appropriate level. It also enables the lending function to devote more time to business development.

Furthermore, a professional analysis function helps ensure that all pertinent information has been assembled and evaluated. Often, banks find a separate analytical function is desirable because the direct involvement of lending officers with their customers, while contributing to a more complete understanding of the credit, can lead to the loss of some objectivity.

Thus, it would seen desirable for the smallest bank to have a separate analytical function, even if it is performed by one individual on a part-time basis. And, in those banks with more complex credits, an analyst should have both the uninterrupted time and the technical skills needed for this detailed and and time-consuming work. Also, a specialist is likely to be aware of changes in accounting principles and other factors that may affect financial statement analysis.

Another common answer to the question of who should perform the work is to have the credit analysis function serve as part of credit training or loan officer development programs. In many banks, most credit analysts are in some phase of training; therefore, it is unrealistic to expect their work to equal that of highly trained specialists who make a career of credit analysis. However, with proper supervision and careful selection of tasks, trainees can participate in credit analysis. This involvement not only benefits the trainees but also the lending function as a whole and the entire bank. Some banks have a two-tier analytical staff organization, differentiating between junior and senior analysts, in which senior analysts may be permanent credit department employees or in the advanced phases of training. In smaller banks, the credit department manager often assumes the role of the senior analyst.

Which Loans Should Be Analyzed

Second, it must be determined which loans are to be analyzed. Before a loan is granted, some analysis must be done. Depending on the nature of the loan request, the analysis may be perfunctory or it may be sophisticated and complex. Also, the distribution of lending authority in banks varies widely. This authority can range from the individual lending limit system (loan officers can approve loans within specified lending limits) to committee approval systems (all new loan requests must be considered by committee before approval). Thus, the proper role of credit analysis in a specific bank's environment must be determined by management.

Obviously, loan volume, complexity of the financing under consideration, and staff availability are major factors to be considered in deciding on loan analysis. While it is possible that all loans will be analyzed, it is equally possible to decide that credit analysis should be performed only on certain types of loans.

For example, unsecured lines of credit of $100,000 and over might always be subject to detailed analysis prior to approval. Or if a bank has experienced significant losses in lending to certain industries or with certain types of accommodations, such as accounts receivable financing, these loans might receive top priority.

Procedures should also be formulated to cover analysis of loans that have been extended or renewed. While these functions may be performed by analysts or loan review personnel, it is essential that extensions and renewals are not permitted to slip by the system.

All loan authorization forms, for example, might indicate the number of extensions or renewals that have been made. This information could appear as a notation on the bank's "made and paid" list or other report of loan activity. Frequently, such reports are issued by the note department. The analytical section or the loan review unit might review extensions or renewals that deviate from the agreed-upon repayment schedule and verify they were approved by the proper loan committee or officer(s). Loans that have been extended many times may never appear on the past due list; however, they could prove to be serious problems for the bank. As a rule, lines of credit should be reviewed at least annually.

When to Analyze Loans

Third, it must be determined when loans are to be analyzed. Obviously, there are advantages in fully analyzing a loan situation before extending credit. And many bankers believe it is essential for all analytical work to be completed before funds are advanced. In reality, customer demands, high volume of loan requests, lack of analytical staff, and the need for prompt service may reduce the time available for an in-depth, before-the-fact credit analysis.

Therefore, follow-up credit analysis, performed after the fact, can be used effectively, and some bankers prefer this method. Since the loan has already been made, the pressure associated with reaching a prompt lending decision is gone, and more time is available for in-depth analysis.

Furthermore, many bankers believe loan officers are entitled to approve credits within their lending limits without waiting for other analytical comments. If a follow-up system is used, procedures must be established so that all loans are analyzed within a reasonable time.

In some banks, a combination of both systems will be preferred. For example, in-depth analysis could be required before certain types or dollar amounts of loans can be granted. In other cases, after-the-fact analysis will be permitted. A number of decisions must be made regarding the timing of loan analysis, and they can only be made in view of a particular bank's operations.

Analytical Standards

Fourth, the depth and emphasis of the credit analysis must be considered. For example, a short-term loan that is to be fully secured by highly liquid collateral might not warrant the time involved in preparing four years of spread sheet presentations. On the other hand, loans secured by accounts receivable might merit the time and expense involved in a full investigation and a complete presentation.

The depth of analysis required should probably not be related only to the dollar amount of the loan since many losses on smaller credits can be just as serious as one larger loan loss. Rather, analysis should attempt to define the degree of risk involved in the extension of any credit.

Determining the depth of analysis is also related to availability and expertise of staff, lending authority system used, volume of loans, customer base, and the complexity of various financing arrangements. In some cases, the loan officer may specify the scope of the credit analysis. In other banks, the loan officer, credit department manager, and the analyst may all conduct a cursory analysis of a credit and then reach an agreement on the most suitable analytical approach. If staff size and expertise permit, all credits can be fully analyzed and then selectivity will not be a problem. Generally, this ideal condition does not exist, so some standards of analysis for all credits should be adopted and priorities for certain loan situations identified.

Analyzing Existing Credits

Fifth, procedures should be developed to cover analysis of existing relationships. This aspect of the analytical function is fully discussed in

Chapter 5 under loan quality control. However, it is mentioned here because loan review is sometimes included among the responsibilities of credit analysts.

Establishing Responsibility

Sixth, the reporting responsibilities of the analysis function and the individual analysts must be clearly defined. Basic considerations include defining to whom the analyst reports, who assigns work to the analyst, and how the analyst's summaries or reports are reviewed and distributed. It must be determined whether the analytical function is ultimately the responsibility of the credit department manager, the senior analyst, the senior line officer, or the individual loan officers.

In larger banks, it is possible that specific analysts would be assigned to and would be responsible for working only with certain loan officers. In other banks, all requests for analysis might be initiated by the loan officer and directed to the manager rather than to a specific analyst. The manager may then actually perform the work or assign it to an appropriate analyst. In smaller banks, the only analyst might also be the credit department manager. After the work is completed, it should be reviewed and distributed according to designated procedures, and, again, there are many possibilities to consider.

Many bankers think that the analyst and the loan officer should discuss the preparation of the analytical report. Misunderstandings or disagreements about the significance or interpretation of certain data can often be resolved at this point, and both the loan officer and analyst can benefit from a dialogue that takes place during the evaluation of a credit. Furthermore, the loan officer is better prepared to anticipate and address questions that may be posed by the senior loan officer or a loan committee.

Other bankers may feel it is not prudent for the loan officer to have an opportunity to influence the contents of the report or the interpretation of the financial data. Rather, all the data might be presented to the analyst with limited comment from the loan officer. If there is disagreement, the loan officer should state his or her viewpoint in writing. This is a procedural decision made only after considering how a particular bank perceives the analytical function.

In some banks, the manager or senior analyst reviews the analysis before its release by the credit department. This departmental review is an especially good idea if the analysts are involved in a training program. In other banks, analysts begin distribution on their own initiatives. It may be decided that the completed analysis should be forwarded only to the loan officer involved, the analyst's supervisor, and to the credit file. In other systems, all participants at a loan committee meeting may require a copy of the analysis, and the senior loan officer may wish to review it before the committee meeting.

Whether the loan officers are involved in the preparation of the report, it is a good idea for the analyst to make certain the appropriate loan officer receives the complete document in enough time to prepare for a special meeting, reach a timely decision, and prepare any additional comments.

It must also be determined whether the analyst will attend loan committee meetings to discuss a presentation and whether this attendance is to be automatic or by invitation only. Obviously, credit analysts will sometimes disagree with the conclusions reached by the loan officers, and reporting procedures should attempt to ensure that such differences can be expressed. If the manager or the analyst or both attend loan committee meetings, the probability of a full discussion of all relevant issues increases. By clearly defining reporting responsibilities and procedures, a bank can formulate policies that ensure analysts' reports are available to appropriate personnel. At the same time, these policies can reduce the friction that sometimes occurs when instructions aren't clear and viewpoints and interpretations differ.

Recommendations and Ratings

Seventh, banks must also decide whether analysts are required to reach conclusions, assign ratings, or make recommendations. In some banks, analysts are required to state only facts and offer no opinions. This approach is based on the belief that facts are sufficient for decision-making and that potential conflicts between staff and line personnel will be reduced. Sometimes, analysts are to refrain from offering opinions but have to assign a letter or numerical rating symbol to a credit request. In other systems, analysts are expected to form opinions; offer recommendations for accepting, rejecting, or improving a credit; and provide an overall rating.

Whether analysts make recommendations should depend on the expertise of the analytical staff as well as the bank's preferences. If only junior analysts with limited experience are available, it might be wise to restrict the analysis to factual observations only. If senior professional analysts or advanced trainees are part of the staff, then the analysts and the loan officers may prefer the presentation to include a documented opinion.

Related Functions

Eighth, it may be decided that the credit analysis function should be responsible for reviewing other aspects of the loan portfolio, as they relate to specific borrowers and to the bank's lending posture as a whole. To cite a few illustrations: In addition to studying individual loan situations, the analysis function could be responsible for studying and reporting on profitability and monitoring loan commitments and related use of funds. A credit analyst could monitor, study, and evaluate relevant economic trends. Furthermore, certain analysts may specialize in selected industries and be responsible for analyses in those fields. Also, specific personnel might be in charge of monitoring and explaining to others the relevance of new accounting and reporting procedures as they affect credit analysis.

In summary, if the composition of a bank's loan portfolio and the procedures for approving loans are well defined, it becomes easier to formulate and implement a logical system of credit analysis. The importance of clearly defining the responsibilities and goals of the analytical function cannot be overestimated. This process ensures that all loans are analyzed according to both the lending policy and the credit analysis policy of the bank.

Follow-Up and Control Systems

For a credit analysis system to be effective, it must ensure that all the relationships management wants analyzed are, in fact, analyzed. It may be desirable to have a loan reporting system identify all new loans so that they may be analyzed within a short time. Many banks have daily or weekly reports of new loans. If this is the case, the list should be checked so no new loans escape the analysis system. Also, it may be advisable to devise a "request for credit analysis" form. The loan officer or other authorized person who requests an analysis can provide special instructions and also document the credit files (see Exhibit 4.1).

Furthermore, follow-up systems should be designed so that all credits that need to be analyzed are accounted for. Good control systems should record when a loan analysis was requested or scheduled; the name of the person requesting the analysis; the name of the analyst assigned to complete the project; the planned or required completion date; the actual completion date; and to whom the final analytical report is sent. Follow-up systems can range from a simple file card tickler system to a sophisticated computerized program.

Division of work, as well as monitoring individual progress and performance, is more easily accomplished if adequate control systems exist. Control systems can be used to ensure that an analyst is exposed to a variety of credit situations and industries, and they can also help the supervisor direct selected work to a specialist. Frequently, control systems can highlight potential bottlenecks such as typing, photocopying, or possible "rush" situations. In addition, the systems often help identify the steps that can be taken to solve such problems.

Exhibit 4.1 — Request for Credit Analysis

To:

From:

Date: / /

Subject:

A credit analysis is requested on the above subject in regard to:

☐ existing loan(s)

☐ contemplated loan(s) as follows:

amount:
purpose:

terms:
rate:
source(s) of repayment:

collateral:

guarantees/endorsements:
other:

☐ other purpose, as follows: ____________________

Please provide: ☐ short form analysis ☐ long form analysis

☐ financial statement analysis only ☐ other:

☐ spread sheet for / /

Special instructions:

The completed review is required by / / for distribution to:

The analyst is requested to contact the undersigned by / / to discuss the credit.

____
signature

Selection of Staff

The individual responsible for the analytical function must first determine the tasks to be performed and then how the staffing requirements can be met. Considerations include bank size; budgetary constraints, which do not always correspond to bank size; training requirements; whether the analysis function is assigned to lending officers or to staff; and allocation of time and resources. In selecting personnel to perform credit analysis, individual capabilities and interests must be carefully matched with the realities of the bank's analytical tasks. Furthermore, special consideration should be given to the needs of trainees, while utilizing the skills that they possess.

Although a natural tendency exists to select individuals with strong analytical ability, credit analysis also requires an appropriate combination of personal characteristics and technical skills. As in most banking positions, a willingness and ability to make decisions, as well as accepting the responsibility that goes with those decisions, are required. Credit analysts must be self-motivated, confident, and oriented toward obtaining results; however, these qualities must be blended with a willingness to seek advice, to admit mistakes, to appreciate and attend to details, to be an open-minded listener, and to recognize an acceptable compromise when opinions differ.

The technical skills desirable for a credit analyst or a loan officer may be acquired through formal education, self-education, experience, and training programs. Many banks seek candidates whose educational backgrounds and other experience have provided them with at least a minimum technical background. These skills could then be supplemented by specialized training and in-bank experience. The professional analyst should be willing to devote a reasonable time to independent study because accounting principles and standards do change, thus affecting the interpretation of financial data. Although the subject of training is beyond the scope of this chapter, it should be emphasized that the credit analyst must have a thorough understanding of accounting, finance, and economics and must display a high level of expertise in applying this knowledge. In addition, an understanding and awareness of a bank's policies and objectives are especially important in performing credit analysis, and this area must not be neglected in the analyst's training.

Supervision of the Analytical Function

Personal supervision in the development of credit analysts is important. The effective supervisor should be both a leader and a teacher and might have lending and credit experience. It is essential that he or she understands credit department goals and objectives and develops a good rapport with bank management, the loan officers, and the analysts.

Depending on the size and scope of the bank's analytical function, the manager or senior analyst may be expected to organize the work flow, train analysts and future loan officers, perform the actual analysis, establish sources of information, and submit recurring reports to management. This individual must also evaluate the skills and performance of the staff, including trainees. Within the credit judgment area, the analyst should be evaluated on knowledge of sources of information, as well as abilities to:

- Identify the key elements of the credit
- Evaluate risks
- Reach a supportable and logical conclusion
- Recognize and assume a reasonable risk
- Estimate the borrower's willingness and ability to repay
- Comprehend and present financial data

The analyst should also be evaluated on the thoroughness, accuracy, clarity, and timeliness of the analytical reports. As a part of this evaluation process, there should be a frequent and regular dialogue between supervisor and analyst, especially if the analyst is involved in some phase of training. In addition, the supervisor may provide a written appraisal to help an individual focus on areas which need improvement. Some standards for evaluating analytical reports are presented below.

Evaluating Quality of Analytical Reports

To clarify the evaluation procedures for trainees and others in the analysis function, the supervisor may institute a quality evaluation for credit analysis reports. The standards are valued 1 to 5, with 5 having the highest possible value. The definitions used for the 1-5 numerical classification follow.

Class 5: Analyses of highest quality which explain concisely and completely the purpose of the loan, bank relationship, financial standing, and business development opportunities. These memoranda should require no editing by the supervisor of the analytical function or the loan officer. Obviously, analytical reports rated 5 comprise a relatively small percentage of the total number of presentations. These analyses demonstrate a complete understanding of financial conditions of the company and outline all extraordinary developments. Information contained in these reports helps supplement loan officers' understanding of a company's financial condition, bank relationship, and possible future developments within the company. The reports also focus on improvements that could be made in structuring, securing, or enhancing the information available on the credit.

Class 4: Other sound analyses denoting clear and concise thinking and expression. The difference between a 4 and 5 classification is the amount of in-depth analysis.

Class 3: Reports considered to be adequate but which do not provide any new information. This classification should be considered the average and will be adequate for purposes of documenting the loan request and the credit file.

Class 2: Analytical reports that have omitted one or two major points from the standpoint of financial analysis and exhibit a lack of understanding on the part of the analyst. These memoranda need corrections in order to present a fair picture for future reference.

Class 1: These memoranda are inadequate from the standpoint of financial analysis or business development. These must be redone.

The Analytical Process

The analysis itself will invariably encompass much more information than is put in the final written report. An analysis will usually begin with a review of the credit file and supporting information.

The analyst will then read and spread the financial statements. Although one needs to analyze and question each item on the balance sheet and income statement, naturally, all these items do not have to be included in the written analysis. The analyst must ask: What is significant? What is relevant? What is omitted or overlooked? And any conclusions drawn should be fully supported by the facts. Materials on which the analysis was based must be condensed into a standardized form to save reading time. But the complete information must be readily accessible in the files in sufficient detail so that other personnel can draw their own conclusions or verify the data.

Scope of the Analysis

As a practical matter, the scope of analysis will depend on many factors. Among these are:

1. Form of business organization
2. Borrower's financial condition
3. Amount of the loan request
4. Type and terms of the loan
5. Creditworthiness as demonstrated by the borrowing history
6. Quality and consistency of the data provided by the customer
7. Security, guarantees, or endorsements for the loan, if any
8. Ability to identify borrowers and secure information about them
9. Demonstrated ability and experience of management
10. Acceptability and marketability of the company's product(s) or service(s)
11. Outlook for the company and prospects for its industry, including external factors
12. Quality and quantity of the borrower's customers and suppliers
13. Inconsistencies or events that require investigation

Given these factors, the objective of the credit analysis is to determine or confirm the amount, term, and purpose of the loan; sources of repayment; and the probability that the loan will be repaid as agreed. Obviously, the scope of the analysis will be affected by whether a new or existing relationship is being considered; nevertheless, these and other relevant factors should be considered even when a well-established relationship exists.

Sources of Credit Information

Those in charge of the credit function must ensure that personnel have the necessary support materials and equipment to perform their duties effectively. In addition to financial statements, many other sources of information are normally used in in-depth credit analysis, and the analyst must have access to such information. In-house and external data may be needed to identify the borrower accurately, present a clear picture of the borrower's credit history and ability to repay obligations as agreed, and document that any proposed collateral is, in fact, the property of the borrower. The data also should provide enough information to develop a complete picture of the company, its operations, and its management. The scope of credit analysis requires that sufficient verified and consistent data be available on which to base a decision. And checks need to be made to catch inconsistencies or inadequacies that may affect the credit decision.

The analyst should know how and when to gather additional information and be familiar with sources of many types of information. Even though the analyst may not be directly responsible for certain commercial credit information gathering functions, such as placing credit inquiries with other banks, he or she should be aware of the types of information that can complete or verify a loan request. Some analysts will be responsible for conducting special research projects or analyzing an entire industry from a credit standpoint. The selection and compilation of data require both initiative and familiarity with the information available from various sources.

Gathering Credit Information

There are many sources of commercial credit information, both in the bank and outside. The following sources are described in some detail:

1. Information obtained directly from the borrower
2. Bank and trade checkings
3. Credit reporting agencies
4. Reference materials and periodicals
5. Comparative analysis tools

6. Public records
7. Government agencies
8. Other sources

This list is illustrative only and should not be considered to encompass all available sources of credit information.

Information Directly from the Borrowers

Essential information is obtained directly from management of the borrowing company. Financial statements, credit references, loan proposals, and other necessary data are usually provided by the borrower. In addition, the bank can develop this information by visits to the business operation, in personal interviews, and through discussions with the company's accountant or attorney.

Bank and Trade Checkings

A credit analyst or a credit investigator should make sure that appropriate bank records are checked. These include internal bank records in the case of an existing or previous customer and inquiries made to the borrower's other banks of account. Direct trade checkings should be done both with suppliers of the borrower and on its major customers. The commercial credit exchange function is covered in Chapter 6.

Credit Reporting Agencies

Trade payment information will be found in credit agency reports and can be ordered on a contractual basis. Companies such as Dun & Bradstreet and National Credit Information Service (NACIS) are major agencies that provide commercial credit reports. Regardless of the agencies used by particular banks, the analyst should be thoroughly familiar with the significance of these reports, their strengths and weaknesses, and how to interpret them. Investigative services also provide information on corporations and executives.

Reference Materials and Periodicals

The credit analysis department or the bank's library might accumulate some general reference materials including directories of the "who owns what" type that provide reasonably current biographies of individuals managing various companies. The analyst should also have access to at least one book describing sources of information, usually arranged by industry type. For example, *The Encyclopedia of Associations*, published by Gale Research, could assist the analyst in obtaining information about various industries through the appropriate association. Many other companies, including Dun & Bradstreet, publish reference books that identify a company and its principals, its operations and sales, and financial strength.

Other publications that may be useful in analyzing companies include those designed primarily for use by institutional investors, such as the Standard & Poor's or Moody's manuals for publicly held companies. Many other reference books are available to help analysts study and evaluate specific industries, such as utilities, agriculture, health care, and insurance. Because there are so many sources of information on companies, reference books have been developed solely to assist the analyst in locating appropriate data. For example, *How To Find Information About Companies*, published by Washington Researchers, provides detailed lists of sources including the government, the courts, the private sector, reference books, and a section on foreign companies.

Since some reference books, indexes, and directories are costly and updated frequently, smaller banks may find it more economical to use such materials at the local library. Some states also publish industrial directories and reports with which the librarian may be familiar. A trip to the local library can provide data on principals, plant sites, number of employees, estimated financial strength, bond ratings, annual sales and other figures, subsidiaries, affiliated firms and parent companies, and local economic trends. College or university libraries also have a wealth of information. Analysts should also have several reference books available on financial analysis and accounting. The bibliography at the end of this book more fully identifies some general reference volumes.

Analysts should have access to business newspapers and magazines, daily newspapers, and trade periodicals covering industries important to them. Selected articles from newspapers and magazines should be clipped for reference and filed according to type of industry or subject. Any articles pertaining to a particular customer should be placed in that customer's credit file. Articles that relate to interpretation of financial data should be circulated to all the credit analysts.

Comparative Analysis Tools

Robert Morris Associates publishes the *Annual Statement Studies* which contains financial data for over 300 lines of business engaged in manufacturing, wholesaling, retailing, services, and contracting. Financial statement data on each industry are shown in common size form and are accompanied by widely used ratios. The *Annual Statement Studies* also contains a useful bibliography of other sources of composite financial data which may be ordered from the respective publishers. For example, the bibliography includes Dun & Bradstreet's *Key Business Ratios in 125 Lines, Cost of Doing Business—Corporations*, and *Cost of Doing Business—Proprietorships and Partnerships*. It also mentions the *Almanac of Business and Industrial Ratios*, published annually by Prentice-Hall. The bibliography also encompasses many industry groups, such as apparel manufacturers, retail grocers, and mortgage bankers to name a few, which publish statistics of great value to the analyst.

Public Records

Credit analysts should be thoroughly familiar with the information in public records. The credit analyst should know how to order and interpret searches, understand the significance of litigation bulletins, and be able to ascertain what filings have been made in accordance with the Uniform Commercial Code. Competent analysts should also be familiar with procedures involving such special situations as liens on yachts and airplanes.

Government Agencies

The Small Business Administration, the U.S. Department of Commerce, state departments of commerce, health departments, and many regulatory agencies offer publications and resource materials of interest. For example, the Securities and Exchange Commission in Washington maintains many documents filed by companies that sell stock to the public. Copies of these documents are available to the public and include Form 10-K, Form 10-Q, and Form 8-K. In addition, the IRS permits examination of returns filed by nonprofit organizations. The Superintendent of Documents, U.S. Government Printing Office, Washington, DC 20402, provides publications on many subjects. Publications are listed in various subject bibliographies, and most are inexpensive, although cost varies with the publication. For example, the subject bibliography on *Banks and Banking* is free of charge.

Other Sources

Other sources of information include such groups as banking associations, certified public accounting firms, insurance agencies, and bonding companies; documents such as appraisals and contracts; economic bulletins issued by banks, business firms, and the government; and various legal journals and bulletins issued by the bank's legal department or prepared by bank counsel.

Compiling an Inventory

No one analyst can know all sources of information in detail; therefore, it will be useful if the analysis function as a whole maintains an inventory of credit information sources. The completed inventory, which lists the information resources used by the bank, should reflect the collective knowledge, experience, and evaluation of the loan officers and the analysts. It should be updated periodically and should promote knowledge of available sources and their efficient and uniform use. If the list is maintained properly, it will also pinpoint sources which are frequently inaccurate, superfluous, or not worth the cost.

The Credit Analysis Format

Every bank should develop formats or outlines for preparing analytical reports. A standard format facilitates consistent presentations and serves as a checklist to help the analyst cover all major areas. Credit analysis formats can also be used by the loan officer to assist in compiling the information to make a sound credit decision. In fact, some forms could be used as an application for credit in the initial loan interview. A copy of the completed analysis should be placed in the credit file to give a complete picture of the credit transaction to senior management, loan review personnel, credit investigators, and new loan officers who may be assigned responsibility for the account. It may be advisable for a bank to develop two basic formats, one a short form, the other a long form.

Short Form

The short form can be used for preliminary analysis, analytical reviews of requests for renewals of well-established, acceptable credits, or as a time-saving cover sheet for presentations to loan committees. A long form attached would provide more detail. An example of a concise loan presentation summary form is presented as Exhibit 4.2. A sample of a completed brief outline is presented as Exhibit 4.3.

Long Form

In the case of new borrowing relationships, complex credits, or troublesome situations, a very detailed credit analysis format may be preferable. The following is a suggested outline for developing a long form analysis presentation.

1. Cover sheet
2. Debt sheet
3. Services used form
4. Background of the company
5. Spread sheet and pro forma projections
6. Company conditions, both operating and financial
7. Customer profitability analysis
8. Bank debt and the total relationship
9. Collateral, documentation, and policy
10. Optional special section for unusual situations

11. Strengths, weaknesses, and the proposed plan
12. Summary and recommendations
13. Exhibits as required

Exhibit 4.2 — Loan Presentation Summary

1. DATE: ____
2. OFFICER: ____

3. NAME: ____
4. ADDRESS: ____
5. LINE OF BUSINESS: ____
6. MANAGEMENT: ____
7. LENGTH OF TIME IN BUSINESS: ____ 8. UNDER PRESENT MANAGEMENT: ____
9. FORM OF BUSINESS: ____ 10. DATE ACCOUNT OPENED: ____
11. AMOUNT OF REQUEST: $ ____
12. TYPE: ____
13. RATE (INCL. FEES): ____
14. COMPENSATING BALANCE REQUIREMENTS: ____
15. EFFECTIVE DATE: ____ 16. MATURITY DATE: ____
17. IF SECURED, DESCRIBE: ____
18. IF ENDORSED OR GUARANTEED, DESCRIBE: ____
19. TOTAL CREDIT: ____
20. PURPOSE OF LOAN: ____
21. REPAYMENT PROGRAM & SOURCE: ____
22. BORROWING HISTORY: ____
23. BALANCES: ____
24. OTHER: ____

FINANCIAL STATEMENT REVIEW

25. AUDITOR: ____
26. OPINION: ____
27. FISCAL DATE: ____
28. STATEMENTS: ____
29. COMMENTS: ____
30. APPROVED: ____ 31. DATE: ____

Robert Morris Associates, Form No. C-129
Carried in Stock by Cadwallader & Johnson, Inc., 5170 Northwest Highway, Chicago, Illinois 60630
312/286-4500

Exhibit 4.3 — A Sample Format for an Analytical Report (Completed)

Loan Summary Sheet

Branch main **Loan Officer** T. Smith **Analyst** M. Richards **Date** 2/25/X8

Loan Request Details

Date funds required	Amount of loan
3/10/X8	$25,000
Term	**Rate**
120 Days	Prime + 1½
Fee	**Rating**
N/A	B+

1. **Full Name** George's Garden Supply Co., Inc.

   Address 472 East Street

   Phila., PA 19002

   (SIC No. 5261)

2. **Form of Organization (identify related companies)** Closely held corporation; incorporated 19X6. No related companies

3. **Purpose of Loan** To purchase spring inventory — garden equipment, fertilizer, nursery stock, etc.

4. **Repayment Plan(s)** Through sale of inventory. (Note prior year's retained earnings and limited guarantee.)

5. **Renewal Instructions** One 90-day renewal permitted without approval of committee. No additional advances of funds permitted.

6. **Endorsers/Guarantors** George H. Kaiser, President

   Amount Limited personal guarantee of $15,000

7. **Collateral**

	Type	Appraisal/Valuation	Prior Liens
Applicable To this Request	N/A		
Applicable To	N/A		

8. **Deposit Balances**

   Demand Deposits **One-Year Average Book** $8,241 **Average Collected** $5,430 **ODS** 1

   Time Deposits $5,000 corporate CD

   Related Accounts Personal checking—one-year average collected $934

   New Accounts to be Opened N/A (approach for truck leasing)

continued

Exhibit 4.3 continued

9. **Loan Data**

		Type	Date Made	Original Amount
Amount this Loan Request	$25,000	120 day note		
All Other Loans Outstanding (itemize)	$ 6,100	term loan	10/X7	$ 6,850
Total Direct Loans	$31,100			
Contingent Liabilities				
Total Liabilities	$31,100			

10. **Loan History**
High Credit $10,000 **Date** 5/X7 **Customer Since** 3/X7
Date of Last Clean Up on Line: **From** N/A **To**

11. **Financial Statement of** George's Garden Supply Co., Inc.
Date: From 1/1/X7 **To** 12/31/X8 **Preparer:** Geo. Little, CPA
Opinion Expressed "clean" opinion
(Spread Sheets Attached)

12. **Comments** Reasonable request and acceptable risk despite drop in net profits last fiscal.

13. **Reviewed in Credit Department by** M. Richards
(signature)

This format could be used for a brief analytical report or used as a cover sheet for an in-depth review. The major topics in this format could also be used to develop an outline of the essential components of an in-depth analysis. In this example, the form is completed in a concise manner to provide highlights without detailed written commentary.

Cover Sheet

The purpose of a cover sheet is to summarize pertinent information. It should provide the name of the company, its principal officers, the profitability rating of the account, a summary of the borrowing relationship, and the dates and types of financial information provided and should also cite security or guarantees for the loan. An example of a cover sheet format is presented as Exhibit 4.4.

Debt Sheet

A debt sheet may be included to outline each borrowing relationship, state the compensating balance requirement if any, indicate usage of lines of credit, and report any contingent liabilities to the bank, letters of credit, or open commitments. An example of a debt sheet is presented as Exhibit 4.5

Services Used Form

The analyst may complete a form of the type shown as Exhibit 4.6 to summarize the bank services used by a customer and pinpoint those services that could be developed in future officer calls. It is possible both the marketing and the lending functions would benefit from a services used form.

Company Background

This section should briefly describe what the company does and its history. Topics such as products, market, pricing, competition, and other related subjects would be pertinent, as well as mention of any significant changes in company management or operation. Management's experience and the bank's assessment of management's ability to run the company satisfactorily should be discussed. The analyst should avoid restating material on the cover sheet or giving an unduly long company history, especially if it is already in the credit files.

Exhibit 4.4 — Credit Analysis Cover Sheet

Name/Address of Company: Date:

Loan Officer:

Type of Organization:

Principal Officers:

Operating Since:

Profitability Rating:

Borrowing Summary (indicate amount and date of high credit):

Financial Information Provided:
- Period(s) covered:
- Type of statement:
- Accounting firm:
- Opinion:

Amount, Purpose, and Terms of Proposed Loan:

Collateral/Guarantees, Endorsements:

Exhibit 4.5 — Debt Sheet

Date:
Name of Customer:

Detail of Commercial Loan(s) Outstanding:	**Loan #1**	**Loan #2**	**Loan #3**
Type of loan/facility			
Date made			
Original amount			
Loan balance/amount in use			
Term			
Rate			
Maturity date			
Amount past due			
Date of last payment			
Amount paid — principal			
Amount paid — interest			
Collateral			
Guarantees/endorsements			
If line, date of last clean up			

Commercial Loans Outstanding (itemize):	**Total Current Debt**	**Total Long Term Debt**	**Total Debt to Bank**
1.	$	$	$
2.			
3.			
Total Installment Debt:			
Total Lease Obligations:			
Overdrafts:			
Other (describe):	______	______	______
	$ ______	$ ______	$ ______

Contingent Liabilities (itemize for company, principals, related companies):	**Total Contingent Liability**
1.	$
2.	
3.	______
	$______

Unused Commitments (itemize all commitments including lines of credit or portions of lines available):	**Total Unused Commitments**
1.	$
2.	
3.	______
	$______

Exhibit 4.6 — Services Used

Customer: ______________________ Savings Account Number

______________________ Checking Account Number

Related Accounts

Date:

Date of Last Officer Call:

Commercial Services	Used	Discussed	Comments
Loans:			
Commercial			
Real estate			
Construction			
Line of credit			
A/R financing			
Small business term			
SBA			
Leasing			
Other			
Deposits:			
Demand			
Savings			
Certificates			
Tax account			
Other			
Other Services:			
Trust services			
Safe deposit/vault			
Other			
Consumer Services Used by Principals:			
Loans			
Deposits			
Other			

Spread Sheet

The nature of the presentation should help the analyst determine the number of years that the spread sheet should cover and whether year-end spread sheets, interim spread sheets, or both are appropriate. Any pro forma projections should follow the spread sheet.

Company Condition

Major changes in the company's basic operating condition should be discussed. Mention should be made of unique characteristics, operating or financial, that make this company successful or unsuccessful. In this section, the type and quality of financial statements that were analyzed may be discussed. Important accounting assumptions and practices, or any deviation from previous practice, should be outlined.

A complete analytical report must include a written financial analysis to clarify and enlarge on the figures as spread. The primary purpose of the written financial statement analysis is to investigate and clarify any confusing aspects of the figures. It should also identify any pertinent information not apparent in studying the spread sheet but which may be significant in overall credit decision-making. The experienced analyst's skills are tested in this work, for the qualitative and quantitative aspects of the financial data must be considered. The qualitative aspects, of course, include the timeliness and the source of the statistics and reports. Credit analysts should be wary of making assumptions on the basis of stale or unverified data.

A written analysis of the major items on the balance sheet, income statement, and other financial data should be included. It is not sufficient to point out that figures are high, low, better, or worse than the previous year's figures. The analyst should study the numbers and, when relevant, attempt to explain why changes occurred, why the changes are important to the analysis, and how they affect the company. The challenge facing the analyst is to extract as much relevant information as possible about the company's operation from the financial statements. This may seem obvious, but too often the analyst seems to forget that the company, not the statements, is being analyzed. Once the review of the balance sheet, income statement, and other financial data is completed, the analyst should then proceed to discuss the source of funds, use of funds, and other aspects of the statement, including significant changes in net worth.

Another important factor to consider is cash flow analysis. If the borrower has submitted a pro forma cash flow statement or other type of forecast, the analyst should test and report on whether the projections are realistic. A pro forma cash flow statement is an essential tool to assist the analyst in evaluating the borrower's ability to repay.

Finally, cross-sectional industry analysis could be performed to determine whether the company differs significantly from others in the industry either in method of operation or in financial condition. The analyst should endeavor to explain any unusual variations from so-called industry norms.

Customer Profitability Analysis

This section highlights the average borrowings, average collected balances, interest and fee income, and all expenses of the relationship to determine loan profitability and return on funds. It is important for a bank to develop a standardized format for customer profitability analysis so that the same benchmarks may be used in evaluating loans and setting rates, fees, and compensating balances accordingly. A format for loan profitability analysis is presented in Chapter 5.

Bank Debt and the Total Relationship

This section should be the focus of the credit analysis. It includes a statement of the purpose of the debt. It attempts to determine whether the bank can be repaid. It also analyzes the methods by which the bank can be repaid and when and with what degree of certainty. Thus, this section tries to evaluate the risk inherent in the lending situation. In the case where loans to an existing customer are already on the books, this part of the analysis might consider whether the bank's previous method of financing was appropriate. Has the bank lent the company too much money or not enough in the past? Is the bank now considering a short-term loan when long-term financing is required? Have the terms of repayment been correctly chosen? In short, will the company be "banked" properly?

The analyst might next consider whether additional funds will be required in the near future, for what purposes they might be required, and the amount the company will probably need. The analyst should also consider whether the bank will be willing to extend more credit and the form that the loans would take.

The analyst should then consider whether the bank is being adequately compensated for the total relationship. The customer profitability analysis should be reviewed in relation to the exposure and the risk taken by the bank.

Collateral, Documentation, and Policy

This section must be developed according to the bank's policy on the credit analysis function. In some banks, analysts will only consider the type of collateral and its adequacy for the purposes of risk evaluation; they will not review documentation or verify availability or existence of the collateral in question. Frequently, verification of collateral and documentation are functions of the loan review or other quality control sections. However, in other banks it may be necessary or desirable for the analysts to incorporate a detailed collateral and documentation review in their reports.

In any event, the analyst must determine the adequacy of the security for the loan and either state that collateral is satisfactory or offer suggestions for its improvement. Analysts may also be charged with reviewing or even suggesting proposed loan agreements and evaluating the loan's conformity with bank lending policy.

Questions involving compliance with the various laws, including usury laws, and federal regulations affecting extensions of credit may also be raised by the analyst. Because most regulations are complex, some analytical reports could be forwarded to the compliance officer for review. Again, bank policy should clearly delineate the responsibility for monitoring these highly technical areas.

Optional Special Section

If appropriate to the analysis, this part can be used to discuss economic conditions, both past and projected; major regulatory or accounting changes which may affect the company; recent industry trends; the effects of various energy problems and needs; and any other items that affect the bank's position in relation to its customer.

Strengths and Weaknesses

This part of the report should outline the major strengths and weaknesses of the credit. It could provide an operating plan for future handling of an existing loan. Also, this section could identify those conditions under which additional funds might be advanced or steps taken to protect the bank from facing an unfavorable situation.

Summary and Recommendation

This section allows the analyst to summarize the analysis of the credit. It provides a place to restate important facts or reach conclusions concerning the bank's method of handling the relationship, the company's basic condition, and the profitability of the relationship. No factual information should be included in the summary that is not presented in the body of the report. Comments should focus on the major issues that concern the company and the bank's relationship.

It is also important that responsibility for the report be established. By signing the document, those who actually prepared the analysis indicate they are satisfied that the information is accurate and adequate and that the conclusions drawn represent their views. The conclusions of the credit analyst as expressed in the presentation may differ from those of the loan officer. If so, the account officer may choose to comment in rebuttal. Those who prepare or recommend the presentation indicate by their signatures that they consider the information to be accurate and adequate. If this is not the case, the presentation should clearly state that a decision was reached or deferred on the basis of incomplete information.

Reviewing the Report

Before distributing the analytical report, the analyst should take some time to review its contents for accuracy, clarity, and thoroughness. While conducting this final review, these 11 basic questions should be kept in mind:

1. Does the purpose of the loan seem satisfactory? Is it legitimate, reasonable, and well defined?
2. Do the proposed sources of repayment seem realistic?
3. Is the company's form of organization understood? Has the report established whether the applicant is a proprietorship, partnership, limited partnership, corporation, holding company, etc.? If affiliates, parent companies, or subsidiaries are involved, is their relationship to the borrowing entity clear?
4. Is the borrower's line of business sufficiently understood by the analyst? Were the statements read with sufficient knowledge of the practices followed by the industry under consideration?
5. What types of financial statements were presented? Do they support the request? Are projections available? Are they realistic?
6. If collateral is involved, what is its condition and estimated liquidation value? What lien position would the bank have? Is insurance in order?
7. Would the loan be consistent with bank policy and regulatory and statutory requirements?
8. Were sufficient sources of information used to confirm and complete the borrower's credit history and investigate industry trends?
9. Are any significant pieces of information or documentation missing?
10. Is the loan rating appropriate to the risk involved?
11. Is any written commentary unnecessarily verbose or confusing?

If the analyst is uncomfortable with the answers to any of these questions, the report should not be released until an attempt has been made to resolve points of confusion. Any matters that remain unresolved at the time the analysis must be distributed should be itemized in the report.

Summary

This chapter has discussed organization, staffing, analytical processes, and formats important to the credit analysis function. As indicated, the analysis function seeks to support the loan officers and loan committees by providing all information relevant to credit evaluation. Credit analyses should be accurate, thorough, timely, logical, concise, and well written. Whether the analysis function is performed by loan officers, one part-time analyst, or a large staff, the importance of the function to the decision-making, record-keeping, and training processes of the bank cannot be overestimated. If the analytical function is properly organized and staffed and if the analyst's responsibilities are clearly defined, the professional analytical reports that result should be reflected in the high quality of a bank's loan portfolio.

5

Loan Quality Control and Compliance Functions

The core of a bank's various loan quality control functions will normally be found in the credit analysis area. These functions, such as loan rating and profitability analysis, are performed in the preparation of the credit department's analytical work and reports. Naturally, credit analysis can be expanded to incorporate as many quality control points and procedures as desired; it may also be broadened to include evaluating the composition of the bank's loan portfolio as well as the individual loan.

A sound loan quality control program begins with the initial credit analysis and extends to an ongoing loan review system. Many procedures and decisions involved in the analysis of new credits also provide valuable information for performing loan review. However, the objectives of these two functions are different. In credit analysis, the goal is to provide the loan officer with data to support his or her decision. In loan review, the objective is to monitor and maintain the quality of the existing loan portfolio.

In many banks, the credit department staff will be expected to perform various quality control functions. In fact, the analysts in moderate-size banks may be expected to change hats and perform the functions of a loan review department when evaluating existing credits. As bank size increases, however, it usually becomes both necessary and preferable to assign specific quality control duties to selected departments or individuals. By doing so, control points, objectivity, and staff expertise in certain areas can be increased.

Regardless of who oversees the quality control procedures, all managers should consider the importance of establishing and using some key control functions. They should also decide which functions can and should be incorporated into credit department responsibilities. Furthermore, the credit department manager and bank management must consider the cost-benefit relationships of various aspects of quality control. The more control points or greater depth of review performed, the higher the cost of loan administration. Responsibilities must be clearly delineated so that any overlap or duplication in control procedures is the result of conscious selection and planning, not chance.

Since loan quality control procedures may be performed in several areas of the bank, it is imperative that the credit department manager know what functions are performed in other areas and who is responsible for their performance. When other areas are involved, the credit department manager will almost invariably find this will complicate scheduling of credit work. Therefore, communications must be maintained to keep all the departments apprised of activity which may significantly affect their work loads.

Key Aspects of Quality Control

The following procedures are basic to loan and portfolio quality control, whether they are assigned as part of credit analysis work or as a completely separate function such as loan review. The duties may be performed within or outside the credit department. Where they are undertaken is secondary, however. What is more vital is that these basic controls are instituted, the areas of responsibility are defined, and suitable reports are made available to appropriate parties.

Recognizing that a number of quality control and compliance responsibilities must be assigned to specific individuals, the manager must make some decisions. He or she must consider what tasks are to be performed, how they relate to the credit department, and the procedures by which other departments performing credit-related functions will provide information to the credit area.

Conformity to Bank Policy

A written loan policy constitutes one of the basic tools used in loan quality control. Without such a policy, loan quality control is a much more difficult task. Every bank should adopt a written loan policy that establishes:

- Individual lending authority
- Procedures for the credit approval process
- Lending strategies, including definition of types and terms of desirable and undesirable loans
- Definition of the bank's market area
- Pricing policies and other matters

All loans should be reviewed for compliance with loan policy and to ensure proper approval procedures were followed. Reports may be generated at this point that provide management with a clear picture of, and state any known reasons for, deviations from accepted standards. The individuals who monitor compliance with loan policy may be requested to compile reports of any loans that do not meet policy standards; furthermore, the same individuals may maintain reports of loans by categories—geographical area, industry type, dollar amount, or maturity date. These reports may also include descriptions of types, terms, and rates of loans.

This kind of reporting, of course, enables management to identify concentrations of loans to a specific industry or area and to assist in the analysis of liquidity as affected by maturity schedules. Such data are often prepared so that they may be retrieved in different modes through the use of computer programs. Each bank must determine the types of reports that should be prepared and designate specific parties to receive them. Another basic decision here involves determining whether loans should be analyzed for compliance with loan policies before or after the credit has been extended.

Documentation and Collateral Controls

Someone in the bank must review loan documentation and inspect collateral to make certain documentation is in order and that collateral valuation is current and accurate. The responsibility for reviewing loan documentation may be assigned to in-house legal counsel or a specialist. Naturally, trainees or other personnel may be responsible for basic functions such as pricing securities held as collateral. However, although trainees should learn documentation and collateral evaluation procedures, the final control should rest with an experienced person.

While no bank should plan to look to collateral for loan repayment, the numerous instances of inadequate documentation contributing to loan losses underscore the importance of this function. Someone in the bank must also ensure that margin requirements are met, insurance policies are current and the amounts are adequate, and Uniform Commercial Code filings are updated. While in some banks these functions may be performed by a special unit, such as the note department, procedures must be in effect to promptly inform appropriate parties, such as analysts and loan officers, of any deficiencies.

Concerning accurate collateral evaluation, banks often require timely and accurate appraisals. Someone in the bank should fully understand real estate and other valuation techniques and establish a working relationship with several reliable appraisers.

Compliance with Loan Agreements

Many loans are subject to various affirmative or negative covenants that are detailed in loan agreements. These agreements should be reviewed as often as necessary to verify that there has been compliance with all covenants. Where violations are noted, appropriate action should be initiated to ensure they are corrected. Since a loan can sometimes be called, the rate increased, or other measures taken if a violation occurs, the importance of the timely performance of this function is clear. Events of default should also be identified and monitored so that prompt action may be taken.

One useful device in monitoring loan agreements is to place a cover sheet in the credit file, or the loan agreement file, that specifies the affirmative and negative covenants and the events of default as set forth in the agreement or the note. An example of such a form is presented as Exhibit 5.1. The individual who monitors compliance with loan agreements may also keep a log citing violations of covenants. This may be accomplished quite easily by filling in a sheet of the type presented as Exhibit 5.2.

By keeping a date log of violations over a period of time, compliance can be monitored as often as necessary, and repeated violations will stand out. Bank policy, the individual loan situation, and the seriousness of any violation will assist in determining what action is to be taken. Reporting procedures should be instituted to keep all appropriate parties informed.

Profitability Analysis

The bank must define who is responsible for analyzing the profitability of accounts. If a standard formula has been adopted for profitability analysis, one person could perform this task, perhaps assisted by a computer program if the bank is large enough to warrant the expense. It is possible to design basic formulas for calculating profitability so that one person can quickly process a large volume of credits or several individuals can apply the same formula independently and achieve consistent results. An example of a basic, effective method of analyzing profitability is presented as Exhibit 5.3.

Furthermore, a bank could arrange for complex profitability analysis to be performed by computer time-sharing. Whatever method is used, it is important that the profitability calculation be standardized so that all personnel will understand the significance of the resulting yield indexes. In addition, required or compensating balances must be monitored periodically as must the receipt of any fees in connection with credit extensions or commitments. Banks may wish to evaluate all profitability reports periodically for marketing and other purposes, including identification of the types of customers and services that are, in general, most satisfactory to the bank.

Exhibit 5.1 — Cover Sheet-Loan Agreement Summary

Customer: ______________________ Loan Number(s): ______________

Date of Agreement: ______________________ Loan Officer: ______________

Frequency of Review Required: ______________

A. **Affirmative Covenants:**
1.
2.
3.
4.
5.
6.

B. **Negative Covenants:**
1.
2.
3.
4.
5.
6.

C. **Defaults:**

Events:
1.
2.
3.
4.
5.
6.

Remedies:

Exhibit 5.2 — Loan Agreement Follow-Up

Customer: ______________________________ Loan Number(s): __________

Date of Agreement: __________

Affirmative Covenants (Refer to Loan Agreement Summary Sheet)
Indicate "C" for compliance and "N" for noncompliance

Date																	
A 1																	
A 2																	
A 3																	
A 4																	
A 5																	
A 6																	

Negative Covenants (same as above)

Date																	
B 1																	
B 2																	
B 3																	
B 4																	
B 5																	
B 6																	

Defaults (indicate "D" for default)

Date																	
C 1																	
C 2																	
C 3																	
C 4																	
C 5																	
C 6																	

Compliance with Regulations and Laws

The nation's banks are subject to many laws, rules, and regulations that substantially govern how they operate. Many of these rules are issued as regulations by the Board of Governors of the Federal Reserve System under power vested in them by the Federal Reserve Act and other laws. Certain regulations directly affect commercial credit granting procedures. For example, Regulation U covers extensions of stock-secured credit for the purpose of purchasing or carrying margin stocks.

Since the enactment of the Consumer Credit Protection Act in 1968, the banking industry has faced a virtual flood of consumer credit legislation. Therefore, credit department managers must be sure their departments are aware that some of this legislation goes beyond consumer credit and affects commercial credit granting practices and pro-

Exhibit 5.3 — Profitability Analysis

This formula is provided only as an example of a method that worked well for a particular bank. Each bank should develop a program suited to its own needs and purposes.

Name: JHK Company

Period: 1/1/X8 to 12/31/X9

Loan Officer: F. Timbrooke

Average Deposit-Book	$77,331
Average Deposit-Collected	49,220
Average Loans Outstanding	51,595
Loan Grade(s)	A
Revenue:	
1. Interest Earned on Loans	$ 5,675
2. Earnings Credit on Collected Deposits (at 90-day Treasury Bill rate 9%)*	4,430
3. Other	N/A
4. Total Revenue	10,105
Costs:	
5. Deposit Activity Cost	$ 906
6. Loan Handling and Officer Time	858
7. Other	N/A
8. Total Cost	1,764

Yield = Revenue Less Costs ÷ Average Loan Outstanding

$$\frac{\$10{,}105 - \$1{,}764}{\$51{,}595} = 16.2\%$$

(*Readers are reminded that the Treasury Bill rate changes frequently. The rate used in this exhibit is for illustrative purposes only.)

This method of analyzing profitability is based on one developed by the Central Carolina Bank in Durham, North Carolina. Basically, revenues received from a commercial customer are added, costs associated with generating those revenues are subtracted, and the difference is compared with the customer's average outstanding loans.

---

cedures. For example, the Equal Credit Opportunity Act, implemented by Regulation B, applies to all credit, both consumer and commercial, with some specific exemptions granted for business credit. Regulation Z, or Truth in Lending, must be complied with if an accommodation loan is made in the commercial credit department. Various state laws are frequently as strong or stronger than federal laws; interest and usury rules are primarily matters of state law, and someone must verify adherence to the controlling statutes.

The *Comptroller's Handbook for Consumer Examinations* contains some excellent suggestions and observations which would be applicable to any bank, state or national. For example, Section 1.5 of the *Handbook* states: "Compliance with consumer laws can only be accomplished by the Board of Directors and bank management acting together to adopt written policies and procedures. Proper internal control programs to insure compliance with all federal and state consumer laws cannot be overemphasized in the examiner's review with management." Furthermore, the *Handbook* states that "to minimize the potential for loss, the bank should designate an officer to insure compliance with consumer laws and regulations and with its written policies."

The importance of establishing a control point for monitoring compliance with various laws, rules, and regulations is obvious. Still, the relevance of this function to the satisfactory performance of the commercial loan unit is often overlooked. Unless compliance with various statutes is achieved by every bank employee in all cases, total compliance cannot be achieved by the bank. Periodic reports on the state of compliance should be made to the board of directors. The compliance officer should also be responsible for keeping loan officers and other bank employees informed of developments in this important area.

Loan Review Function

If a bank is small or staff size is limited, the analysis function that is described in Chapter 4 may encompass virtually all the loan quality control activities, including loan review. Some specific control areas, such as reviewing documentation and compliance with laws and regulations, are quite technical and require particular skills. Therefore, specialists hired or trained within the credit department may be needed to perform these functions.

However, as the bank's portfolio grows in size and diversity, it becomes difficult to maintain an ongoing evaluation of portfolio quality and composition. Therefore, throughout the banking industry, the development of an independent loan review function is becoming more important.

The first separation of loan quality control responsibilities usually means establishing an independent loan review section or unit. The loan review function may be performed by a unit within the credit department. However, some banks, particularly larger ones, may create an autonomous loan review department, completely separate from the credit area. While the credit analysis function services the information needs of loan officers, loan review is expected to be both objective and critical of the loan itself.

Organization

There are many possibilities for organizing the loan review function in a bank. The function may be supervised by the credit department manager or consist solely of one full- or part-time loan review officer. It could also fall under the responsibilities of the audit department, or it could be a large and highly specialized unit that reports directly to the president or the executive committee.

If the credit department manager is responsible for supervising or actually performing the loan review function, the following basic questions must be addressed:

- What are the objectives of a loan review?
- What should be the scope of the loan review operation?
- To whom is the unit responsible?
- What reports should be prepared?
- Will there be loan review meetings to discuss findings with management and loan officers?
- Who will staff the unit?

Obviously, as in the credit analysis function, all these organizational and operational aspects and more must be considered in view of a specific bank's loan portfolio and its staff size and expertise. But some general considerations apply to all loan review units.

Objectives

Broadly stated, there are five objectives of loan review:

1. Ensuring that bank lending policies are adhered to
2. Identifying actual or potential problem loans as soon as possible
3. Indicating what action is needed to correct problems promptly
4. Providing management with knowledge of the quality and structure of the loan portfolio
5. Enabling management to ascertain the adequacy of the bank's loan loss reserves and of the bank's capital.

Scope of Loan Review

The appropriate scope of a loan review program that will accomplish these five primary objectives must then be determined. Obviously, the scope of the loan review responsibilities will be affected by cost and staffing factors as well as by the size and condition of the loan portfolio. Basic considerations include determining which loans will be reviewed, when they will be reviewed, and the specific duties to be performed. In some banks, a review of all loans may not be feasible;

other banks will decide that all loans must be reviewed at least annually, with problem loans receiving more frequent attention. If the composition of a bank's portfolio is analyzed, it then becomes easier to formulate and implement a logical system of loan review that considers desirability, feasibility, and necessity. A report listing the number, dollar amount, repayment status, and types of commercial loan relationships in a bank will assist in organizing the function.

After the process of identifying the composition of the portfolio is completed, it may be determined that all loans can be reviewed at least once a year. Or it may be determined that priorities must be established in view of loan volume and staffing. Perhaps a minimum dollar limit on the size of relationships to be fully reviewed can be set. Or loans that have had a certain number of extensions or are past due could receive top priority.

In some banks, the complexity of the financing arrangement will indicate how often a review is required. The determination of which loans should be reviewed, and how often, may also be influenced by the bank's unfavorable experiences with certain types of loans. Another factor that might be considered in establishing priorities is the type of collateral, if any, securing the loan.

While each bank's loan review priorities will be unique, every logically organized loan review system should start by analyzing the core information in the active loan portfolio. This system should be designed to include all new loans so that they will be properly scheduled for review and to eliminate promptly those loans that have been paid out or transferred to other loan departments.

Next, the specific duties to be performed in the loan review program must be identified. Some loan review departments will be responsible for a variety of quality control functions. These range from the evaluation of each loan from a risk analysis standpoint to the analysis of and reporting on the composition of a bank's loan portfolio as a whole.

Within specified limits, the loan review function may be required to review all loans in the bank, grade them individually, and then evaluate the entire portfolio in terms of trends, concentrations, profitability, and risk. Obviously, some of the credit analysts' work will be duplicated in the loan review process, but the viewpoints of those performing loan review should be different. And the opinions expressed and the recommendations made may be reported to different levels of management.

When evaluating an individual credit, the unit will normally be expected to review the complete credit and collateral files. The loan review function is usually responsible for a thorough study of documentation, evaluation of collateral, and financial statement analysis. The areas which are frequently included under loan review responsibilities are enumerated in Exhibit 5.4. While the list is not all-inclusive, it points out some less glamorous—but nonetheless important—duties performed by the loan review unit.

The grading and rating of individual loans on a consistent basis are often a loan review function. There are many types of loan grading systems in use, and two samples are presented as Exhibits 5.5 and 5.6. The establishment of a well-defined rating system will have loan pricing and frequency of review implications.

Furthermore, identifying standards against which credits can be measured or evaluated helps eliminate conflicts between line and staff functions. It is one thing for loan review personnel to form a subjective opinion or to reach no conclusion at all. However, if the loan review staff can point toward objective criteria for credit evaluation, the presentation is likely to be more favorably received and more useful.

Responsibility and Authority

Persons engaged in loan review should have the freedom to form independent opinions. Therefore, they should not report to the individuals whose loans are being reviewed. Ideally, the person who is responsible for the loan review program should have complete authority to administer an autonomous function. This person should report as directly as possible to senior management, to a special loan or executive committee, or to the bank's board of directors. Each bank must also determine the weight that the recommendations made by loan review personnel will have in managing the loan portfolio. And each bank must recognize the importance of management support for the objectives of the unit.

Whoever is ultimately responsible for the performance of loan review must be in a position of authority. Then opinions and recommendations made by qualified loan review staff will not be overlooked or potentially hazardous situations neglected. The loan review unit may also be responsible for recommending that loans be referred to a workout unit, legal counsel, or the appropriate loan officer for restructuring or collection.

Even though a bank may create a special review function, the ongoing credit administration responsibilities of the loan officers should continue to be recognized. The officer who makes or administers a credit also has an obligation to identify and act on a troublesome situation. Although the loan review unit should not report to the loan officers, it does have a responsibility to notify the appropriate officer as

Exhibit 5.4 — A Loan Review Checklist

The areas that a loan review unit frequently attempts to cover when evaluating an existing credit are listed below. All loan review units will not be required to perform every function listed, while other units' duties will exceed those enumerated here. Nevertheless, most of these procedures should be performed by all loan review departments.

A. **Evaluation of Credit Quality** — Including analysis of:
   1. Ability and willingness to meet loan obligations to the bank as agreed
   2. Handling of other bank relationships such as checking accounts
   3. Ability and willingness to live up to the terms of loan agreements
   4. Financial condition, including evaluation of cash flow, liquidity, earning power, etc.; report any improvement or deterioration of financial condition
   5. Degree of dependence on secondary sources of repayment
   6. Management capability
   7. Effects of external factors, such as competition, shortages, legislation, etc.
   8. Information — is it current and complete? Are credit memoranda in good order? Any unusual correspondence or clippings? Has special research been done?

B. **Conformity with Bank Loan Policy** — Covering type of loan, security, terms, rate, type of business, geographical area, proper approval processes, and other stated policies.

C. **Documentation** — Including a physical inspection of all documentation and collateral files. A few questions are:
   1. Are notes properly drawn and signed?
   2. Is collateral properly pledged? Are Uniform Commercial Code filings correct?
   3. Are guarantees correct and properly signed?
   4. Is a landlord's waiver necessary?

D. **Collateral** — Basic questions include:
   1. Is collateral safely located? Where is it?
   2. Is the collateral the same as that stipulated in the loan agreement? Any releases or substitutions?
   3. What is the quality of the collateral? What is its condition? Is there a market for it? What is liquidation value?
   4. If securities, accounts or notes receivable are pledged as collateral, what is the credit quality of the entity who issued them?
   5. What other liens exist against the debtor? What is the bank's lien position?
   6. Are securities or other collateral restricted in any way?

E. **Credit Checks**
   1. Are credit checkings current?
   2. Should additional inquiries be made?
   3. Were any unusual inquiries received, unusual either in nature or volume?
   4. Are agency reports current?
   5. Are payments to other creditors, both business and bank, current?

F. **Compliance** — Does the loan comply with various laws and regulations, including Regulations U, B, and Z; usury laws; real estate lending requirements; others?

G. **Profitability Analysis** — Is the loan profitable to the bank? If not, what can or should be done?

H. **Loan Rating** — What is the overall risk evaluation (or quality rating) of the credit?

I. **Action Required** — Determination of appropriate report to be issued or action taken based on the evaluation of the credit and recommendations made.

Exhibit 5.5 — A Commercial Loan Grading System (Using Four Ratings)

Loan Rating	Review Schedule	General Description	Specific Circumstances
A	360 days	Top Grade	1. Unsecured loans to very substantial companies with unquestionable financial strength.
			2. Loans adequately secured by cash surrender value, government bonds, CDs, or savings accounts.
			3. Loans well secured by listed stock.
B	180 days	Good	1. Loans where the risk is reasonable but the overall situation is less desirable than grade A.
			2. Loans adequately secured by listed stock.
			3. Loans generously secured by receivables, inventory, and other readily marketable collateral.
C	90 days	Marginal	1. Loans that require more-than-average service and attention to collateral and financial information or counseling.
			2. Loans where collateral values are less than standard.
			3. Loans that are not conforming to the repayment schedule but are not seriously past due. Creditworthiness or collateral values are in evidence.
D	30 days (minimum)	Workout Doubtful Loss	1. All loans classified by bank examiners.
			2. Unusually high credit risks that require constant supervision.

soon as a problem loan or a potentially troublesome situation is identified. Conversely, a loan officer should be able to request that a thorough and prompt review be prepared if indicated. The loan officers and the entire bank benefit if problems are promptly detected and acted on.

The earlier the recognition of problem loans, the greater the options available. Therefore, the loan review unit should be flexible enough to accommodate unanticipated requests for reviews and be aware of the need to keep loan officers informed of developments that affect a credit. By establishing good communication between these staff and line functions, the loan review unit that is normally viewed in a "policing" role can also be perceived as a support function.

Exhibit 5.6 — A Commercial Loan Grading System (Using Seven Ratings)

Loan Rating	General Description	Specific Circumstances
0	Unrated	A. This rating is used solely for computer purposes if no other rating has been assigned. When the credit is evaluated, a specific rating will be issued. B. A loan that was previously assigned a rating that cannot be confirmed or changed due to lack of information; includes loans where documentation is in the process of completion.
1	Prime Quality	A. Unsecured loans to borrowers with highest credit ratings and financial strength. Loans have a definite repayment schedule and are being handled as agreed. B. Loans fully secured by acceptable and highly liquid collateral, including properly margined listed stocks. Loans have a definite repayment schedule and are being handled as agreed.
2	High Quality	A. Unsecured loans to borrowers with entirely satisfactory credit ratings and financial strength. Repayment schedule is definite and being handled as agreed. B. Amply secured loans with a definite repayment agreement in effect.
3	Satisfactory Quality	A. Unsecured loans to borrowers with satisfactory credit ratings and financial strength. Loans require a reasonable amount of attention. All these loans should be paying as agreed, with a satisfactory repayment schedule. B. Revolving loans to borrowers who demonstrate entirely satisfactory credit ratings and financial strength. The ability to repay is evident. C. Loans partially secured by acceptable collateral with a definite repayment schedule in effect and being adhered to. Supported by satisfactory financial statements and cash flow sufficient for debt service. D. Loans that are amply secured by acceptable collateral but without a definite repayment agreement in effect. E. Other satisfactory loans that fall short of the requirements for grade 1 or 2 credits, yet are not considered marginal.

Exhibit 5.6 continued

4	Marginal Quality	A.	Unsecured loans to borrowers with limited ability to secure credit elsewhere or exhibit a lack of financial strength. A repayment schedule is in effect.
		B.	Partially secured loans, not properly margined. Total debt is large in relation to worth, and cash flow available for debt service is marginal. Loans may or may not have a definite repayment schedule in effect.
		C.	Loans to a weak borrower with a strong guarantor or endorser.
		D.	Loans where repayment has not been satisfactory or where terms of a loan agreement have been violated. If these loans were paying as agreed, they would be rated satisfactory or better.
		E.	Loans requiring constant attention to maintain a set repayment schedule.
5	Critical Quality	A.	Secured and unsecured loans where repayment is questionable and concern exists over the possibility of full or partial loss.
		B.	Loans classified by the bank examiners.
		C.	Workout loans on a liquidation basis, even if a loss is not expected.
6	Loss	A.	Loans considered uncollectible and of such little value that continuance as an active asset of the bank is not justified; may have some recovery or salvage value.

Reports

A formal system of reports, replies, and follow-up procedures is essential for the smooth operation of a loan review unit. Copies of loan reviews are generally sent to selected bank personnel, such as the loan officers affected by the report and their supervisors. It is also important that periodic reports prepared by those responsible for loan review be directed to persons with authority and responsibility for managing the bank's portfolio. Such reports might be directed to the board of directors, the audit committee, or the credit committee.

The contents of the reports will vary considerably depending on the recipients as well as the preparers. Often, higher level personnel might receive more general, broader-based reports than the more specific reports distributed to lending personnel and their immediate supervisors. It is good practice to have reports standardized as much as possible, but there should be some flexibility to accommodate unusual or complex circumstances.

A very basic loan review format is presented as Exhibit 5.7. Of course, this format does not present the loan relationship in great detail. It should usually be accompanied by supporting information, such as the complete analytical review from which the comments and recommendations were extracted. This format often works well as a cover sheet for a complete loan review package. It is also useful for distribution to those bank employees who want only an overview of a particular credit. Of course, some banks will wish to develop much more complex forms, while others will provide only an outline of topics to be covered when performing loan review.

Loan reviews directed to lending personnel sometimes require that the recipient respond within a specific time as to action taken and results obtained. These responses might be directed to all parties who received the original loan review report. The unit may also be responsible for noting "exceptions" or matters that require correction and for maintaining a follow-up list that identifies all corrective actions.

Loans that have been charged-off must also be reviewed to determine if payment is being pursued or if the note is uncollectible at that point. The loan review officer or other staff may be responsible for preparing follow-up reports on the condition of previously charged-off loans.

Loan Review Meetings

There are several ways to arrange loan review meetings so that all appropriate parties are informed of required action and developments are reported. For example, some banks schedule monthly loan review meetings with the senior loan officer, the loan officer assigned to the credit, and the loan review staff or officer in attendance. All the parties discuss the loan review report, share their knowledge of the credit, and formulate a plan of action if necessary.

In some cases, the loan officer is requested to prepare an independent review of the credit and present recommendations before such a meeting. If a bank has in-house counsel, the presence of an attorney at these meetings, at least on a selective basis, can be advantageous.

Another approach is to call special meetings to discuss troublesome loans with members of the board, the audit committee, senior management, bank attorney, and lending and loan review personnel. Less serious situations may be handled by a system of written reports and informal discussions as needed.

Those formulating review meeting procedures should consider a loan officer's possible reactions when made aware of a problem credit.

Exhibit 5.7 — Commercial Loan Review Fact Sheet (filled in)

Customer: XYZ Company **Date:** 4/19/X9

Last Reviewed: 9/18/X8 **Prepared by:** J. Kane

New Review: 3/X0 **Loan Officer:** M. Higgins

Line of Business: Wholesaler, hardware & paints

Commercial Loans Presently Outstanding:

Original Date of Note	Original Amount of Loan	Present Balance	Collateral	Collateral Value	Loan Rating	Prior Rating
3/21/X5	$50,000	$32,000	N/A	N/A	B1	A2
6/30/X6	25,000	25,000	A/Rs	$374,000 (book)	A2	A2

Guarantors: N/A

Loan Status: Current on principal and interest payments (✓)
Past due on principal or interest payments ( ) (describe)

Other Related Loans (itemize):
1. N/A
2.
3.

Corporate Deposits:
12-month average DDA: $43,100 (book)
37,250 (collected)
Time: $15,000 CD

Financial Statements Dated: 12/31/X8 **Annual** (✓) **Interim** ( )
Opinion Expressed: "Clean" opinion; full audit

Total Assets:	$1,247,700	**Net Working Capital:**	$295,500
Total Liabilities:	$701,000	**Current Ratio:**	1.46
Net Worth:	$546,700	**Net Profit (loss) for latest fiscal:**	$32,000
Debt/Worth:	1.28	**Net sales:**	$643,300
		Profits/Worth:	10.9

Profitability Index: 10.7

Credit Department Comments and Recommendations (highlights):
1. Net worth has increased 22% in past three years.
2. Last fiscal was most profitable year in company history.
3. Sales have expanded 33% in past three years.
4. Above has led to decline in current ratio and increase in debt/worth.
5. All other trends favorable; continue to monitor sales growth.
6. Accounts receivable agings not being received in timely manner (required quarterly).
7. H/C $85,000 in 19X4 and $130,000 in 19X2.
8. Recommend obtaining projected figures from management regarding plans for relocation/expansion.
9. Checking account handled in satisfactory manner.

Loan Officer's Comments: Date: 4/5/X9
Met with principals at their request to review operations for past five years. Company plans to relocate and hopes our bank can finance the building. Principals aware of potential working capital problem; receptive to our advice.

Some officers might react defensively if one of their loans turns sour, while others might overract to a situation that can, in fact, be corrected or worked out. Obviously, tact and consideration are required to encourage a cooperative and realistic attitude on the part of the officers involved. It is suggested that each loan officer attend only that portion of the meeting which applies to his or her loan.

One good way to educate all loan officers is for the loan review unit, or workout function, to arrange an annual charge-off meeting. At this meeting, all officers receive an abbreviated review of selected loans that were charged off during the year. The primary reasons for the problem loans are cited and discussed so that common oversights and errors will be identified and the officers can avoid repeating them. Such meetings also improve morale since positive action emerges from a negative situation, and no one feels that his or her bad loans were the only failures during the year.

Staffing

Selection of staff for the loan review function is critical since expertise is required in many areas. This is not the proper area of the bank in which to assign trainees or inexperienced personnel any major responsibilities. Some banks have found that experienced credit analysts, loan officers, or former bank examiners make excellent loan review officers.

Loan review personnel must be in a position of authority and should merit the respect of other people in the bank. They should have the ability to remain firm in resolving problems. But, at the same time, they should be able to achieve goals by encouraging—rather than simply demanding—cooperation with other people in the bank.

The Workout Function

The responsibility for handling workout situations, or problem loans, must be assigned to a specific individual or to a special department in the bank. No matter where the responsibility ultimately rests, the task will not be an easy one. Therefore, the combined efforts of the analysts, loan review personnel, and others responsible for performing loan quality control will reduce the work load in this area. The number of problem loans can be reduced through prompt identification and correction of difficulties before loans reach the point where collection efforts or workout situations must be faced.

Nevertheless, even the best run bank will have its share of problem loans. Thus, the workout function should be designed to recognize these situations as early as possible and take proper action. This will be in the best interests of both the customer and the bank.

Loan Officers and Specialists

Workout situations may be made the responsibility of the officer in charge of administering the loan. Keeping the total collection effort in the hands of the original loan officer provides two advantages. First, the officer is probably closest to the credit; second, the officer will also learn which types of loans can be successfully made and collected and which cannot.

However, it is often argued that the loan officer may spend a great deal of time on workout situations, thereby neglecting his or her satisfactory credit relationships and the development of additional business. Therefore, some banks provide special personnel to assist the loan officer. In other banks, this concept is taken a step further. After a certain amount of effort and time has been expended by the loan officer, the problem credit is referred to a designated workout specialist or unit for collection. It is not uncommon for workout loans to be turned over to an attorney for collection.

Credit Department Personnel

In a small bank, the experienced credit department manager may also be in charge of the workout function, assisting and working closely with the loan officer assigned to collect the loan. This method follows the principle that the person making the loan decision should ultimately be responsible for carrying it to its conclusion.

The credit department may also participate in the workout area in other ways. For example, if loan review or credit analysis is performed within the credit area, then the department should promptly identify potential problem loans and convey this information and any recommendations to management. In addition, the analysis or loan review functions may assist the workout officer in the collection effort. Frequent, in-depth analysis work and evaluating collateral from a liquidation or restructuring standpoint are examples of collection effort support. Another is ensuring that documentation is adequate. As noted, problem loans normally require that rapid and thorough action be taken; therefore, competent analytical and review personnel are needed to identify and evaluate these situations.

Naturally, bank size, staff expertise, the availability of legal counsel, and cost-benefit ratios will all influence the many decisions regarding the workout function. Nevertheless, the credit department invariably has a close relationship with this function. This is true even if the credit department is not directly involved in the workout function, subsequent to identifying a problem loan situation. This kinship, of course, may be traced to the credit department's initial research and later analytical work which often brings problem and potential problem situations to light. A high degree of professionalism is required in this area because identification of weak loans is only part of the function. The workout staff must be able to make sound recommendations and suggest alternative actions that the bank and the customer might take to minimize or prevent loss.

The Exception Desk

While this function is relatively new and may be called by different titles, its basic purpose is to detect a potential problem before a loan is put on the books. The exception desk's duties can be accomplished in several ways depending on the organization of the bank.

Defining the Scope

Loans may be analyzed *after* they are booked, as in the case of an emergency accommodation to a valued customer or a loan approved within a loan officer's lending limit. In this situation, the exception desk's function is especially important, and it might encompass many facets of quality control. However, when all loans are thoroughly analyzed *before* approval by the officer or the loan committee, this final checkpoint might only verify that events occurring subsequent to the original analysis have not adversely affected the credit.

For example, a loan committee might have imposed additional conditions on the contemplated credit extension, and the exception desk should verify that they were met. The exception desk, or a documentation control function, might be responsible for inspecting all documentation and correcting errors or noting any deficiencies. Furthermore, credit analysts may have identified specific conditions that needed correction or pieces of information that should have been obtained. This final control point may be used to check that the analysts' recommendations were followed or subsequently waived by the officer. If the credit analysts also act as exception desk personnel, perhaps with the assistance of a documentation expert, they would be in a good position to ensure that any missing pieces had been included and other problems resolved.

If exceptions are noted or still exist, it is essential that timing procedures be adopted. These procedures should provide a prompt determination of whether to book the loan "as is" and should establish responsibility for taking any required action or making corrections. One technique sometimes used by exception desk personnel is to prepare a control sheet for each loan that is reviewed. This sheet should include exceptions noted, follow-up required, and a recommendation on whether to book the loan.

Those responsible for this quality control function could then discuss any problems with either the loan officer responsible for the credit or with another designated officer who can determine whether to book the loan. If a loan is made regardless of the certain exceptions cited, exception desk personnel may ensure proper follow-up is taken by the loan officer.

In some banks, a separate exception desk function may not be practical or cost-efficient. This type of in-depth review will be performed only on an after-the-fact basis. However, other banks have regularly experienced loan losses attributable to faulty documentation, irregularities in following recommendations of the loan committee, or loan conditions waived at the last minute. These banks may find it worthwhile to consider at least some exception desk quality control functions, such as documentation review.

The Compliance Function

Designation of a Compliance Officer

The formal designation of someone at the bank as compliance officer is important. The function can only be performed by an individual with the time and ability to keep up-to-date on the many areas that the examiners will test for compliance. The compliance officer must be knowledgeable about lending procedures in effect at the bank and should be familiar with all areas of the bank including internal operations, deposit, and loan functions. He or she could be an attorney or have legal training, but generally the employee will work closely with legal counsel.

A partial list of the numerous state and federal laws and regulations requiring strict compliance are Federal Reserve Regulation Z (Truth in Lending Act), Regulation B (Equal Credit Opportunity Act), Regulation Q (controlling payment of interest on deposits), the Consumer Leasing Act, the Fair Credit Reporting Act, the Real Estate Settlement Procedures Act, the Financial Institutions Regulatory and Interest Rate Control Act, and various laws and regulations on interest, usury, and advertising.

As bankers are only too aware, this list could be greatly expanded. As a result, the designation of a compliance officer is vital to a bank. This is especially true given the growing importance of the compliance examination and the perennial threat of litigation. A well-managed compliance program requires a determined effort on the part of bank management and the board of directors.

Responsibilities

The compliance officer should report to the board of directors. Even if performed on a part-time basis, the compliance function must be an independent one that provides periodic reports on the state of compliance as well as the results of periodic compliance audits to the board. The compliance audit program should include such duties as the periodic review of Regulation Z disclosures and verification that interest has been properly calculated. It also should include a review of denied and approved credit applications to verify that credit is granted in accordance with bank policy. And the audit should also check compliance with the Fair Credit Reporting Act and Regulation B.

All advertising and required notices must be checked for accuracy, and the compliance program should also include the review of any complaints registered with the bank. The officer should also be responsible for reviewing forms and replacing those that are obsolete.

Education

The compliance officer is responsible for educating bank personnel, and this must be an ongoing function. For example, loan officers and other personnel who take applications for credit need training in complying with Regulation B. They must know what questions may or may not be asked and when it is appropriate to make certain inquiries. Loan officers must also be aware of property laws which affect the bank's obtaining a spouse's signature on various loan documents. The compliance officer must also provide training in the area of nondiscriminatory lending criteria and may assist in establishing bank policy.

As regulations, statutes, and laws are revised, amended, or introduced, the compliance officer will be responsible for providing continuing education. Different methods will make personnel aware of the various regulations and will undoubtedly vary with bank size. Some banks will conduct special seminars for large groups of employees; others will rely on individualized instruction in combination with written memoranda.

The bank's compliance officer must have sufficient time available to perform this responsible function and to keep current with new regulations, proposals, and laws. The officer should also have a complete compliance library that is kept up-to-date. By being on the mailing lists of the bank's examining agencies, the bank can directly receive copies of new regulations, proposals, and laws. Some suggestions for a compliance library are included in the bibliography.

Commercial Credit and Compliance

By its nature, the compliance officer position is usually associated with the consumer credit function; however, the compliance function is also important in the commercial lending area. As previously mentioned, there are many instances of present and proposed laws and regulations that affect both the consumer and commercial loan areas. Furthermore, especially in small banks, the consumer and commercial loan functions may be combined or accommodation loans may be made for consumer purposes but handled by the commercial loan area.

Commercial loan officers must know the effects of laws and regulations on such matters as taking and processing applications, setting rates, and notifying a customer of adverse action taken. They must also know when consumer loan documentation is required for a loan processed in the commercial division. While the compliance officer, and bank counsel, must educate and assist all those involved in the lending functions, the credit department, too, can play an integral role in ensuring effective performance of the compliance function.

Since commercial loan personnel may not work regularly with documents such as right of recission and various disclosure statements, a critical piece of documentation may be overlooked when a consumer loan is being prepared. Thus, it is advisable for the compliance officer or compliance staff and commercial credit personnel to monitor commercial loans for instances of noncompliance. The individual who serves as the compliance officer may, in a small bank, also function as the credit manager. Or the bank's documentation or consumer loan expert could be designated to perform this function.

If the credit manager does not also serve as the commercial loan compliance officer, the manager must at least be familiar with applicable laws and regulations. The manager needs to know when to seek advice from the officer and when assistance is needed in reviewing or recommending specific types of documentation. The credit manager should also know when to request a compliance review before a loan is approved, booked, or reviewed.

Summary

Control is certainly a basic C of credit, and an inadequate system of controls is likely to be one of the problems contributing to loan losses. Of course, there are many quality control points that can be included in the organizational structure of the bank and many ways to allocate the performance of these controls. The credit manager must consider what control responsibilities are to be assumed by the credit area. He or she must also be informed of other control points within the bank that influence the work of the credit department.

Qualified credit personnel can help provide the skills and perform the ongoing loan monitoring functions that contribute to a high-quality loan portfolio. The credit department can help reduce loan losses by identifying potential problem credits and by recommending appropriate action. Especially in a small bank, the credit department may be involved with a loan from its inception to the day it is paid off.

Bank management must consider the types, degree, and scope of controls in relation to their costs, staff availability, and benefits to the bank. Management must also ensure that the control functions of the credit department are clearly defined and supported.

6

Commercial Credit Information Exchange

The exchange of commercial credit information is of vital importance in the business world. Comprehensive, accurate, and timely credit information, exchanged on a reciprocal basis, assists banks, their customers, and business credit grantors in making sound business decisions regarding the creditworthiness of their clients.

Although the credit department is not usually thought of as a profit-generating operation, its function can have a direct effect on the bank's profitability. For example, the scope, timeliness, and accuracy of the information compiled by a credit information unit will ultimately contribute to the quality of the bank's loan portfolio and therefore to its profits. Also, the caliber of service which a credit investigation function provides could be a major consideration in determining whether customers maintain a relationship with the bank. This is especially true in metropolitan areas where many banks employ professional credit inquiry and investigation staffs and where the excellence of one bank's service compared with another's could provide a definite competitive advantage in attracting new business.

Some banks charge for conducting credit investigations, by direct charges and fees or by analysis. In such cases, larger banks may organize the credit investigation unit as a separate profit center. On the other hand, many banks, particularly smaller ones, only charge for the direct costs of conducting an investigation, such as telephone charges. But whether the credit information exchange function is technically regarded as a profit center, its impact on the profitability of the bank can be significant.

The character of the credit department will be as individual as the bank in which and for which it functions. Of those banks able to have a separate credit department, some will choose to maintain a large staff whose responsibilities include all the functions necessary to compile and disseminate credit information. These functions range from the maintenance of credit files and a resource library to credit and loan analysis and the training of prospective loan officers. Others, by choice or necessity, have a smaller staff of specialists whose duties primarily consist of answering inquiries, conducting investigations, ordering agency reports, and searching the public records. Whatever decision is made regarding the size and character of the credit department, it should be remembered that the department and its output can have a significant impact on the bank's standing, image, and reputation in the community and the industry.

Guidelines and Standards

If the free flow of credit information should cease, our present credit-based economic system would be seriously impaired. The exchange of credit information depends on the trust placed in all parties involved that the information has been requested for a legitimate business purpose, will be kept confidential, and will not be used indiscriminately. Since the effectiveness of the exchange of credit information is predicated on mutual trust between inquirers and respondents, adherence to a commonly accepted set of standards or guidelines is important.

Code of Ethics

In 1916, Robert Morris Associates formulated a *Code of Ethics for the Exchange of Commercial Credit Information Between Banks* for use by its members, outlining acceptable practices and norms for the exchange of credit information. The *Code of Ethics* has undergone several revisions since it was conceived, but its essence remains substantially unchanged. Although intended to apply to information exchanged between commercial banks, the precepts of the *Code of Ethics* serve as the foundation for all commercial credit information exchange.

Today, the RMA *Code of Ethics* remains a valuable guide to the management of the credit inquiry and investigation function. (The Code is printed as Appendix A.) Familiarity with its articles and respect for its tenets should be emphasized by the credit department manager as essential to the commercial credit information exchange function.

Of course, there is no legal requirement demanding adherence to the Code; however, membership in RMA requires acknowledgment that the member has read and agrees to abide by it. Furthermore, the credit department manager must impress upon his or her staff that failure to comply with this requirement could result in a bank or individual forfeiting membership in RMA.

Statement of Principles

The credit department manager should also recognize another set of guidelines which has proved invaluable in facilitating the free and responsible flow of commercial credit information. This is the *Statement of Principles for the Exchange of Credit Information Between Banks and Business Credit Grantors*. (The Statement is presented in full as Appendix B.)

Robert Morris Associates and the National Association of Credit Management (NACM) originally adopted the *Statement of Principles* in 1955, and it was revised in 1978 to include explanatory comments for each of the principles. The Statement reiterates many of the points made in the RMA *Code of Ethics*, but its language is more applicable to extensions of trade credit. Both NACM and RMA encourage their members and others with whom credit information is exchanged to become familiar with and respect the *Statement of Principles*.

Foreign Credit Information

This chapter concentrates on the exchange of domestic, rather than foreign, credit information. Managers responsible for conducting foreign credit inquiries should consult RMA's *Guidelines for the Exchange of Foreign Credit Information*. These Guidelines*, published in 1978, are designed to assist investigators in responding to credit inquiries on foreign account relationships and to increase the effectiveness of credit interchange.

---

*The *Guidelines*, the *Code of Ethics*, and *Statement of Principles* are available from RMA, 1616 Philadelphia National Bank Bldg., Philadelphia, PA 19107.

Inquiries and Investigations—Vital Factors

An inquiry is a request for credit information directed to the bank of account or trade supplier which has a direct relationship with the subject of the inquiry. An investigation is a request for credit information which results in the information being supplied by a third party. For example, a bank conducting an investigation on behalf of a customer would develop credit information from sources other than its own records and would contact the bank or trade supplier who had a relationship with the subject of the investigation.

Since this book is not designed to serve as a procedures manual, detailed discussions of rules and guidelines in replying to inquiries and conducting investigations will not be included here. The purpose of this section is to review the qualities which make a good credit report and to discuss several factors contributing to a quality product.

A proper inquiry should fully identify the subject, state the purpose and the amount involved, provide a summary of experience with the subject, be specific about the information needed in response, and disclose any other relevant factors. The qualities of an effective response are these: It must be timely, comprehensive, accurate, and appropriate to the inquiry. The first three of these qualities are fairly straightforward; the fourth merits some explanation.

How Much Information?

One important question in conducting investigations and replying to credit inquiries is "how much information should be compiled and subsequently released?" The *Code of Ethics* and the *Statement of Principles* provide some excellent guidelines to determine the amount and scope of information to be provided. The determination is dependent on various factors, the first of which is proper identification of the inquirer.

It is necessary to emphasize the importance of being as certain as possible about the identity of the inquirer, including the source of the inquiry (such as a bank, a customer, a collection agency, or a credit reporting agency) and the name of the individual responsible for conducting the inquiry. Written inquiries which supply the name and address of the inquirer and provide the manual signature of the authorized signer usually pose no difficulty.

Telephone inquiries, however, frequently create problems since, at the time of the call, there is no way of verifying whether the inquirer provided proper identification. In such situations, it is best to record the inquiry and inform the inquirer that the information will be compiled and telephoned back at a later time.

A return call will provide some assurance that information is being released to the proper party. The respondent now has time to verify the inquirer's name and number in the telephone or other commercial directory. Furthermore, the inquirer's telephone should be answered in a businesslike manner, providing additional identification. If the identity of the inquirer cannot be satisfactorily established by phone calls, correspondence, or other verification procedures, it is wise not to answer the inquiry.

The purpose, amount, importance, and specific questions posed by the inquirer will normally determine the amount of information to be provided. The inquirer may further emphasize the importance of the inquiry by providing information on the amount and its relationship to the size and financial position of the subject. Descriptions of proper inquiries are set forth in Article 2 of the Code, and general guidelines for responding to the requirements of a legitimate inquiry are presented in Article 3. Naturally, situations will occur when the Code provides little assistance and special handling is required. It is on these occasions that good channels of communication between the credit department manager and loan officers, the availability of specific bank policies, and an investigator's training, experience, and judgment are of great value.

Policy Considerations

In addition to applying the guidelines in the *Code of Ethics* and *Statement of Principles*, each bank will have to make many internal policy determinations. The credit department manager or the supervisor of credit information exchange should develop a written statement that clearly sets forth the bank's policies and procedures for handling inquiries and investigations. This statement should provide detailed operational procedures and should also identify who is authorized to conduct and respond to inquiries. Such a document is essential to the smooth operations of a credit department; it helps eliminate confusion, encourages uniform operating standards, and establishes responsibility for the function.

Furthermore, bank customers should be treated equitably, and inquirers should receive consistent responses. If a policy statement were not developed, the bank might find that some personnel released insufficient information while others released information that exceeded the industry norms or ran counter to the opinion of legal counsel. To be successful, such a document must be supported by senior management, and all employees who are involved in the function must be appropriately trained.

Some specific areas must be covered in formulating a policy on the exchange of credit information. For example, decisions will have to be made on releasing the following kinds of information:

- Recommendations
- Financial statement data
- Unfavorable information
- Information involving litigation

Other policy considerations include who should receive credit information, when to accept inquiries by telephone, and so forth. These main ideas are discussed separately in the following sections.

Recommendations

One important management decision relates to making recommendations on a customer's reliability for a particular amount or transaction. Many banks decline to make recommendations regarding a customer's creditworthiness and confine their responses to strictly factual, ledger-type information. The reasons are twofold: First, the final credit decision should be made by the inquirer after factual information has been gathered from various sources; second, undue reliance on any one source or on comments not based strictly on fact would be unwise. Furthermore, banks must take into account the legal implications of making recommendations. Therefore, one should not be surprised when banks provide all relevant facts but offer little, if any, interpretation of them.

There is another school of thought regarding this question, however. Many bankers believe they should make recommendations if requested because the credit recommendation is a valuable service which a bank provides *for*, as well as *to*, customers. After all, it is argued, a bank will be quite familiar with a customer's creditworthiness, so why not make a recommendation if asked. For example, many banks will make recommendations on their own customer's creditworthiness for a specific amount when that customer attempts to secure trade credit.

Thus, there are two sides to this question. And it is left to the discretion of the bank to determine whether to provide recommendations regarding creditworthiness for a specific amount or to provide an opinion of management. As an aid in reaching such a decision the manager might find it useful to prepare a list of pros and cons. Some opinions on the topic of recommendations are presented as Exhibit 6.1.

By setting forth both sides of a policy question, the manager is in a better position to reach a logical and supportable conclusion that is appropriate for the particular bank. If bank policy permits the release of opinions and recommendations, the credit department manager should impress upon his or her staff that the account officer should be consulted unless the person answering the inquiry is specifically authorized to provide such information.

Financial Statement Data

Another matter of bank policy involves the release of financial statement data. Although some guidelines for release of such information are offered in the RMA *Code of Ethics*, each bank should provide its investigators with specific policies that meet with the approval of bank management and, of course, legal counsel. Some banks provide no financial statement data, some will confirm figures supplied by an inquirer, while others provide analytical information. In addition, banks may differentiate between information released about publicly held and nonpublicly held companies.

Obviously, there are many approaches to the subject, and bank policy must establish the proper procedures for its credit department staff and officers to follow. The pros and cons of providing financial statement data to an inquirer are presented as Exhibit 6.2.

Exhibit 6.1 — Pros and Cons of Providing an Inquirer with a Recommendation

Explanation: A recommendation involves making and conveying a judgment about the creditworthiness of a customer to an inquirer. For example, the respondent might state that he or she believes the subject of an inquiry is "good for" a specific amount of credit or a certain performance.

The *Code of Ethics* states: "It remains at the discretion of the responding bank to provide the inquirer with recommendations . . . If a recommendation or opinion is asked for, the account officer should be consulted unless the person answering the inquiry is authorized to provide this information."

PROS:

1. The credit recommendation is a valuable service which a bank provides for, as well as to, its customers.

2. Recommendations serve to reinforce a satisfactory credit rating.

3. A recommendation assists an understaffed or inexperienced credit grantor in reaching a difficult credit decision.

4. The need to formulate a recommendation causes the respondent to fully analyze the situation and draw a conclusion.

5. A favorable recommendation expresses confidence in a customer's abil-

CONS:

1. The final credit decision should be made after factual information has been gathered from various sources. A recommendation might encourage an inquirer to rely on only one source of information.

2. Recommendations may not always be reached by a bank's application of consistent standards. Depending upon the procedures in effect at a bank, various personnel could provide different recommendations on the same credit.

3. Banks should not try to act as credit managers for other concerns.

Exhibit 6.1 continued

PROS:

ity to handle the transaction under consideration, and helps customers establish or continue to receive credit. On the other hand, an unfavorable recommendation alerts an inquirer to a potential difficulty. However, it may hamper the customer's ability to obtain credit.

6. A recommendation adds to the overall summary of experience with a customer.

7. Based on its knowledge and experience with a customer, a bank should be in a position to know whether a specific amount of credit is within the subject's ability to repay.

8. Agency and trade reports may not provide support for a credit. However, the banker may believe that the specific type and amount of credit presented by the inquirer may be justified and within the customer's capabilities.

CONS:

4. Banks that provide recommendations do not always furnish enough other factual details of the relationship and may express the viewpoint that the recommendation is sufficient. A recommendation that is not supported by other factual information is not appropriate.

5. A bank's experience may not reflect a customer's overall condition. For example, a customer may pay the bank promptly but run slow with trade suppliers, or vice versa.

6. A bank may not have sufficient analytical staff to fully evaluate the situation prior to providing a recommendation.

7. The reasonable duty of a respondent is to provide factual information, not recommendations or opinions.

8. Some banks only provide recommendations for larger customers with whom they have an extensive relationship. This leads to inconsistencies in bank policy. Some customers may feel discriminated against if they are not considered large enough to merit the formulation of a recommendation.

9. Banks that provide recommendations may find that litigation is initiated by an inquirer who claims to have relied on the recommendation.

Exhibit 6.2 — Pros and Cons of Providing Financial Statement Data to an Inquirer

Explanation: Disclosure of financial statement information may include a description of the financial condition and trends of the subject, dates of the statements and the period they cover, and the type of auditor's opinion given.

The *Code of Ethics* states: Financial statement data. Where the subject is a publicly held company publishing current financial information, the release of financial statement data will normally be in compliance with the securities laws. When financial statements of nonpublicly held companies are submitted to the bank, with no instructions to the contrary, a general summary of the data may usually be disclosed. This disclosure should be tempered by the respondent's confidence in the inquirer and by the amount and nature of the inquiry. The summary may consist of:

- Dates of the statements and the period they cover.
- Auditor's opinion.
- A description of the financial condition and trends of the subject, which should include current assets, total assets, current liabilities, net worth, sales, and an

Exhibit 6.2 continued

indication of profitability. It is the option of the responding bank to disclose this data in actual figures or in RMA General Figure Ranges (see *Code of Ethics*, Appendix A). Even when financial statements are submitted in confidence, a brief general description of the company's strength, size, and trends may usually be disclosed.

If comments are made regarding the financial standing of the subject, they should be based on the bank's analysis of the company, pointing out to the inquirer that "our analysis shows" or using other such wording.

PROS:

1. Disclosure of financial statement data provides the inquirer with a more complete understanding of the subject's condition and ability to pay.
2. If the figures have been spread by the bank, the inquirer receives the benefit of this analysis.
3. If the bank discusses the significance of financial statement data, then the inquirer may get a better feel for the company's financial condition.
4. Disclosure of financial statement data will enable an inquirer to verify the accuracy of information previously obtained from a customer or other source.
5. When given as part of a credit history, financial data may assist an inquirer in reaching a sound and prompt credit decision.
6. Faced with the need to expedite an order, business credit grantors may not have sufficient time to obtain and analyze the subject's financial statements. Therefore, comments from the bank of account can be helpful to the inquirer and the customer.

CONS:

1. If a bank provides financial information, it may discourage an inquirer from obtaining financial statements and performing an independent analysis.
2. When only highlights of the financial picture are released, the inquirer may be misled.
3. Analysts utilize different methods and techniques in performing statement analysis; therefore, comparisons of ratios and other calculations may not be uniform. Misunderstandings could occur.
4. The figures presented on the most recent financial statement may not represent the company's present condition.
5. There may be risk involved if a bank provides data from a statement that has not been made public. A privately owned company may not want the details of its financial condition revealed.
6. An inquirer may place undue reliance on financial statement data when reaching a credit decision.
7. Personnel who release financial data must be trained and experienced. Without sufficient knowledge of financial statement analysis and accounting, an employee could unintentionally misinform an inquirer.
8. Release of financial data is time-consuming for the bank. This is true even if data is provided from only one financial statement. The problem is magnified if a trend review over several years is needed when a large or complex credit is being considered.
9. Some inquirers could construe certain analytical comments to be recommendations or opinions.

Unfavorable Information

The release of unfavorable information may also pose a problem for the manager. If a bank's relationship with a customer has been unsatisfactory, the bank has an ethical obligation to report that fact to inquirers. A bank should not mislead an inquirer by reporting only favorable information and omitting unfavorable information, despite the fact that reporting unfavorable information may pose a problem for both the bank's customer and the bank. It is essential that the credit department manager emphasize this point to staff, trainees, and loan officers.

Further, it should be stressed that when in doubt, advice of legal counsel should be sought. For example, if a bank reports factual (but unfavorable) information honestly and accurately, it would seem that the bank would not be liable for any loss of business such information might cause its customer.

This conclusion would seem consistent with interpretations of the Fair Credit Reporting Act. These explanations suggest that the law permits banks to report information on customers if that information is a true reflection of the facts of the bank's relationship with its customer. Yet the law is not always clear, and it is dangerous to try to generalize about specific situations. Thus, advice of counsel should be obtained in setting policy in this area.

The method and wording used to report unfavorable information can sometimes be a problem. Some banks choose to release such information over the telephone, but there are occasions when it is preferable or necessary to put unfavorable information in a letter. In these cases, it is often best to keep the data as concise and factual as possible, while providing adequate and complete information which the inquirer can use to help formulate a credit decision. For example, if a customer is past due on a 90-day unsecured note, the credit reporter might include a statement of this type in the letter:

> "On Jan. 3, 19XX, we extended an unsecured loan of a low five-figure amount to the XYZ Company. The note matured on April 3, 19XX, and the entire balance is outstanding at this time. No interest or principal reductions have been made at the date of this letter nor has the maturity date of the note been extended."

This language is free of confusing or misleading jargon, gives the inquirer a clear picture of the facts, and makes it quite plain that the note is delinquent. However, the bank has not indicated how it thinks the situation might be resolved and has not provided a recommendation on the transaction in question. The inquirer should be capable of reaching a suitable decision on the basis of the information given.

Information Involving Litigation

Another major policy consideration involves handling requests for information based on actual or contemplated litigation. As stated in Article 5 of the *Code of Ethics*, considerable judgment must be used in responding to inquiries of this nature. They can, among other things, place the bank of account in the difficult position of providing information while protecting its customers. Although reply, if any, is at the discretion of the respondent, every bank should adopt procedures for handling such requests.

Bank policy could state that no information is to be provided in response to such inquiries, and that the loan officer should be informed of the inquiry. Or another bank might want each inquiry of this type referred to the account officer for evaluation. In many cases, advice will be sought from bank counsel both about formulating bank policy and in responding, if at all, to certain inquiries on troublesome loans. Some considerations useful in this area are presented as Exhibit 6.3.

Other Policy Considerations

When writing a credit information exchange policy, the manager must consider when to accept an inquiry over the telephone and when to require that an inquiry be made through correspondence. For example, some bankers may prefer to receive written inquiries to assist in identifying an inquirer and to document the request in the credit folder. Others believe that the delays involved in handling written inquiries could injure a customer and that the cost of preparing credit correspondence would create additional, unwarranted expense for the bank. Most banks will accept telephone inquiries from sources who are readily identifiable, such as other banks. Others follow a "written inquiries only" policy for all or selected types of inquiries.

It must be determined if information will be given at all to certain types of inquirers, such as collection agencies. It should also be remembered that a customer may request that no information be released to anyone on his or her accounts; honoring such a request would require appropriate controls to be in place.

In addition to determining the scope of credit information the bank will release, the bank must consider the policies it will follow when it requests credit information. For example, it would be unfair to expect another bank to provide financial statement data if the inquiring bank will not reciprocate in the future. Policies must be adopted both for requesting and responding to requests for credit information, and these policies should be consistent.

Exhibit 6.3 — Pros and Cons of Responding to Requests for Information Based on Actual or Contemplated Litigation

Explanation: Such requests may involve problem loans, collection activities, or skip accounts; an attempt to locate assets; and various types of actual or contemplated legal action.

The *Code of Ethics* states: "When the purpose of a request for information is actual or contemplated legal action, full disclosure of this fact by the inquirer is necessary. It is clearly unethical to disguise the purpose of any inquiry. This could be detrimental to the parties involved, especially when legal action is associated with an inquiry. Under those circumstances, the potential for damages is such that all parties must exercise considerable judgment before conducting an investigation or answering an inquiry of this nature.

"Whenever the bank of account is placed in a conflicting position of providing information and, at the same time, protecting its customers, the amount of information, if any, will be at the discretion of the responding bank."

PROS:

1. By exchanging credit information in such instances, both parties will have a better indication of the subject's position.

2. If it is a bank's policy to respond to such requests, that bank is more likely to receive a full response when it requests similar information.

3. When an inquirer knows that it is a bank's policy not to respond to inquiries of this nature, it is unlikely that the inquirer would contact the bank. Thus, the bank may lose a valuable source of credit information.

4. If a full response is not provided by a bank, an inquirer might interpret this as tacit acknowledgment of a problem situation. This, in fact, may not be the case.

5. If a bank responds with a full story, the creditors may develop better channels of communication and reach more timely solutions. Furthermore, the bank is in a better position to administer and service its loans if it is aware of other creditors' relationships with its customers.

6. An unduly concerned inquirer might decide to postpone litigation or other actions that could damage a mutual customer if the bank reports information that is favorable or clears up a misunderstanding.

7. Banks choosing to respond to such inquiries may hold that it is proper to fully answer any reasonable credit inquiry that discloses the material facts.

CONS:

1. The bank should not function as a collection agency for customers or outside sources.

2. A response to such a request could assist an inquirer who seeks to attach a bank customer's account.

3. A bank has an obligation to protect its customers and may not wish to risk providing information that could be used in litigation.

4. If a bank responds to such inquiries,

factual. Once a bank decides to respond, failure to provide a complete picture could have serious repercussions.

5. If a bank's response is unfavorable to a customer and the party contemplating litigation decides to take action, the bank could find its own position weakened. For example, an inquirer could learn that the bank is unsecured and take an advantageous lien position.

6. A bank may be more likely to become involved in litigation if it responds to an inquiry of this nature.

7. Many respondents who consider supplying such information may want to confer with legal counsel prior to the release of specific data. While this could be helpful, it may be a costly and time-consuming procedure.

8. If it is decided to respond in these matters, care must be taken to ensure that all requests are handled consistently throughout the bank.

It is important that each bank establish, write, and distribute internal policy guidelines for credit information exchange. Policy should be formulated with the assistance of individuals having a variety of expertise. In a moderate-size bank, for example, legal counsel, the credit department manager, an experienced investigator, the bank's compliance officer, and senior management might well be involved. Their combined expertise can ensure that no important considerations are overlooked and that the bank and its customers are protected. One element of this policy—"who should answer inquiries?"—is discussed in the next section. It is one of the most important determinations that a bank must make.

Organizing the Credit Function

Each bank should specifically authorize certain personnel to handle credit inquiries and investigations. However, several factors must be considered before this responsibility is delegated. To aid in the decision-making process, the matters of receiving, responding to, and initiating inquiries and investigations should be viewed separately.

Incoming Requests for Credit Information

In regard to who should receive incoming requests for credit information, three options may be considered:

- Each loan officer could receive inquiries related to his or her own customers.
- Credit inquiries could be received by the branch that is handling the account.
- All credit inquiries could be received at one central location.

In the smallest banks or in banks serving a limited customer base, some credit department functions may be virtually nonexistent or staff few in number. In this situation, loan officers may receive credit inquiries on their accounts directly and, of course, are immediately aware of the details of an inquiry. They will be able to spot any unusual developments, and they are generally able to supply a full response. However, this approach may lead to poor record-keeping practices, inconsistencies in the application of bank policy, and delays if the officer is not available.

In multioffice banks, the branch system approach is sometimes used: Inquiries are received by or directed to the branch at which the account is maintained. In this case, central credit files will probably not exist. If this method is followed, each branch may be responsible for training credit inquiry and investigation staff and keeping accurate records. While this procedure works well in some banks, others have experienced difficulty in directing inquiries to the correct branch. A master list of accounts by branch location usually helps overcome this problem.

The third method of handling inquiries, the centralized approach, has become increasingly popular in recent years for several reasons. First, all inquiries can be logged, monitored, and recorded in one location for better control. Second, all authorized personnel will be specifically trained and supervised to perform this function. Third, policies can be implemented on a uniform basis; fourth, loan officers and others are not constantly interrupted by requests for credit information.

The centralized approach may be used in both large and small banks. Even when only one person is in the credit department, that individual might receive and record all requests for information. All other bank personnel would be instructed to transfer calls and correspondence to that person. As the credit function expands, several individuals might be answering the credit department phone and recording inquiries, but the basic duties performed remain the same.

Responding to Requests for Credit Information

After an inquiry is received by the bank, someone must answer it promptly and accurately. Many banks recommend that credit department personnel respond to credit inquiries for the four primary reasons cited under the centralized approach to recording inquiries. It is important, however, that the credit reporter's responsibilities be clearly defined so that he or she knows when to refer inquiries and seek advice from the manager, loan officers, and others.

In a small credit department, the person receiving inquiries may be responsible for answering routine inquiries directly. Naturally, advice can be sought from the account officer in special cases, such as inquiries involving large amounts, solicitations, or reported slowness. Other banks prefer that all inquiries be referred to account officers before a response is made. In this case, credit department staff might furnish the officer with a copy of the inquiry with the proposed response attached and request that any comments or corrections be made within an appropriate time.

In some credit departments, the manager may review all inquiries, decide if special action should be taken, and direct inquiries to the proper credit reporter, investigator, or officer for response. In many cases, credit department personnel will be responsible for responding to both telephone and written inquiries. In other instances, especially in unusual situations or when the inquirer has requested to speak with the account officer, the loan officer will choose to respond.

Requesting Credit Information

Procedures should also be adopted for proper handling of investigations and inquiries conducted by the bank. In addition to using the guidelines in the RMA *Code of Ethics*, each bank will need to identify who is permitted to request credit information for use by the bank or its customers. Frequently, credit department personnel are responsible for requesting information since they "speak the language," understand bank policy for the function, and are usually available to accept return telephone calls.

In most cases, loan officers will request that credit department staff, or the manager, conduct an inquiry. They should also provide complete details, including inquiry purpose and amount involved. Depending on bank policy, an internal inquiry or investigation request may have to be written to establish responsibility. In some banks, loan officers will be authorized to conduct credit inquiries. This decision often depends on the staffing, organization, and size of a particular bank.

Banks must also decide how requests for investigations on behalf of customers should be handled. If investigations are conducted, basic considerations include whether to charge the customer, the basis on which the charge, if any, should be made, and who the customer should contact to request an investigation. To conduct an efficient investigation, competent credit department staff should be trained to obtain all the information required from a customer during the initial phone conversation. Since banks do provide different services to their customers at varying costs, a consistent policy, uniformly applied, is important to good customer relations.

Record-Keeping

Whatever internal policies and procedures a bank adopts, the importance of keeping complete and accurate records of inquiries, investigations, and responses cannot be overemphasized. A bank must be able to follow the pattern of inquiries on its own customers; know what was said, who said it, and when it was said; and be able to produce satisfactory records if a problem, such as litigation, should occur.

Scribbled notations of a response may be adequate to meet immediate needs but will be difficult to interpret or produce in a few days. Inquiries placed by the bank should also be documented so that, among other things, staff will know when follow-up action is required and who should be contacted if a timely response is not received. A sample credit inquiry-investigation form is presented as Exhibit 6.4.

Exhibit 6.4 — Sample Credit Inquiry/Investigation Form Side 1

Credit Inquiry

(internal use only)

Inquirer ______________________ Phone ______/ ______________

Individual Calling ________________ City ________________ State ______

Subject ____

Address ____

Bank ______________________ Branch ________________

Address ______________________ Phone ______/ ______

Principals ______________________

Purpose of Inquiry

Purpose ____

Amount ______________________ Terms ________________

High Credit __________________ Outstanding ____________

Payment ______________________ Experience ____________

Details of Mutual Revision ______________________________

____

Comments ____

Internal Investigation

Deposit Accounts

	A/C#	Opened	Closed	Experience	Office/ Branch	Average Balance	Savings Balance
Checking							
Checking							
Corporate Savings							
Other							

Loans

(attach additional sheets as needed)

A/C# ______________ Opened ______________ Terms ______________

Outstanding __________ Purpose ______________ Type ______________

Security ______________ Guarantees/Endorsements ______________

High Credit ______________ Rating ______________ Amount Past Due ________

Previous Paid Out Loans ______________________________

Received by ______________ Date ______________ Time ______________

Instruction Due ____ Method ________ Investigator ________ Log No. ________

Answered by ______________ Date ______________ Time ______________

Referred to ______________ Individual ______________ Time ______________

Exhibit 6.4 continued—Sample Credit Inquiry/Investigation Form Side 2

Outside Investigation—Bank to Bank

(internal use only)

Bank ______________________ Phone ________/ ____________

Individual Contacted ______________________ Date ______________________

Checking A/C Opened ________ Average Balance ________ Experience ________

Corporate Savings A/C Opened ____________ Present Balance ____________

Loan Experience:

Opening Date ______________________ Type of Accommodation(s) ____________

High Credit ______________________ Present Outstanding ____________

Security (describe) ____

Guarantees/Endorsements ______________________________________

Terms ____________ Maturity Date ________ Clean-Up Period ________

Approval Date ______________________ Expiration Date ____________

Paid Out Loans ____

Overall Experience ____

Other:

Principals ____

Affiliates ____

Comments ____

____

____

____

____

Financial Statement Data

Statement Prepared By ______________________ Date ______________________

Fiscal ☐ Interim ☐ Opinion Expressed ______________________

Total Current Assets ____________ Total Current Liabilities ____________

Total Assets ____________ Total Debt ____________

Net Worth ____________

Sales ______________ Net Profits ______________

Statements are held in confidence ☐

Comments on Profitability ______________________________________

Additional Information ______________________________________

____

____

____

Credit Correspondence

Several examples of credit correspondence are presented at the end of this chapter starting on page 168. These sample letters are not designed to cover every possible situation. However, they are provided as guidelines that may be adapted for various types of inquiries and to suit the needs of a particular bank. For example, the first sample letter designed for bank to bank use is followed by five different lead-in paragraphs suitable for use with various types of requests for commercial credit information; similar formats are included for information exchange between banks and business credit grantors.

In addition, a sample letter of reply provides a full response to a letter requesting credit information. Three examples of form letters provide ideas for replying to credit inquiries.

Use of Form Letters

Whether to use form letters or formal typewritten letters has been the subject of much discussion among credit professionals. Typewritten letters are generally considered to be the most professional manner of handling credit correspondence and may be the only way of describing complex situations. However, cost considerations, time and personnel limitations, and economic realities may make it both necessary and desirable to use form letters for credit information exchange. Therefore, form letters should be as thoroughly and carefully prepared as typewritten letters. Naturally, both form and typewritten letters must appear on bank letterhead.

Bank credit personnel should be familiar with Form 19, presented here as Exhibit 6.5. This form is widely used by business credit grantors to request commercial credit information from banks. Developed jointly by the National Association of Credit Management and RMA, the form provides sufficent space for a routine trade inquiry and a bank response on the same page.

Manual signatures are essential on all credit correspondence, including form letters. Signatures are evidence that reasonable procedures were used to ensure the accuracy of the information. In addition, the title, if any, and the name of the authorized signer should be typed or printed on the correspondence. This practice facilitates correct addressing of responses and identifies the person to contact if questions arise. Remember that a facsimile signature stamp or presigned form letter may fall into inappropriate hands.

Exhibit 6.5—Form 19

REQUEST FOR BANK CREDIT INFORMATION

Please provide bank credit information on the account below. This information is requested for use in the extension of credit for business purposes only and will be held in strict confidence. We are providing a summary of our experience with the subject of the inquiry.

TO: ______ (Bank Name)
______ (Street Address)
______ (City, State, Zip)

______ (Date)

FROM: ______ (Your Company Name)
______ (Street Address)
______ (City, State, Zip)
______ (Inquirer's manual signature)
______ (Print or type name of inquirer)
______ (Inquirer's title)

SUBJECT: ______ (Company on which inquiry is made)
______ (Street Address)
______ (City, State, Zip)

INQUIRER TO COMPLETE THIS SECTION

The purpose of the inquiry is:
☐ Initial order $ ______
Anticipated requirements $ ______
☐ Established customer; increased requirements to $ ______
☐ File revision.
☐ Change in payment experience from ______ to ______
☐ Other (describe) ______

We are referring this inquiry to you because:
☐ Your bank was given as a reference (provide branch/account no. if possible) ______
☐ We are checking with other area banks and information from your file only will suffice.
☐ Other (describe) ______

Our experience with the subject has been:
Sold since ______ Amount Owing $ ______
Last Sale ______ Terms ______
High Credit $ ______ Amount Past Due $ ______
Collateral (describe) ______
Are there guarantees, endorsements? ______

Our file contains:
☐ Current trade credit reports.
☐ Financial statement dated ______
Year end ( ) Interim ( )

The last time we made an inquiry of your bank on the subject was ______
Comments ______

BANK TO COMPLETE THIS SECTION

Our experience with the subject has been:
Depository accounts: Date(s) opened ______ Average Balances ______ If closed, when? ______
Aggregate balances used? ☐ yes ☐ no
Experience and comments ______

Loan Accommodations: Describe, including length of borrowing relationship, high credit, types of loan accommodations (line of credit, term loan, mortgage, installment, etc.), amount outstanding, amount past due (if any), collateral, guarantees and endorsements (if any).
______

Loan Experience/Comments: ______

Financial Statement: Date ______ Period Covered ______ Audited: ( ) yes ( ) no

NATIONAL ASSOCIATION OF CREDIT MANAGEMENT NACM

rma

This form and the "Statement of Principles" (See Reverse Side) have been approved by the Robert Morris Associates and the National Association of Credit Management.

______ (Manual signature of banker)
______ (Print or type name of banker)
______ (Banker's title)
______ (Date)

Form 19
Published by NACM
To be submitted in duplicate.
Bank to retain one copy.

Disclaimers

None of the sample letters includes a *statement of disclaimer* that is frequently printed at the bottom of credit department stationery. A majority of banks use disclaimer statements, or nonresponsibility notices, when responding to credit inquiries. This device notifies inquirers of the confidential nature of the communication and discourages recipients from misusing the information. Some banks believe that a disclaimer affords protection to the bank or at least discourages litigation. Others use the notice on a selective basis or not at all.

Robert Morris Associates cannot recommend a disclaimer that would be suitable for general use. A single, standardized statement would not be applicable for all banks because of varying bank policies and procedures, special circumstances, differing legal opinions and interpretations, and state laws. Furthermore, there is no definitive body of case law that directly comments on the use of disclaimers and the protection they may or may not afford.

A particular bank's legal counsel is in the best position to evaluate the use of disclaimers and construct a meaningful statement. Therefore, it may be advisable to review a disclaimer with counsel with the following thoughts and questions in mind:

> Is it possible that disclaimers which include a blanket statement denying *all* responsibility by the bank or its officers could be held to be meaningless? Can a bank disclaim to the point where its disclaimer, which may also include specific factual information, becomes invalid in its entirety? While opinions may differ on this, legal counsel should consider whether a broad statement of nonresponsibility is desirable.
>
> If the disclaimer states or implies that the bank or its officers attest to the accuracy of the information recited, counsel may wish to consider softening the language to reduce the responsibility assumed by the bank.
>
> Is the disclaimer up-to-date? If references to the Fair Credit Reporting Act, securities laws and regulations, and any applicable state laws or other technical points are included, have they been reviewed recently for accuracy? If such references are not included, the bank might want to explain that credit information is provided subject to the requirements of such laws. Of major importance are the Fair Credit Reporting Act and the federal securities laws—particularly Rule 10b-5, promulgated under the Securities Exchange Act of 1934—dealing with material representations and omissions in connection with the purchase or sale of any security.
>
> Does the bank choose to include a statement that deals with providing additional information in the future? Should a bank specifically inform an inquirer that it will *not* undertake to update a response by providing additional or further information that may be obtained, received, or discovered unless another inquiry is initiated? In this connection, counsel may

wish to review the *Heller* case. (*First Virginia Bankshares v. Benson, et al*, 559 F. 2d 1307 [5th Cir. 1977].)

Phrases such as "for your use only," "at your request," "subject to change without notice," "business purposes only," and "information contained herein is strictly factual" are often used in disclaimers. Bank counsel might wish to review these phrases to make certain that they are used appropriately and accurately reflect the bank's current practices. Review is strongly recommended if the disclaimer was merely copied from a statement used by another bank.

Staffing

Bank management and the credit department manager should determine how the credit inquiry and investigation functions are to be performed. Then they need to consider staffing requirements in view of specific responsibilities and estimated volume of work. A centralized credit unit will record and respond to all inquiries, conduct investigations, maintain records, and issue credit correspondence. Its staffing requirements will be quite different from those of a system in which each account officer responds to and initiates most requests for credit information.

Some banks will receive many more inquiries than others with a similar dollar amount of loans outstanding because of differences in their customer base. Certain account officers will initiate a high volume of credit inquiries, perhaps because they are developing new business. Therefore, it may be useful to monitor the volume of work, in terms of items processed and time expended, in order to evaluate staffing requirements.

Qualities and Skills

In selecting or appointing individuals to credit posts, the department manager should keep in mind the principal duties of a credit investigator and the qualities or skills necessary for successful performance of those duties. Examples of these duties may be summarized as follows:

- The investigator must determine the depth of response appropriate for each inquiry and must determine which inquiries take precedence over others. The employee must therefore be a self-starter, an individual capable of working without constant supervision. The investigator must demonstrate organizational abilities enabling him or her to set priorities.
- The investigator must gather information from various sources including agency reports, other banks, business credit grantors, and the

public records. An employee must therefore demonstrate an ability to extract pertinent information from appropriate sources.

- The investigator may be responsible for analyzing the data compiled and citing inconsistencies and irregularities. If this is the case, the employee should demonstrate an analytical ability to interpret data and to weigh the importance of positive and negative information.
- The investigator may be required to compile financial data, both from published reports and from data received in the information exchange process. Therefore, a working knowledge of accounting principles is useful at the entry level and essential as the investigator takes on additional duties.
- The investigator must assemble, organize, and document the information compiled and relay the information to the appropriate party. Good oral or written communication skills are important, and accuracy is essential.
- The investigator will occasionally meet with problems, both in communicating with others and in obtaining credit information from a respondent. A good investigator should be tactful but firm. Persistence is often needed to follow-up on requests for information.
- In gathering and reporting credit information, credit department personnel will communicate with many individuals who have varying responsibilities in banking and other industries. Therefore, it is important to choose staff with sufficient self-confidence to deal successfully with all management levels.
- The investigator must understand and respect the confidential nature of credit information.

Personnel Management

Since no manager finds it possible or practical to remain in the department at all times, it is necessary to develop a staff member or members who can assume responsibility during absences. Some managers accomplish this by establishing a "senior credit investigator" position. This staff member should be developed carefully so that he or she can process inquiries requiring unusual sophistication or knowledge. The senior credit investigator should be groomed to control the department in the manager's absence. In some banks, the senior investigator is given some responsibility for supervising other credit investigators. This key staff member should also be qualified to answer other investigators' questions and to share in training new personnel.

The way a credit inquiry department is organized varies depending on its size. Regardless of department size, the manager will find it helpful to maintain an up-to-date organization chart and have it available for all staff. The reasons are twofold: First, the chart will ensure that all personnel are aware of the organization of the department;

second, it will clearly indicate the lines of accountability in the manager's absence.

In distributing work to investigators, a manager must not forget that processing routine inquiries is tedious. Accuracy could suffer if an investigator were assigned only the most routine work. Unless an investigator has an opportunity to handle a variety of inquiries, development and morale could be seriously impaired.

A manager must develop a knowledge of the strengths, weaknesses, motivations, and personality of each staff member as well as special talents in order to delegate work properly. A consistent program of evaluation is essential. Each individual bank will undoubtedly have its own system and format for evaluation. If a bank has no system, one should be developed because it is vital these evaluations be performed regularly.

Training

After appropriate personnel have been selected, it is essential to provide adequate training so they can become successful investigators. Although the specifics of training are covered in Chapter 7, there are special requirements worth mentioning here. Banking is a dynamic industry, and changes occur regularly. Improvements in methods and services and new developments in credit legislation will require constant training and updating to maintain high-level performance. Thus, a primary responsibility of credit managers is to keep informed of any developments in the banking industry and in their banks' operations to ensure that this information is transmitted to the staff. In this manner, a manager can integrate training with the performance of regular duties.

Formal procedures for answering inquiries and conducting investigations are essential aids in training credit department staff. They must be in written form and must be readily available to all staff members. The procedures should reflect any new developments in applicable legislation and any changes in bank policy. They should give explicit instructions for processing the most common types of inquiries and investigations in clear, concise language and also indicate what inquiries should be referred to the manager or loan officer. The procedures can be an important training aid during the first critical weeks of an investigator's training. Thereafter, written procedures can eliminate an investigator's uncertainty about how to respond to particular inquiries. The procedures can also eliminate the investigator's need to consult peers or superiors for answers to routine questions.

Another training aid that could be developed by the bank would be a glossary or list of terms commonly used in the exchange of commercial credit information. A basic glossary is presented as Appendix C. A bank could expand this glossary to include terms that are unique to its operations, such as special designations for various types of loan arrangements, and terms that are often used in its particular geographical area.

Each credit investigator will eventually develop a style in responding to inquiries by letter. But until that happens, it is helpful to keep a manual containing sample replies to inquiries. Copies of actual replies could be used for the manual, illustrating appropriate responses in particular situations. All credit investigators have spent time searching for the proper phrases to use in responding to an unusual or difficult inquiry. Circulating actual letters which demonstrate good style and complete information is a training device many managers find helpful.

An investigator should be given ongoing guidance to develop the additional assurance and knowledge needed to handle difficult situations. For example, when the senior investigator or credit manager has processed an unusual or particularly difficult inquiry, the method and rationale used should be communicated to other investigators. It is incumbent upon the manager to encourage senior personnel to take full advantage of such occasions for training of staff.

In addition, credit investigators must develop an awareness of the cost of conducting an investigation or inquiry in relation to the value of the information compiled. A staff member can be trained to follow guidelines and to comply with the requirements of legislation, but a person cannot be specifically trained to make the appropriate decision in every special circumstance or emergency. Guidance, communication, and evaluation are all necessary for personnel development.

Legislation and Credit Information Exchange

The Consumer Credit Protection Act was signed into law by President Lyndon Johnson on May 29, 1968. Since then, the Act has been amended many times, and most of these amendments expanded its coverage to provide additional protection of the credit rights and privileges of consumers. The Board of Governors of the Federal Reserve System and the Federal Reserve banks now administer more than 24 regulations affecting a wide range of financial activities. These include several regulations established to implement laws pertaining to consumer credit transactions. Historically, these laws and regulations have applied to the exchange of credit information regarding retail, or consumer, credit. However, legislation is periodically considered which would expand coverage to commercial transactions as well.

Failure to comply with the law, either by design or through carelessness, places the bank in jeopardy because it could become the target of lengthy and costly litigation. Moreover, customers' rights could be violated by noncompliance. It is therefore incumbent on bank management to ensure that appropriate measures are taken to achieve compliance throughout the bank. Furthermore, it is essential that the credit department manager:

- Understands how to achieve compliance in the operations of the credit information exchange function
- Is kept informed of developments and procedural changes
- Understands the meaning and implications of the applicable laws and regulations
- Is authorized to seek advice from appropriate parties, including bank counsel, in regard to resolving matters of concern

The credit department manager should make certain that his or her staff's understanding of the laws and regulations is sufficient to prevent noncompliance. Ideally, such material should be incorporated in the department's policy guidelines.

While it is impractical here to detail current state and federal laws and regulations which affect the exchange of credit information, they are important considerations in credit department operations. Therefore, a few comments concerning the background and constraints of selected federal laws may help the manager focus on some of the more important questions in this area.

Fair Credit Reporting Act

During the 1960s, with the growth of consumerism, concern was often voiced that credit data were improperly compiled and indiscriminately sold by some credit reporting agencies. In addition to information regarding credit performance, reports sometimes contained data referring to the subject's character and mode of living. Frequently, the information compiled by these agencies was gathered without the subject's knowledge. Moreover, the subjects had no legal right to receive disclosure of the information compiled and released by consumer reporting agencies.

The Fair Credit Reporting Act (Public Law 91-508, Title VI of the Consumer Credit Protection Act), effective April 25, 1971, was passed to respond to this situation. The May 1971 publication *Financial Institutions and the Fair Credit Reporting Act*, jointly distributed by several bank regulatory agencies including the Federal Reserve Board and the Office of the Comptroller of the Currency, stated:

"It [the Act] is designed to insure fair and accurate reporting of information regarding consumers. It restricts the use of reports on consumers, and in certain situations requires the deletion of obsolete information. It requires notice to consumers when the use of a credit report contributes to the denial or increase in the cost of credit or insurance, or denial of employment. Disclosures must also be made when credit is denied or the cost is increased on the basis of other information from third parties, and when investigative consumer reports are used. Under the Act consumers are entitled to disclosure of the information maintained in their files by consumer reporting agencies, and procedures are provided for the correction of erroneous information. The collection, use, and referral of information on consumers for credit, insurance, employment and other purposes by financial institutions is directly affected by this Act.

"Financial institutions are likely to be subject to the Act as credit grantors, purchasers of dealer paper, issuers of credit cards, and employers. In some instances, a financial institution may even be a consumer reporting agency under the Act as a result of the type of information about consumers that it provides to others. In general, the Act does not apply to commercial transactions."

A consumer reporting agency was defined as "an entity which, for monetary fees, dues, or on a cooperative nonprofit basis, *regularly* engages in whole or in part in the practice of assembling or evaluating consumer credit information or other information on consumers for the purpose of furnishing consumer reports to third parties, and which uses any means or facility of interstate commerce for the purpose of preparing or furnishing consumer reports."

Furthermore, if a financial institution regularly passes on information in its files about a consumer, other than information that relates solely to its own transactions or experiences with a customer, it may be considered a consumer reporting agency.

Thus, in some cases a bank could be included in this classification. And if it is considered a consumer reporting agency, there are many responsibilities that must be assumed, including proper disclosure requirements, record-keeping practices, and handling of disputes. If it is bank policy to avoid being considered a consumer reporting agency, experience would suggest that the credit department confine itself to relaying purely factual reports on its own consumer credit transactions with its customers and avoid relaying information received from a third party. But conditions and laws change, and advice of counsel should be sought on this matter.

There are several ways in which bank credit departments, even if they are not considered consumer reporting agencies, are affected by the Fair Credit Reporting Act. For example, if a financial institution uses consumer reports, it must follow specified procedures to obtain such reports for legitimate business purposes. Also, there is a responsibility to make certain disclosures to the consumer if information obtained from an outside source contributed to a denial or increase in the cost of credit.

Many banks utilize magnetic tapes from their computer systems to transmit reports of consumer credit transactions to credit reporting agencies. This method virtually eliminates reporting consumer transactions directly to inquirers. However, there are many bank credit departments which do not use tapes and do release credit information on both consumer and commercial transactions to inquirers. Therefore, credit investigators and reporters must be certain when they are dealing with a consumer, rather than a commercial, transaction.

For example, it is easy to understand how a credit reporter could inadvertently release credit information for third-party use if a loan was made in the commercial loan department to an owner of a business for personal reasons and was not clearly earmarked as being a consumer transaction. Precautions should be taken to enable credit reporters to differentiate clearly between consumer and commercial transactions, including checking accounts and loans. Such definition can avoid inadvertent reporting of consumer transactions in response to inquiries made on behalf of third parties.

Federal legislation is periodically introduced to expand the Fair Credit Reporting Act to include certain aspects of commercial credit transactions. If such legislation were passed, banks could then face the decision of whether to become "commercial reporting services," by regularly providing commercial credit information for use by third parties. This could be a difficult decision for many banks, and it could have a significant impact on the credit information process and related record-keeping and disclosure practices.

Equal Credit Opportunity Act

Another Act that has an impact on the exchange of credit information is the Equal Credit Opportunity Act (ECOA). Regulation B was issued under the authority of ECOA in October 1975 and was subsequently revised to carry out the 1976 amendments to the ECOA. Very broadly stated, Regulation B prohibits creditors from discriminating against credit applicants, establishes guidelines for gathering and evaluating credit information, requires that notification be furnished when adverse action is taken on an application for credit, provides for notification of reasons for adverse action, and sets forth procedures for furnishing certain types of credit information and for record retention.

Regulation B affects many bank operating procedures including the taking and completing of applications, compilation and use of data in evaluating credit requests, and record-keeping practices. It is beyond the scope of this chapter to discuss Regulation B, about which volumes have already been written. However, the credit manager should pay particular attention to requirements for furnishing credit information as set forth in Section 202.10 of Regulation B. In essence, the Regulation's impact on the exchange of credit information has been primarily as follows: When credit information is being gathered or relayed in connection with evaluating an application, any accounts for which the applicant was contractually liable must be considered. Also, any account in which the applicant participated with a spouse or former spouse and which can be shown to demonstrate the applicant's creditworthiness must be evaluated. Therefore, banks must design their information retrieval systems so that pertinent information is available and can be accessed in the name of the individual about whom credit information was requested. Quoting from Regulation B, Section 202.10, Furnishing of Credit Information:

> Regulations under the Act give married persons the right to have credit information included in credit reports in the name of both the wife and the husband if both use or are responsible for the account. This right was created, in part, to insure that credit histories will be available to women who become divorced or widowed.

To highlight restrictions on gathering credit information, a creditor is prohibited from making any inquiry about race, color, religion, or national origin of the applicant or any other person in connection with a credit transaction. In addition, there are specific restrictions on inquiries with regard to the applicant's sex, age, and marital status.

Financial Institutions Regulatory and Interest Rate Control Act of 1978

On Nov. 10, 1978, the Financial Institutions Regulatory and Interest Rate Control Act (FIRA) was signed into law by President Jimmy Carter. Title XI of FIRA is called the "Right to Financial Privacy Act of 1978" (RFPA) and governs the procedures to be followed by a bank when the federal government seeks access to records of customer transactions. The law covers access to information on a bank's present and former customers but does not protect corporations, large partnerships, associations, or trusts.

Since credit information exchange personnel are often partly responsible for assembling customer records in response to requests by federal government agencies, the manager should become familiar with the RFPA procedural requirements with which a financial institution should comply. All staff should have operational guidelines so that records are not incorrectly released.

In essence, Section 1102(a) of RFPA provides that no employee of a financial institution may provide any federal government authority access to, copies of, or information contained in a customer's financial records except in accordance with RFPA. Also, the institution must obtain written certification of RFPA compliance before it may release the requested records to the government authority. This relieves the bank of liability for government failure to comply with RFPA. Credit department managers should review the law with legal counsel to determine the procedures to be followed and to establish, or learn how to participate in, a record-keeping system that keeps track of government requests.

Manager's Responsibilities

While only three of the many consumer protection laws have been discussed, it should be apparent that consumer credit reporting creates some special problems for the credit department manager. It is essential that federal and state laws are followed in order to protect the bank from costly lawsuits as well as protect the legitimate rights of customers. Credit department staffs must be well aware of these facts. They should fully recognize the need to maintain accurate documentation on all responses given and received in order to comply with record-keeping and disclosure requirements. In this regard, it is essential that management define the responsibility of its commercial credit department in regard to both consumer and commercial customers. This definition is important whether or not consumer credit reporting is a commercial credit department function.

At the time this chapter was written, Alaska had the only statute guaranteeing privacy of bank records for both consumer and commercial accounts. If this type of legislation should become widespread, it could have serious implications for the exchange of credit information. For example, an inquirer might have to obtain and relay to the bank of account a customer's written authorization that credit information can be released.

The primary purpose of mentioning these possibilities is to emphasize that the credit manager must recognize his or her duty to monitor proposed federal and state legislation affecting the credit area. Legislators are kept well informed on positions maintained by organized consumer groups in regard to legislation affecting credit practices. Their arguments are often strong and persuasive. Thus, it is to the bankers' advantage, as professionals, to be sure lawmakers and regulators are made equally well aware of the possible deleterious effects restrictive legislation could have on business.

It is also incumbent on credit professionals, in both banking and industry, to ensure that legislative and regulatory requirements are met. Furthermore, adherence to the generally accepted guidelines for exchanging commercial credit information as presented in the RMA *Code of Ethics* and the NACM-RMA *Statement of Principles* should help prevent the conditions which led to the Fair Credit Reporting Act.

If credit information exchange is conducted in a professional and ethical manner, protecting the interests of the customer as well as the creditor, there should be no need for additional legislation.

Customer Involvement

Educating Commercial Customers

Those banks which have not already done so should consider instituting formal procedures to educate commercial borrowers about the credit information exchange process. Typically, existing customers, as both seekers and grantors of credit, have used or are familiar with traditional credit inquiry and response procedures. However, first-time borrowers and others may benefit from an education program.

By encouraging customers to become more informed in this area, banks may find business relationships are improved. For example, customers who realize that their bank of account can conduct investigations on their behalf may screen their own applicants for credit more readily. Also, customers can acquire an insight into how credit information exchange assists businesses both in obtaining and granting credit. Customers will also learn what the bank does to protect their privacy.

Customer education can be accomplished in many ways. For example, RMA's *Commercial Credit Information Exchange: A Two-Way Street* pamphlet contains basic information about the process. It can be used as a customer handout, or its ideas can be incorporated in other customer information material. In addition to explaining credit information exchange, the pamphlet pinpoints areas of interest that commercial customers might discuss with their bankers. Banks desiring to explain their policies and procedures in more detail could develop a more specific brochure or information statement. The statement could list and describe the sources of credit information generally used by the bank to complete and confirm a credit history. The circumstances under which credit information is normally released could also be explained.

Notification

Where applicable, banks could formally notify customers that credit information is exchanged in accordance with the *Code of Ethics* and the *Statement of Principles* and offer to provide copies of these guidelines. For notification purposes, banks might include an appropriate statement on documents such as signature cards, loan agreements, applications for credit, or the like. Some banks may ask the customer to sign a notification statement, acknowledging he or she has read the notice. As in many policy matters, it would be wise to seek advice of counsel in connection with a notification program

Customer Authorization

Many bankers logically assume that implicit authorization to exchange credit information is provided by the customer when credit references are supplied. However, there is now considerable discussion about the concept of explicit customer authorization. In essence, it might require a bank to obtain written permission from a customer before credit information about that customer is released or sought.

Explicit authorization, like many other privacy-related issues, is still being evaluated. Therefore, no attempt will be made to weigh the various arguments or explore the operational procedures that might be involved. Furthermore, the specific effect that some procedures would have on the free and responsible exchange of commercial credit information is difficult to predict. Nevertheless, such procedures could result in considerable additional paperwork and costs and might create serious problems if a customer could not be reached or if a credit were deteriorating.

Obviously, these difficult issues are important to bank loan and credit officers. Since notification, authorization, and other privacy-related issues are becoming increasingly significant, credit department managers should review them with bank counsel and with management. RMA recommends the current status of any legislation related to privacy be examined carefully before policy decisions are made. It might also be worthwhile to discuss these issues with commercial customers to obtain their reactions and ideas. In any event, credit department managers and bank management should be aware of and monitor these issues. These concerns are relevant to the customer, to bank operations, and to the smooth and professional handling of the credit information exchange process.

Summary

Professional management of the credit information exchange function will have a positive effect on the bank's profitability. This is true whether the bank charges for these services. An investigations staff that obtains timely, accurate, and complete credit information for the bank and its customers will improve the lending process and could be a major factor in attracting new business.

The credit manager has many opportunities for professional development since the information exchange function is not static. The manager must keep up with the privacy issue and various laws and regulations that affect performance of the function. In addition, he or she can make important contributions in developing a credit department policy statement and in training employees to become credit professionals.

The free flow of commercial credit information is vital to our credit-based economy. Since the effectiveness of the system is based on trust between inquirers and respondents, adherence to the guidelines and standards set forth in the *Code of Ethics* and *Statement of Principles* is essential.

EXAMPLES OF CREDIT CORRESPONDENCE
Sample Letter Formats—Bank to Bank Use

Loan Request — Existing Customer

TO: DATE:

SUBJECT:

Dear :

We are seeking credit information on the above subject for our own use, and your name has been obtained as a reference. This inquiry concerns an additional loan request involving the following amount and type of credit extension:

Our experience with the customer is as follows:

We would appreciate receiving the following information: opening date of the relationship, history of the subject, demand deposit information, a complete summary of the borrowing relationship, financial statement data if available, overall experience with the subject, and other comments relevant to the relationship.

You may be assured that all information you share with us will be handled with discretion, and your reply will be held in strict confidence.

We are enclosing a stamped, self-addressed envelope for your convenience. If we can reciprocate at any time, please do not hesitate to contact us.

Sincerely yours,

____

(signature)

____

(print or type name and title)

The format of the sample letter for "Loan Request — Existing Customer" may be modified for use in different situations by changing the first paragraph. Some suggestions are offered below.

Initial Loan Request

Dear :

We are seeking credit information on the above subject for our own use, and your name has been obtained as a reference. This inquiry concerns an initial loan request involving the following amount and type of credit extension:

Mutual Exchange

Dear :

We are in the process of updating our credit file on the company identified above, a mutual customer. The following is a summary of our experience with the subject:

Customer Investigation — File Revision

Dear :

We have been requested by one of our customers to obtain credit information on the above subject, and your name has been given as a reference. The purpose of the investigation is a file revision. A summary of our customer's experience with the subject follows:

Customer Investigation — Customer First Order

Dear :

We have been requested by one of our customers to obtain credit information from you on the above subject. Our customer stated that the investigation is requested in regard to a first order in the amount of:

Fish — On Behalf of Customer

(Note: While RMA discourages fishing, unusual circumstances may make it necessary.)

Dear :

We have been requested by one of our customers to obtain credit information on the above subject. Unfortunately, our customer did not know the bank of account, and we would be grateful if you would investigate in your area on our behalf.

Sample Letter Formats—Bank Inquiring to Trade

File Revision — Bank Use Only

TO: DATE:

SUBJECT:

Dear :

We are in the process of updating our credit file on the above company. Your name has been obtained as a reference. The following is a summary of our experience with the subject:

The form on the reverse side of this letter may be used for your response. We would appreciate receiving the following information: opening date of the relationship, date of last sale, recent high credit, present outstanding, amount past due, terms of sale, collateral, and the existence of guarantees and endorsements, if any. Also of importance would be comments on your overall experience with the subject, including the manner of payment.

We have enclosed a stamped, self-addressed envelope for your convenience. You may be assured that all information you share with us will be handled with discretion and that your reply will be held in strict confidence. If we can reciprocate at any time, please do not hesitate to contact us.

Sincerely yours,

____
(signature)

____
(print or type name and title)

Form that would appear on reverse side of "File Revision — Bank Use Only"

Opening date of relationship: ______________________________

Date of last sale: ______________________________

Recent high credit: ______________________________

Present outstanding: ______________________________

Amount past due: ______________________________

Terms of sale: ______________________________

Collateral: ______________________________

Guarantees/Endorsements: ______________________________

Manner of payment: ______________________________

Other comments: ______________________________

____

____

____
(signature)

____
(print or type name and title)

____
(date)

The format of the sample letter for "File Revision — Bank Use Only" may be modified for use in different situations by changing the first paragraph. Some suggestions are offered below.

New Customer — Bank Use Only

Dear :

We are seeking credit information on the above subject for our own use, and your name has been obtained as a reference. This inquiry concerns an initial loan request involving the following amount and type of credit extension:

Customer Investigation — Customer First Order

Dear :

We have been requested by one of our customers to obtain credit information from you on the above subject, and your name has been given as a reference. Our customer stated that the investigation was requested in regard to a first order in the amount of:

Customer Investigation — File Revision

Dear :

We have been requested by one of our customers to obtain credit information on the above subject, and your name has been given as a reference. The purpose of the investigation is a file revision. A summary of our customer's experience with the subject follows:

A Typical Reply to a Credit Inquiry — Full Response

Mr. T.S. Adams, III
Vice President
Flatbrush Fifth National Bank
P.O. Box 492
Chicago, IL 94370

Dec. 14, 19X9

RE: Gladstone-Rittenhouse, Inc.
225 South Garrett Lane
Newfield, Connecticut 47209

Dear Mr. Adams:

We are pleased to reply to your inquiry of Dec. 11, 19X9, concerning Gladstone-Rittenhouse, Inc.

The subject has maintained an account with us since July 20, 19X3. Average deposit balances are in the moderate six-figure range, and the account is handled in a satisfactory manner. In addition, the subject maintains a corporate savings account with a present balance of a low six-figure amount.

At present, we extend a moderate seven-figure line of credit to the subject, secured by accounts receivable and inventory and guaranteed by the principals. The line was originally approved in July 19X9 for a low seven-figure amount and has been reapproved annually through July 19X9. The line was increased to moderate seven figures in July 19X3. Since the line is secured, there has been no annual clean-up requirement. This accommodation is handled according to terms, and a low seven-figure amount is presently outstanding.

We also extend a low six-figure, five-year term loan to the subject secured by the equipment. This loan was made on May 12, 19X9, and is being handled according to terms. Present outstanding is a high five-figure amount.

The subject recently paid off a medium five-figure unsecured loan for working capital purposes which was handled as agreed.

Financial statement information has been given to us in confidence; however, we can state that the subject's latest financial statement dated 6/30/X9 reflects profitable operations.* We suggest that you contact the subject for details of its financial condition.

Incorporated under Connecticut laws in 19X3, the company is a manufacturer of patio and garden furniture. Management includes Frederick A. Buck, Chairman of the Board; Robert D. Burns, President; and Megan Miller, Treasurer.

Our experience with the subject has been entirely satisfactory. If we can be of further assistance, please don't hesitate to contact us.

Sincerely yours,

____
(signature)

____
(print or type name and title)

*When a bank releases financial statement data, Article 3 of RMA's *Code of Ethics* should be consulted.

Sample Form Letters

Reply to Credit Inquiry — Nonborrowing Relationship

TO: DATE:

SUBJECT:

This is in reply to your inquiry dated ____ regarding the above subject.

Checking Account Relationship	**Time Deposit Relationship**
Account Opened ____	Corporate Savings Opened ____
Average Balance ☐ Low figures / Moderate figures / Medium figures	Present Balance ____
Aggregate Balances ☐ High figures	CD ☐
Satisfactory ☐ Generally Satisfactory ☐	
Unsatisfactory ☐	

Remarks:

We have searched our records and are unable to locate a borrowing relationship with the subject. If we can be of further assistance, please feel free to contact us.

Sincerely yours,

____
(signature)

____
(print or type name and title)

Reply to Credit Inquiry Correspondence — Borrowing Relationship

TO: DATE:

SUBJECT:

This is in reply to your inquiry dated ____ regarding the above subject.

Checking Account Relationship	**Time Deposit Relationship**
Account Opened ____	Corporate Savings Opened ____
Average Balance ☐ Low figures / Moderate figures	Present Balance ____
Aggregate Balances ☐ Medium figures / High figures	CD ☐
Satisfactory ☐ Generally Satisfactory ☐	
Unsatisfactory ☐	

Borrowing Relationship

Opening date__________ Type of accommodation(s) __________

High credit __________ Present outstanding __________

Security (describe) __________

Guarantees/Endorsements __________

Purpose(s) of accommodation(s) __________

Terms __________ Maturity date __________ Clean-up period __________

Approval date __________ Expiration date __________

Summary of paid out loans __________

Overall experience __________

Other comments __________

____

If we can be of further assistance, please don't hesitate to contact us.

Sincerely yours,

____

(signature)

____

(print or type name and title)

Reply to Credit Inquiry Correspondence — No Record and Miscellaneous Responses

TO: DATE:

SUBJECT:

This is in reply to your inquiry dated regarding the above subject:

- ☐ We have checked with several areas in the bank and have been unable to locate a relationship with the subject. Please supply us with any additional information that may be helpful, and we will be pleased to investigate further.
- ☐ Our files show a different address from the one you provided for the subject. Please verify the address that was given to us.
- ☐ Information given is insufficient for us to identify the subject properly. If you will provide us with additional information such as __________, we will be pleased to investigate further.
- ☐ In order for us to provide credit information, the purpose for and the amount of the inquiry must be provided.

☐ Other: __________

____

Sincerely yours,

____

(signature)

____

(print or type name and title)

7

The Training Function

In many banks, the credit department no longer has the primary responsibility for training lending and credit personnel. Nevertheless, the credit area typically remains the center of a bank's overall commercial loan training activities, expecially in small-to-medium-size banks. The credit departments in such banks are often the only units capable of providing well-rounded training experiences for employees involved in the credit and lending functions.

Given the logical relationship between credit and lending skills, the credit department offers many opportunities for employees to develop expertise in these areas. Furthermore, the credit area is well suited to provide on-the-job training since certain credit skills may be rapidly developed. And within a relatively short time, trainees may also be able to perform necessary tasks

Few bankers would argue that the credit department should be the only area to provide commercial loan training programs. Often the commercial loan or credit officer is responsible for the entire banking relationship with a customer. This responsibility requires skills in areas such as management, interviewing, financial counseling, negotiating, loan administration, marketing, and written and oral communications. The credit department may not be able to offer training in management skills or in such bank operations as proof and transit or in marketing techniques. But it can provide exposure to a variety of lending and credit tasks, the mastery of which is essential to the development of competent commercial loan officers, branch managers, analysts, statement spreaders, and credit investigators.

Role of the Credit Department

Assume that a bank has decided to institute or upgrade its training program. The credit department's contribution may be very limited, or its manager may be responsible for developing, instituting, and administering virtually all the bank's commercial loan training opportunities. In choosing between the alternatives, one must take into account the size of the bank, the number of trainees, the experience levels and expected career paths of the trainees, the funds and time available for training, the expertise and teaching capabilities of the trainers, and educational resources available within the community but outside the bank.

The following three situations illustrate some possible roles of the credit department in relationship to the bank's training program.

Minimal Involvement

Especially in a very large bank, all training could be accomplished in a formal training program completely removed from ongoing bank operations. In such programs, large numbers of students may be trained in groups. The training department, complete with classrooms and resources, functions full time.

In this case, the credit department manager's contribution would be minimal. But it might include suggestions on curriculum content and some specialized presentations for the class on such topics as credit information exchange, proper use of credit files, analytical techniques, and analysis of special industries.

Primary Responsibility

In this situation, the credit department manager could be fully responsible for developing, instituting, and administering the entire training effort for commercial loan and credit personnel. The manager would be required to work with bank management to define training goals, develop the curriculum, and gather resources. When necessary, he or she could request other bank departments and experts to contribute in their areas of expertise. Particularly in smaller banks, the credit department manager often has been assigned this responsibility, especially if that person is a good instructor with a strong commercial banking background.

Shared Responsibility

Another possible role for the credit department is to share training responsibilities with other areas of the bank. In this case, the credit department manager might contribute to the development of the overall curriculum by working with other department heads. For example, bank management and department heads could decide that trainees should spend four to eight weeks in various areas of bank operations, each with its own curriculum. However, the credit department would be responsible for credit training.

Those responsible for the other areas would provide instruction in such topics as general ledger, proof and transit, bookkeeping, and various functions of bank tellers. This training would provide a basic understanding of how these functions contribute to overall bank operations. Trainees could then spend as little as a few months or as much as a year or two in the commercial credit department, with the designated amount of time related to each trainee's previous banking experience and expected career path. Finally, all potential loan and credit officers could conclude the program by spending a few months working closely with the loan administration trainer or with a selected loan officer on a one-to-one basis.

For the purposes of this chapter, the credit department manager in a small-to-medium-size bank has been assigned the overall responsibility for developing, implementing, and administering a complete training program for all commercial lending and credit personnel. Therefore, the manager must not only consider the curriculum to be offered in the credit department but also the goals of the bank regarding identified needs, time, personnel, costs, and the scope of training required in other departments.

Essential Ingredients of Successful Training

Any serious training effort must consider who is to be trained, objectives of the training, and methods used to accomplish the stated goals within the time available. A number of training methods can introduce the trainee to the knowledge and skills needed to become a competent commercial banker. Specific methods that work well within one bank might not be suitable in another; nevertheless, there are certain common elements. These essential ingredients include management support, a competent and enthusiastic trainer, and trainees who want to progress in a business environment. Each item merits closer examination.

Management Support

The training program, be it existing or contemplated, must be fully supported by bank management. If not, frustration and failure will almost certainly result. The first task of the credit department manager is to cultivate tangible, not token, support from the top. Management must be convinced that employee time spent in the training program is not wasted; that a capable employee must possess skills and knowledge in certain subject areas; and that even the most intelligent and experienced individual requires specific training to understand the policies, operations, and expectations of a particular bank.

Management must also recognize that the long-term benefits of a training program may not be immediately apparent. In terms of the time required, a training program may appear to be very costly. However, the costs involved in only one incorrect credit decision that might have been prevented by thorough training may be substantially higher.

The commitment from management should be publicized throughout the bank. Some banks even distribute a statement of support for the program to all bank employees. This statement makes clear to both seasoned bank personnel and trainees that every effort will be exerted to ensure trainees will not be taken out of a training program before it is completed.

Furthermore, the statement frequently gives notice that other departments will not be permitted to "borrow" trainees for purposes unrelated to the learning process. Unfortunately, especially in smaller banks with limited staff flexibility, these standards are hard to maintain.

The Trainer

Another necessary ingredient for a successful program is a competent, enthusiastic, patient trainer. The instructor needs to be a master of the knowledge and skills to be taught to others. The instructor should also recognize his or her own lack of expertise in a given area and know when to call on others for assistance. Regardless of other functions to be performed in the bank, a good instructor should develop teaching skills and familiarity with available teaching materials and aids. It is reasonable to expect instructors to study and understand the principles by which people learn and to apply those methods and techniques which are most useful.

An effective teacher should have experience in the credit area since, by blending theory with practice, personal experiences in banking can be drawn upon to teach a concept or skill. While the teacher should be aware of training materials, he or she should also recognize that good instruction is frequently more important to the success of a training program. No doubt, an innovative individual can find almost unlimited training resources available in a credit department. Nevertheless, the development of training materials is itself an art, and optimum results are achieved when good instruction is combined with quality instructional materials.

A good instructor must express concepts clearly. He or she must not only be sure the trainees understand the subject matter but must also check that training methods, materials, and processes are achieving their objectives.

Some large banks hire individuals specifically to perform the training function. In smaller banks, it would be unusual to find a full-time trainer. But full or part time, the important consideration is the ability of the individual to be a trainer. It is the person's ability to teach, not necessarily his or her position, which should determine who does the training. Often an effective credit department manager may not be a suitable instructor. Therefore, it is important to identify those individuals in a bank who do meet the requirements of a good instructor and use them to their fullest.

In a smaller bank, the credit department manager will probably have to develop some teaching skills. But, for best results, employees from other departments should be involved in both developing and implementing a credit and loan training program. This should be the case even if the credit department manager has primary responsibility for overall training.

The Trainee

The training function in many banks develops the skills and knowledge of trainees who will remain in the credit area and those who will work in other bank areas, particularly in commercial lending. Regardless of the career paths a bank may expect its trainees to follow, there are certain qualities that all credit trainees should possess.

For example, they should be comfortable working with numbers. It is doubtful that even the most competent and enthusiastic instructor could overcome a trainee's basic resistance to working with and comprehending figures. Suitable trainees should also be able to communicate an idea or a concept to others. While the credit and loan training function may not be expected to dictate hiring policies, the desirable characteristics for a trainee should be defined by the credit trainer, bank management, and the person who does the recruiting.

The hiring decision is often subjective, and its result is critical to the success of a training program. Significant training problems can arise if the program is not supported by intelligent hiring practices. For example, the overqualified trainee may quickly become bored with a training program on a level below his or her ability or education. The result may be either the rapid departure of the trainee or the underutilization of the trainee's talents. In either case, much of the training effort will be wasted. On the other hand, underqualified people may become frustrated with training or jobs that they are not equipped to handle from the outset.

It is suggested that a trainee's educational background should be well suited to career goals and that the trainee exhibit a receptive attitude toward training. The more developed a training program is, the more flexibility a bank has in hiring new personnel or in adapting the training program to suit the background and experience of the trainees. If the ability to train is limited, the bank should try to hire more experienced personnel.

It is essential that each bank clearly identify its present and future needs when constructing a program and properly define the areas of training responsibility. And the bank must determine what types of trainees will enter the program. Credit departments usually have at least two primary areas of training responsibility. First, they must train and develop their own staff; second, they must help train employees who will eventually be assigned to work in other areas of the bank.

A third area of responsibility, one sometimes overlooked when training is centered in the credit area, is the need for continuing education. The credit department should be at least partially responsible for refreshing and expanding the skills of seasoned bank employees as well as those of entry-level trainees. This is important, assuming a bank regularly promotes from within. Continuing education is also essential in such subject areas as accounting or compliance where practices or regulations change frequently in application or interpretation.

Defining Training Needs

The bank must carefully review its present and future needs when constructing a training program. The following questions, among others, should be answered if a clear picture of the program is to be established.

- Is our personnel shortage so acute that, at the moment, we must hire the most experienced people we can find and train almost exclusively in such areas as bank policies, procedures, and operations? After the initial need is addressed, what is our long-term plan?

- Are we committed to promoting existing employees? Is there a shortage of promotable talent in the bank? Should our program concentrate on developing present employees, recruiting entry-level trainees, or could the training needs of both groups be addressed simultaneously?

- What are our present and future human resource requirements? How long will it take the bank to train people to meet these needs? How can enough trainees be developed in the time available?

- How many trainees will be involved in the program during an average year?

- How much money should we allocate for the training program?

- Are our existing loan and credit officers being kept up-to-date on changes that regularly occur in certain areas of banking? Is this an appropriate area for in-house training, or would it be more practical to rely on outside assistance, such as workshops and seminars, for continuing education?

Training and the Need to Produce

Some banks, especially the larger ones, hold that production standards and goals are not at all compatible with entry-level training standards and goals. In other words, those banks feel the trainee cannot be expected to acquire a basic skill, nor go through the initial phase of developing that skill, in an environment that is production-oriented. Therefore, some banks have completely eliminated the need for trainees to produce work during their training. This type of "classroom" training provides a favorable learning environment in which the instructor can control the introduction of a new skill. A formal program eliminates the need to make concessions constantly to production goals, standards, and emergencies.

However, there are many banks which claim to have a training program but, in fact, are only instructing their trainees to react to production needs and crises. In this situation, a trainee who knows absolutely nothing about financial statement analysis may be handed a financial statement, a spread sheet, and a request to "get this out by 4:00 p.m. today." The trainee may learn how to fill out the form to meet the deadline but will not learn the basic concepts involved in actually working with financial data. Too much production-oriented training will provide limited opportunities for structured learning. This type of on-the-job training may be dangerous in that trainees may acquire misconceptions that go undetected.

Many banks are unable to provide a formal training program that is completely removed from a production-oriented environment. Others firmly believe that training should not, as a matter of principle, be removed from "real life" situations or the actual working environment.

As a general rule, however, and on a cost-benefit basis, banks that provide only on-the-job training are probably not providing any constructive training at all. In fact, they might as well encourage their personnel departments to hire the most experienced individuals they can find.

Allocating Time

For many banks, it would be virtually impossible to allocate large blocks of time to a formal training and development program. Nevertheless, it is possible to provide a logical, structured learning experience if only small amounts of regularly scheduled time are set aside exclusively for training. The key words here are *regularly scheduled*, that is, the time must be specifically designated for training. The 15 minutes the credit department manager has to spare because a loan review meeting was delayed, for example, is *not* scheduled training time.

Assuming that the credit department manager is responsible for developing the program, one of the first questions to be addressed is how do we find the time? Even the smallest credit department should be able to reserve regular blocks of time devoted exclusively to training. The following suggestions might be considered when time must be budgeted carefully.

- A specific part of each day could be devoted to training. For example, the trainees could be required to meet from 8 a.m. to 10 a.m. every day. Generally, early morning hours are preferred because students are more alert then. In addition, the normal work pressures—often potential sources of interruptions—may be reduced or eliminated during these hours. The training sessions can be reinforced immediately through the careful selection of related production-oriented tasks to be accomplished during the balance of the working day.

- Lunch sessions could be held on a regular basis, perhaps once a week, to discuss informally individual and class progress and problems.

- Formal training sessions, perhaps one-to-two-hour lectures, can introduce students to important concepts. Trainees also could be expected to complete various assignments and solve problems at home. When completed, these assignments could be reviewed on a one-to-one basis, as a group, or both.

For example, the credit department manager might prepare a case study on selecting the most appropriate financing for a customer. Discussion of the methods by which the trainees arrived at possible solutions will reinforce learning and also assist the trainer in evaluating a student's progress.

■ Formal classroom sessions can be conducted by various bank employees or other experts in a specialized area. For example, many bank employees benefit from presentations on the bankruptcy laws made by legal counsel. Or in banks with specialized lenders, the accounts receivable expert might prepare a program to describe the purposes, goals, and methods involved in a field audit of a borrowing customer's accounts.

■ Students should realize that they will be expected to study on their own both during and outside normal banking hours. This independent study could entail solving problems presented in class, reading materials that were suggested or provided by the instructor, or attending night school. Extra time could be devoted to completing tasks required for performing the job at hand—statement spreading, for example.

■ Some banks offer instruction services that can be presented to employees of other banks.

■ Trainers should investigate the various workshops, seminars, and other programs that are conducted by banking associations such as Robert Morris Associates, National Association of Bank Women, and the American Bankers Association. These intensive courses might be the answer for a trainee who requires development in a specific area but cannot leave the bank for any significant period of time.

These are just a few possibilities for integrating training opportunities into the normal work flow of any bank or department. Whatever decisions are made regarding time allocation, certain blocks of time must be designated solely for the purposes of training. It must be remembered that the shorter the time available for producing a competent employee, the more intensive the training effort must be. For example, three trainees who were not expected to produce usable output while in training might require one year or less of intensive classroom study. If the same three students were expected to generate usable work during training and if only a few hours each week were devoted to training, they might require two or three times as long to develop the required skills.

Whether the credit department is responsible for training only a few employees a year or many, there should be a logical program and a commitment to develop each employee as completely as possible within the existing financial and time constraints.

Program Design and Implementation

It is expected that the training curriculum will be well defined and planned. It is not uncommon to see the course content set forth in great detail through the use of complex charts and graphs. While this approach is desirable, it would be a mistake to concentrate only on the subject matter without first considering how to manage the training, define the objectives of the curriculum, and adapt the program to the needs of the trainees.

Managing the Program

Managing and structuring the logistics of the training program is difficult regardless of the number of trainees. Basic operational considerations include the number of trainees that can be accommodated in the department; a time frame for completion of the primary curriculum; and procedures to handle special situations, including remedial or advanced skills development. The most detailed curriculum will not work unless it is logically structured and the topics are presented in a designated order.

For most banks, simplicity and structure are probably the keys to managing the training program effectively. If, for example, the basic curriculum requires 12 weeks to complete and 6 additional weeks for special work as needed, then new trainees should enter the program only at the beginning of the 18-week cycle. The instructor would be hard pressed to present any training program if trainees were to arrive and depart randomly. No trainee should be confused by having to start in the middle, and no instructor can reasonably be expected to train a number of students who are at different stages of the primary curriculum. There must be an understanding that students will participate in the program in the order in which it was designed.

Specifying the Objectives

Before the curriculum is structured, the trainer and bank management should clarify the objectives of the program. The statement of objectives need not be lengthy, but it should be specific. One example of a possible goal would be "to develop an individual's ability to prepare pro forma financial statement projections within two weeks." A more broadly stated but realistic goal might be "to develop a completely trained credit analyst within nine months."

The statement of objectives should also clarify how many individuals are to be trained and the degree of assistance that is expected from other departments. If the bank does not hire a trainee with a specific job in mind, an objective might be "to provide an opportunity for trainees to select a well-defined career position within the commercial banking department."

Individualizing the Program

All trainees should comprehend the basic skills needed by professional bankers; furthermore, all students should be familiar with the bank's specific policies and procedures. These areas of knowledge and skills will constitute the primary, or core, curriculum. To allow for individual differences in skill levels and learning speed, trainers should develop methods to meet any special needs within the basic credit curriculum.

Suppose that all students attended a one-hour lecture on ratio analysis skills. The trainer could build extra time into the program for additional study by those students whose future jobs require more sophisticated ratio analysis techniques. This additional time could also help those students who fail to grasp basic concepts.

Obviously, one-to-one instruction will be required in many instances. As work flows to the credit department, future financial analysts should be given the more difficult analytical tasks. A perceptive trainer should use informal opportunities to begin a dialogue with a student and get a better idea of the individual's goals, progress, and problems.

Another advantage of a well-organized training program is that the needs of present employees can be recognized and accommodated. If the availability of the training program is publicized, those employees who seek refresher courses may attend one or more training sessions as needed. Special sessions also may be developed for them. In addition, management support of continuing education helps overcome employee reluctance to admit deficiencies and should improve the skill levels of virtually all bank personnel.

The Curriculum

The credit and loan training curriculum will vary from bank to bank depending on departmental expertise, skills required by the trainees, number of trainees, and the knowledge deemed necessary for good performance in the bank. If the credit department is to assume the primary responsibility for training throughout the bank, the curriculum should be as broad as possible. If the credit department manager is to coordinate the training effort, he or she will have to establish a close relationship with the personnel and other departments.

Many commercial lending functions can be included in the credit training curriculum, but the scope of the required training must be fully understood before the curriculum can be developed. This is true whether a bank is relatively small, with a part-time trainer and only one or two trainees, or a multibillion dollar institution. This basic need for curriculum organization, regardless of bank size, illustrates again that while there are substantial differences among banks, the general principles of credit department organization and operation apply to any bank.

Identifying General Subject Areas

As an aid in defining curriculum content, a list of areas of knowledge useful to commercial lending personnel should be drawn up. Then those topics should be classified according to their importance in the bank's training program. Examples of such topics to be considered include accounting, money and banking, financial statement analysis, credit information exchange, loan documentation, and so forth. The list of subjects could then be circulated to bank management and various department heads who would rank the subjects according to such classifications as:

- Essential for all trainees
- Essential for some trainees
- Desirable but not required
- Not required
- Do not teach in-house (outside training suggested)
- Make available as continuing education

This technique will help set priorities for the subject areas to be covered in the training program. As a planning tool it is applicable regardless of who has the responsibility for training. Furthermore, if several departments are responsible for certain aspects of training, a logical program that is free of duplication can be developed.

Organizing the Order of Subject Presentation

After the desired subjects have been selected, each skill development or subject area must be placed in a logical order. Few people would agree on what this logical order should be since a number of diversified and sometimes unrelated subjects must be taught. The proper order for structuring the curriculum, or building the desired order of subject presentation, must be determined by each particular bank.

One approach might be to divide the desired areas of knowledge into rather broad categories and develop them in outline form. For purposes of illustration, a general outline is presented as Exhibit 7.1. No time estimates have been indicated for completion of various subject areas; this is a decision that must be made by each bank. Also, continuing evaluation of a new training program will undoubtedly lead to changes both in the individual units of study and in the time required for each aspect of the curriculum.

An outline of the curriculum might also be useful in identifying those departments or experts who might teach some subjects. Furthermore, it helps establish various training units which might be attended by different types of trainees, depending upon their previous experience or education and anticipated career paths.

Exhibit 7.1 — Outline of a Curriculum

The following outline is not presented as an example of all the subjects that could or should be taught in a training program. Rather, it illustrates an organizational approach to structuring the curriculum and suggests topics to be covered.

I. Orientation (for all employees)
- A. Goals of the Bank
  - 1. Market area—relationship to the community and the shareholders
  - 2. Deposit structure
  - 3. Types of loans made
  - 4. How a bank makes money
  - 5. Competition
    - a. Other banks
    - b. Savings institutions
    - c. Credit unions
    - d. Other financial intermediaries
  - 6. Other related topics
- B. Personnel Policies
  - 1. Employee benefits
    - a. Retirement and profit-sharing plans
    - b. Vacation policies
    - c. Illness policies
    - d. Other related topics
  - 2. Expectations of the bank
    - a. Attendance
    - b. Standards for ethical behavior
    - c. Other related topics
- C. The Training Program
  - 1. What to expect
  - 2. Its contents, duration, and schedule
  - 3. Who will instruct
  - 4. What is expected from the trainees
  - 5. Other related topics

II. Bank Operations (for most, if not all, employees)
- A. Money and Banking
  - 1. Basic economic functions
  - 2. Creation of deposits
  - 3. Traditional commercial banking functions
  - 4. Other related topics
- B. Various Deposit Functions
  - 1. Acceptance and proof
  - 2. Collection of negotiable instruments
  - 3. Savings account and other time deposits
  - 4. Other related topics

Exhibit 7.1 continued

C. Various Payments Functions
 1. Bookkeeping/general ledger
 2. Teller training
 3. Other related topics

D. The Audit Function
 1. Responsibilities of the auditor
 2. Methods used
 3. Other related topics

E. Customer Services-Special Services
 1. Safe deposit
 2. Trusts
 3. Other related services

Note: Tellers, bookkeepers, and other employees who are not directly related to the loan and credit function might leave the training program at this point. Others who require expertise in the lending and credit functions will remain.

III. <u>Credit and Loan Function (the basics)</u>

A. The Function of Credit
 1. Nature and definition of credit
 2. Goals of the bank in extending credit
 3. Misuses of credit
 4. Other related topics

B. Economics (introduction)
 1. Economics and the banker
 2. Economic measurements
 3. Economic indicators
 4. The prime rate and other key interest rates
 5. Other related topics

C. The Credit Organization in the Bank
 1. Discussion of the organizational chart
  a. Lines of authority
  b. Staff responsibilities
  c. Other related topics
 2. Major functions performed in the:
  a. Credit department
  b. Loan department
  c. Real estate department
  d. Loan review section
  e. Personal loan department
  f. Other loan areas (e.g., credit cards, special industries, letters of credit, international, etc.)

D. Bank's Loan Policy
 1. Review and discussion of each item in the bank's written loan policy
 2. Importance of adhering to bank policy

E. Elements of Loan Analysis
 1. Interviewing the customer
 2. Site visits
 3. Methods of evaluating management
 4. Understanding the purpose of a loan request
 5. Importance of financial statement information
 6. Sources of repayment
 7. Other related topics

Exhibit 7.1 continued

F. Financial Statement Analysis (the basics)
   1. Understanding statement content
      a. Various types of auditor's opinions expressed
      b. Management prepared statements
      c. What constitutes a full presentation
      d. Reading the footnotes
      e. Other related topics
   2. Items of special importance
      a. Balance sheet
      b. Income statement
      c. Working capital analysis
      d. Sources and uses of funds
      e. Other related topics
   3. Spreading a financial statement
   4. Basic analytical techniques
      a. Ratio analysis
      b. Trend analysis
      c. Comparative data
      d. Cash flow analysis
      e. Other related topics
   5. Research and sources of information

G. Types of Loans
   1. Working capital loans
   2. Term and revolving loans
   3. Accounts receivable and other types of secured financing
   4. Loans to contractors
   5. Leasing
   6. Other types of loans

H. Credit Information Exchange
   1. The RMA *Code of Ethics*
   2. The RMA–NACM *Statement of Principles*
   3. Credit department policy
   4. Types of requests for information
      a. Inquiries
      b. Investigations
      c. Requests from agencies
      d. Special situations
   5. Sources of credit information
   6. Other related topics

I. Credit Files
   1. Importance
   2. Organization
   3. Authorized access
   4. Maintenance
   5. Retention and destruction
   6. Other related topics

J. Basic Loan Documentation
   1. Types and purposes of notes
   2. Guarantors and endorsers
   3. Uniform Commercial Code
      a. Perfection of a security interest
      b. Special types of filings
      c. How to verify a filing

Exhibit 7.1 continued

4. Loan agreements
5. Mortgages
6. Other related topics

K. Communications Skills
1. Written reports
   a. Letters and memos
   b. Credit analyses
   c. Loan reviews
   d. Comment sheets
2. Oral communications skills
   a. Telephone communications
   b. Verbal reports to loan committees
   c. Interviewing techniques

Note: This level of study may be sufficient for statement spreaders, credit investigators, and others who are not expected to become loan officers or perform sophisticated credit analysis work in the near future. Credit and loan trainees who are experienced in certain areas, such as economics or credit information exchange, might skip entire sections of the outline. Those employees who are expected to become credit or loan officers or credit analysts would probably continue to IV Advanced Loan Administration.

IV. <u>Advanced Loan Administration</u>

A. Financial Statement Analysis (advanced)
1. Expansion of analytical techniques to include:
   a. Preparation of projections (various types)
   b. Testing proposed sources of repayment
   c. Additional ratios and their applications
   d. Other related topics

B. Structuring the Loan Package
1. Matching loan terms to the customer's needs and to sources of repayment
   a. Lines of credit
   b. Short-term loans
   c. Term loans
   d. Accounts receivable financing
   e. Other related topics
2. The Loan Agreement
   a. Purpose
   b. Covenants and conditions
   c. Events of default
   d. Monitoring loan agreements
   e. Other related items

C. Loan Documentation (advanced)
1. Appropriate documentation for the particular business entity
   a. Corporation
   b. Holding company
   c. Partnership
   d. Other types of organizations
2. Documentation for specific types of collateral
   a. Accounts receivable
   b. Inventory
   c. CDs and other time deposits
   d. Securities (stocks, bonds, debentures, etc.)
   e. Other related items

Exhibit 7.1 continued

3. Documentation for guarantees, endorsements, and hypothecations
    a. Various types of guarantees and endorsements
    b. When, and when not to, request a guarantee or endorsement
4. Unusual situations
    a. A debtor doing business in many locations, especially out of state
    b. Warehouse financing, trust receipts
    c. Boats, airplanes, etc.
    d. Usury considerations
    e. Other unusual situations
5. Common pitfalls and problems
6. How and when to request legal review and advice

D. Collateral
1. Types of acceptable collateral
2. Securing additional collateral
3. Releasing collateral
4. Marketability and liquidity
5. Understanding the bank's lien position
6. Appraisals and other valuation techniques
7. Other related items

E. Loan Pricing
1. Criteria and considerations
2. Compensating balances
3. Fees
4. Competition
5. Other related items

F. Ongoing Loan Administration
1. Maintaining current information
    a. Customer relations
    b. Documenting the credit folder
    c. Other related items
2. Changing circumstances
    a. Extensions or renewals
    b. Business cycles
    c. Counseling the customer
    d. Raising or lowering rates
    e. Other related items

G. Problem Loans
1. Requesting loan review, analytical report, or audit
2. Loss prevention techniques and early warning signs
3. Calling a loan
    a. Notification of guarantors
    b. Securing the collateral
    c. Offsetting balances
    d. Other related topics
4. Collection techniques
5. Other related topics

H. Loan Review Meetings and Loan Committee Meetings
1. Role of the loan officer
2. What to prepare
3. What to expect

I. Banking Law and Regulations
1. Federal Reserve Regulations
    a. Regulations B and Z

Exhibit 7.1 continued

- b. Regulation U
- c. Other pertinent regulations

2. Federal laws
   - a. Fair Credit Billing Act
   - b. Fair Credit Reporting Act
   - c. Community Reinvestment Act
   - d. Other pertinent laws
3. State laws
   - a. Usury
   - b. Property
   - c. Other laws pertinent to the bank

J. Management Skills
1. Managing your time
2. Personnel management
   - a. Evaluations and appraisals
   - b. Communications
   - c. Management by objectives and other techniques
   - d. Other related topics
3. Art of negotiation

K. Marketing Bank Services and Selling Skills
1. Define bank market area
2. Cross-selling
3. Other related topics

After the fourth level of the curriculum has been completed, those students who are to be placed on the line or those who will serve as credit officers might spend a period of time working on a one-to-one basis with a designated, experienced loan officer. By actually making site visits, assisting in reaching various loan decisions, processing credit applications, and performing other tasks, the trainee will become more confident in making prompt, logical and accurate loan decisions. By answering customer's questions as they arise, deficiencies or areas of uncertainty will be spotted and corrected before the student completes the training program.

Organizing the Subjects

After the order of subject presentation has been established, each instructor must decide how the topic he or she is responsible for should be presented. Most instructors find it useful to prepare an outline for each classroom unit and a list of related training resources. Such an outline helps ensure that the subject is covered in a complete manner, helps the instructor organize the presentation to fit the available time, and helps eliminate duplication. Furthermore, when reading materials and other training resources are readily available, trainees can be better prepared for their training sessions. Such outlines are very helpful when a substitute instructor must teach a class, since the course content and resources are already identified.

An example of an outline for written communications skills is presented as Exhibit 7.2. If a similar outline were prepared for each subject in the curriculum, a complete outline for the training program could be compiled as a working reference guide.

Exhibit 7.2 — Subject Presentation Outline

Written Communications Skills-Credit Communications

Session #1 (2 hours)

I. Importance
  A. To the bank
  B. To its customers
  C. To the examiners and others
II. The Basics (review)
  A. Rules of good English usage
    1. Parts of speech
    2. Punctuation
    3. Paragraph and sentence structure
  B. Clarity of expression
  C. Economy of words
  D. Basic tools
    1. Dictionary
    2. Thesaurus
    3. Other reference books and manuals of style
III. Review of Letters and Formats Frequently Used
  A. Credit correspondence
    1. To the borrower
    2. To an inquirer
    3. To initiate an inquiry
  B. Officer comment sheets
  C. Credit analysis format
  D. Loan request format
  E. Loan review format
IV. Written Assignments and Projects (writing workshop)
  A. Using actual credit reports, letters, and various analytical reports as examples, trainees will discuss qualities of various reports. Qualities of a well-written report compared with a poorly written one will be cited.
  B. Using a fact sheet extracted from a credit file, students will prepare:
    1. An analytical report — to include written financial summary, comments, and recommendations only.
    2. A written response to a credit inquiry made by another bank.

(Projects are to be prepared at home and will be discussed at the next class session.)

Session #2 (1 hour)

I. Review of Assignments
II. Developing Writing Style
  A. Is it clear?
  B. Is it concise?
  C. Is it straightforward?
  D. Is it accurate?
  E. Does it answer the question?

Session #3 (Optional)

I. For Trainees who Experienced Difficulty with the Subject
  A. Private interview with the instructor
  B. Discussion of possible options including:
    1. Individual instruction
    2. Special assignments
    3. Night school
    4. Seminars/workshops outside the bank

Exhibit 7.2 continued

Training Resources for Communications Skills

1. Samples of credit correspondence and various reports gathered by the instructor. Include all commonly used formats.
2. Articles including:
   Ley, Patricia S. "Style in Analytical Writing." *Journal of Commercial Bank Lending*, April 1974, pp. 61-66.
   Mitchell, Dan W. "Linquistic Overkill." *Journal of Commercial Bank Lending*, June 1973, pp. 32-34.
   Morris, John O. and Wilcox, Thomas R. "Well-Written Credit Reports: A Successful Program." *Journal of Commercial Bank Lending*, July 1974, pp. 51-63.
   Stapleton, Tom. "Ten Steps Toward Better Writing." *Banking*, March 1978, pp. 63, 65.
3. Books including:
   Brock, Luther A. *How to Build Goodwill Through Credit Correspondence*. New York: National Association of Credit Management, 1976.
   Crouch, W. George. *Effective English*. Washington, DC: American Institute of Banking, American Bankers Association, 1969.
   Hodges, John C., and Whitten, Mary E. *Harbrace College Handbook*. 8th ed. New York: Harcourt Brace Jovanovich, 1977.

Training Resources and Devices

Every trainer has access to a variety of educational materials. Even if he or she has a limited budget, good instructional tools can be obtained. In fact, the real problem may be in selection, not in accumulation, of materials. It is important that many different resources be compiled—not only to cover important topics in the curriculum but also to develop different methods of presentation. Eleven types of training resources and devices are considered in the following text to provide some ideas for gathering educational materials.

Utilizing the Work Flow

In a production-oriented environment, the instructor will have to identify the learning opportunities within the bank's work flow. This may be difficult since tasks do not always fit training priorities, and pressures caused by deadlines do exist. Nevertheless, a good trainer will be alert to those on-the-job situations that are applicable to the needs of the trainee and will make every attempt to direct suitable work to the appropriate person.

An alert trainer will also be able to spot items that can be used for training experiences at a later date. For example, if a financial statement illustrates some key point or concepts, it would be a good idea to delete the customer's name to assure confidentiality, photocopy the material, and retain it for future training use. Such financial statements could also be modified for use as a case study.

Textbooks

The trainer, perhaps working with a librarian, may begin a search for resources by contacting various publishers who specialize in the banking field. Many are listed in the bibliography at the end of this book. These companies will normally provide detailed catalogs, and many offer cassettes, audiovisual aids, and programmed instruction packages. Also, trainers could write to bankers' associations such as Robert Morris Associates, American Bankers Association, Bank Administration Institute, and Bank Marketing Association to request their lists of available publications and training aids. A visit to one or more banks with established training programs and libraries may also provide a wealth of useful information and ideas.

Certain reference books should be purchased as the basis of the training library. These texts should be selected carefully. Trainers might talk to other bankers and instructors to study the texts they recommend, review the books available at various libraries, and scan bibliographies for additional ideas.

A very basic training library should include an encyclopedia of banking and finance terms; basic, intermediate, and advanced accounting texts; a book on auditing practices; a few texts covering financial statement analysis; a guide to obtaining sources of information on various businesses; copies of and interpretive materials that clarify the relevant laws and federal regulations, including the Fair Credit Reporting Act, Regulation B, and Regulation Z; a guide to the Uniform Commercial Code; a book presenting composite financial data such as the RMA *Annual Statement Studies*; a dictionary; a thesaurus; one or two books on management skills; a text on the commercial banking system; an economics textbook; and a guide to writing business letters and memos. Of course, the bank's policy and procedures manuals should be included among these reference materials.

Periodicals

It is important to impress on trainees that a banking professional must keep current with developments in the field. There are many excellent business and banking magazines and newspapers available, and the trainer should select the most suitable periodicals for use in the program. Articles or selected publications should be circulated to the students. Some leading banks also provide summaries of current periodical literature at a reasonable cost. They also prepare economic reviews which are often free of charge. The instructor may wish to develop files of clippings on various subjects and industries. It may also be worthwhile to subscribe to a periodical devoted exclusively to training skills and techniques.

Sources of Free Materials

Many businesses and service organizations publish free or low-cost materials. For example, the Financial Accounting Standards Board, CPA firms, the Federal Reserve System and each of its 12 district banks, the Comptroller of the Currency, the Federal Deposit Insurance Corporation, the Securities and Exchange Commission, and brokerage houses could be contacted. In addition, the federal government has a voluminous list of publications, and the Federal Reserve Board in Washington makes available a list of its research library acquisitions biweekly. Many industries, such as public utilities, are happy to provide publications useful in training. *The Wall Street Journal* also prepares an annual list of educational materials sent to those interested at no charge.

Programmed Instruction

Programmed instructional packages can be valuable because they reduce the time the instructor must devote to some forms of training and students can progress at their own pace. In addition, programmed instruction can be used as refresher courses for more experienced employees and is often ideal for learning at home. If well designed, this instructional material breaks a subject down into very small components and presents pieces of information in a logical, step-by-step manner. Each fact presented is reinforced, and the student cannot proceed to the next concept until he or she demonstrates that previous facts are understood. Programmed instruction may be costly in terms of purchase price and required equipment, but if it is well prepared, it can be worth the expense.

Case Studies

Many credit departments prepare studies based on actual experience. Good case problems require careful preparation, raise questions that stimulate worthwhile discussion, and make a clear point. Case studies should be detailed enough so that students receive the entire picture of the credit situation, rather than one isolated element. They are useful as take-home assignments when followed up with discussions. An example of a case study, together with an instructor's guide, is presented beginning on page 207 at the end of this chapter.

Site Visits and Interviews

Participating in site visits and interviews can help introduce students to actual banking situations. Ideally, the credit trainee should accompany an officer on occasional site visits and be present at some interviews with borrowing customers. These experiences help trainees learn about obtaining relevant information and the skills of negotiation, persuasion, observation, and communication. Site visits could include one to the municipal building to search public records.

The trainer can also devise hypothetical business calls in which one student plays the role of a customer and another the banker. A tape recorder can help analyze conversations and point out useful techniques; video equipment and sophisticated training materials are also useful in this area. Ideally, case histories and lectures on planning and making effective business calls should precede role-playing situations.

Workshops and Seminars

Many banking associations offer workshops of varying cost and duration. Workshops are valuable training tools, especially when the bank cannot provide in-depth training in a given area. Workshops are designed to eliminate boredom through a change of pace, offer a great deal of knowledge in a relatively short time, and provide an opportunity to become acquainted with other bankers and their policies and procedures. Workshops are also ideal for upgrading the skills of present employees.

If the cost of a workshop seems prohibitive to the bank, the trainer should investigate low-cost and free educational opportunities that may be locally available. In some cases, workshop lectures are sold in cassette form. Various firms also sponsor brief meetings or lectures on a variety of banking-related topics with outstanding speakers. The person responsible for training should not overlook these opportunities.

Bankers and Other Professionals

Every banker knows professionals—in and outside banks—who are expert at communicating knowledge in a particular area. Those individuals in the bank should be assigned specific aspects of the training program. And local attorneys, public officials, business leaders, and university faculty members who can provide valuable information should also speak to the trainees. It is important that trainees be exposed to seasoned professionals whose thoughts and expertise could be a regular part of the program.

Banking Courses

Many courses are available at the university level and through the American Institute of Banking. Formal evening programs offer a good opportunity for personnel development without infringing on the work day.

Formal Classroom Instruction

Every instructor will want to develop well-organized, effectively presented classroom lessons. This is true even if the instructor is responsible for training only one individual at a time, for every student deserves the benefits of a well-devised presentation. Although many facts must be presented formally, this does not mean that formal lessons must be dull. Interest can be created by distributing written materials in advance, by using visual aids, and by incorporating actual work or problem-solving situations in the program.

The subject of statement spreading, for example, might be introduced by distributing sample spread sheets and background information to the trainees before the lecture. After the students have studied the material, the instructor might present a lecture that incorporates completing the asset side of the spread sheet. Subsequently, students would spread the liability columns; discussion and review would ensue. Presentation of the computation and purpose of various ratios might follow a similar method. Moreover, the formats and content of the analysis and spread sheets should be consistent with the bank's policies and practices.

Concepts of Learning

Few credit department managers possess extensive background in education or psychology. Nevertheless, it is important that as instructors they know something about the major learning theories relating to educational practice. Familiarity with some elements of learning will help the instructor make decisions about how the curriculum should be structured and taught; develop a philosophy of training that can be applied consistently; more readily comprehend publications about training; evaluate training programs more critically; and apply elements of learning theory in actual practice.

Improperly designed training programs may increase the time required to train employees without improving their job performance above what might be anticipated through trial and error. Therefore, it is vital that such basic educational concepts as readiness for learning, motivation and goals, retention, and other principles be considered when designing any training program, regardless of the concepts and skills to be learned.

While this section does not attempt to explore major learning theories in detail, some familiarity with these concepts will help the manager understand how learning principles can be applied in the training program. Many excellent textbooks are available on educational psychology and learning theory. Managers should consult with local libraries or universities for advice about books that would be helpful.

Readiness for Learning

It is essential that the trainer recognize the important concept of readiness for learning. The trainee will not progress until his or her skill development needs are identified and addressed or until the instructor finds a way to present the subject at the student's level. Both the maturity of the trainees and their prior learning experiences are important factors of readiness, and so are the methods of instruction. In considering the student's readiness to learn, the instructor should always ask: What must a student know or be able to do before he or she can learn the subject? Do my students possess this necessary knowledge and ability? How can I best present the subject?

The concept of readiness can be illustrated by the futility of teaching statement spreading before the trainee is acquainted with basic accounting terminology. The spreading process would not make sense, and the work would be either extremely frustrating or completely meaningless.

Some other ways a bank training program can help assure that trainees are ready to learn are through:

- Intelligent hiring practices that select trainees equipped with the knowledge, skills, and maturity levels identified as prerequisites for the program. Such practices can save time since the instructor can assume the students possess a common level of knowledge and skills.

- Constructing a systematic training program that presents information logically and increases the student's potential to grasp new concepts. Each concept or skill that the instructor wishes to develop should be broken down into small units that can be presented in a step-by-step fashion. Students progress logically from the least difficult to the more complex units of instruction. Many banking skills naturally lend themselves to this "building-block" approach.

- Formal programmed learning in which certain questions must be answered correctly before the student can proceed. The readiness of the student for the next question is assured by his or her answering the previous question correctly. A similar technique can be used to check for comprehension and readiness to proceed when programmed learning is not used. For example, the instructor can frequently evaluate each student's progress in order to identify troublesome areas quickly. The instructor should review assignments, listen carefully to trainees' responses and questions, and evaluate performance for evidence of demonstrated ability.

- Individualized instruction that addresses identified problem areas. If a student cannot grasp a specific concept, such as cash flow, the time the instructor might spend with the student on a one-to-one basis may well prevent frustration and failure.

Motivation and Goals

Simply defined, a motive is a need or desire that causes a person to act. Our motives direct our activity toward related goals and give purpose to our behavior. Motivation is absolutely essential to learning, and some practical considerations about motivation are presented here.

- Students can be motivated by the need for security, approval, financial reward, recognition, opportunities for new experiences, and many other factors. If, for example, students want to become loan officers and receive the benefits accompanying that position, they will be better motivated to master statement spreading. The successful instructor must make it clear that proficiency in statement spreading is a prerequisite to becoming a loan officer.

- Both positive and negative incentives can be used to motivate students. Positive incentives would include promises of promotions and salary increases during the training program. Negative incentives include fear of failure and possible dismissal. While both types of incentives are used, the positives produce better results than the negatives.

- Motivation that is too intense can be disturbing and destructive. For example, if students are permitted to become too competitive with their classmates, undesirable results may occur.

- Motivation is related to good communication. A pleasant, reasonably calm atmosphere is essential to fostering a favorable attitude.

- If tasks and problems are clearly stated, well defined, and understood, students will be better motivated. If these tasks and problems are directly related to work that is performed in the bank, or if the long-term need to possess such information is understood, learning will be accelerated.

- Students must be satisfied that they are, in fact, learning important things. For this reason, students who are proficient in certain areas might bypass those portions of the training program, thus preventing boredom and a sense of futility that hinders learning.

Retention

It is important that instructors take steps to enhance learning retention. If the initial learning experience is successful, it is easier for a student to recall the information, recognize the material at a later date, or retain the basic principles. Some techniques that can be used to encourage retention of information and skills include the following:

- The instructor should schedule short review periods. These review sessions can be spaced over increasingly longer intervals of time. Periodic review, rather than cramming, contributes to retention.

- If students have to state facts in their own words, rather than repeating or rereading the facts, retention is improved. For example, a review session that requires students to define an asset or state the use of a security agreement in their own words encourages retention.

- If knowledge or an acquired skill is put to use in a practical way, retention is improved. A student who has learned how to spread a statement and then performs this task on a regular basis will retain that skill longer and be able to recall information quicker than the student who learns the technique and never applies it.

Student Involvement

When an instructor merely imparts knowledge, as through a formal lecture, or readily supplies correct answers, student involvement may be minimal. Student participation increases in active learning situations and reaches optimum levels when a problem must be solved.

Just how much guidance the trainer should provide and when and in what form to provide it are fundamental problems. If the task is too complex and no guidance is provided, the trainee may become frustrated and attempt random solutions. One attempt might work, but the learning experience may not be satisfactory. And it will almost always be time-consuming. Conversely, if a problem is too easy, nothing will be learned.

The following five suggestions can create student involvement while providing sufficient guidance.

After the instructor has formally presented certain essential concepts, students could be assigned to read a relevant case study and to offer solutions to the problems presented.

Active participation in situations such as site visits, calls on potential customers, role playing, and the like encourages involvement.

Teaching methods should be varied sufficiently. A good training effort includes different instructional methods since some students will almost always "tune out" if lectures, case problems, or any other technique is used exclusively. Audiovisual aids, reading assignments, discussion groups, new experiences, and other techniques are all useful.

Different techniques not only reduce boredom but can reach each student in the way he or she learns best.

Teachers should not always answer questions directly. Guidance can be given in such a form that the student does something to get the desired answer.

New ideas or approaches to solving a problem are encouraged when students are given the opportunity to postpone the obvious solution and brainstorm. Discussing alternative solutions fosters involvement and creative thinking. When a variety of methods can be used in reaching a solution, students learn the value of flexibility.

As mentioned earlier, every trainer should be aware that there are many, and sometimes extremely complex, theories of learning and education. A full-time trainer would do well to take an educational psychology course to become more familiar with these ideas.

Evaluating the Training Program

Once the program is in operation, there may be reluctance to evaluate its effectiveness. In part, there may be some fear of finding something wrong with a training effort that has been carefully planned. Evaluation is not easy, and there may be reluctance to take the time to reflect on the results of training. A lack of feedback may result in a training program that is resistant to change and, consequently, becomes outdated.

Four primary components of the training program must be evaluated regularly:

1. The trainees
2. The instructors
3. The subjects in the curriculum
4. The curriculum and the overall training effort

Trainees

As an initial step in evaluating the trainee, the instructor should identify the trainee's existing skills and knowledge as well as those likely to be required by this employee in the future. The trainer should also establish those achievements that can indicate learning has occurred.

A useful tool to assist the trainer in becoming more familiar with the trainee's background is the "Individual Educational and Experience Inventory" presented as Exhibit 7.3. By completing such an inventory with a trainee, the instructor can better evaluate a student's progress and individualize his or her training. This inventory also provides space for noting a student's expertise, or the lack of it, while the training is in progress.

Exhibit 7.4 is an example of a performance assessment sheet that could be prepared after a student has completed a specific unit or section of the training program.

Regularly scheduled one-to-one evaluation and review sessions should be an integral part of the training program. To learn properly, people need to know exactly how they are doing at each step in their training. The trainer should make every effort to let the trainees know when they are performing correctly and also when more work is necessary to reach a given skill level. If a conflict exists, it is advisable to have an independent observer present during a review session. This person might be selected from the personnel department or senior management.

Exhibit 7.3 — Individual Educational and Experience Inventory

ARTHUR SAXON
Trainee
P = Partial familiarity
W = Working knowledge
E = Some expertise in field

	Prior Part-Time Employment	Prior Full-Time Employment	High School	College—Major Field	College—Elective Course	Pre-Training Summary	Training Review 5/22/74	Training Review 9/11/74	Training Review 1/13/75	Training Review 3/28/75	Post-Training Summary
1. Accounting—basic				W		W					W
2. Accounting—advanced				W		W					W
3. Accounts receivable loans									W		W
4. Corporate finance									W		W
5. Credit analysis	P					P		W			W
6. Credit information exchange	P					P	E				E
7. Economics—basic			P			P		W			W
8. Equipment lending									W		W
9. International finance										W	W
10. Inventory lending									W		W
11. Leasing									W		W
12. Negotiable instruments					P	P		W			W
13. Sales calls on corporations		W				W				E	E
14. Other—real estate		E				E					E

Interviewer's Comments

(14) Trainee has worked in a real estate office since graduation from college. To obtain his sales license, he has taken and passed courses in real estate appraisal, law, etc., which could prove useful during a banking career.

(5) & (6) Worked three summers as general assistant in credit department of General Merchandise, Inc. WHS 1/14/74

(This chart first appeared in *The Credit Department, Its Role in Training*, by Charles S. Dickerson, published by Robert Morris Associates, 1975.)

Exhibit 7.4 — Unit Performance Report

Dept: Credit Training

Trainee Name	**Supervisor's Signature**	
Name of Unit Completed	**Length**	**Date Completed**

Performance is rated by a 1, 2, 3, or 4. Performance standards for this section are attached.

1 = consistently exceeds standards
2 = meets standards and may occasionally exceed them
3 = needs further development
4 = inadequate/unacceptable

	1	2	3	4
Job Knowledge				
Functional Assignments				
Overall Performance				

General Comments

Job Knowledge—consider overall familiarity with classroom material and learning speed.
Functional Assignments—consider amount of work accomplished, adaptability, initiative, and effective time management.

(This form was adapted from an actual report provided by Seattle First National Bank.)

When commenting on a trainee's performance, the trainer should be careful to avoid personal criticism. Constructive criticism must be specific and should identify the incorrect action and outline procedures to correct it. For example, a trainer might say, "You should always screen prospective borrowers to evaluate their past borrowing history. Redo this assignment being sure to check all possible sources of credit information in this regard. Research should include the bank's own credit files, checkings with other banks, trade checkings, agency reports, and searches of the public records."

Trainees should be asked for their comments on the program. They can provide evaluations through questionnaires and personal discussions at various points during their training. After trainees have performed at their permanent jobs for four to six months, they and their supervisors might be asked to provide additional evaluation.

Instructors

There are several good ways for a trainer to improve and refine his or her teaching ability. First, self-evaluation is essential. In addition to appraising the subject matter and methods of presentation critically, teachers might tape record their lectures, then make improvements based on their presentations. Second, professional educators or bank employees could observe and evaluate selected presentations. Third, the trainees could make suggestions and comments about an instructor's presentation. Of course, these evaluations could be done anonymously. Fourth, teachers should view the progress of the trainees as an indication of whether learning has taken place. If the trainees, on the whole, fail to grasp a specific unit of instruction, then that unit probably should be restructured or taught differently.

Subjects in the Curriculum

The instructor should evaluate each unit of instruction with these questions in mind:

Should the subject be taught at all?

Is the subject relevant to the work that the students will perform?

Is the information up-to-date and accurate?

Are the materials to be used readily available? Have they been re-evaluated recently?

Should the method of presentation be changed?

Is the subject being presented at the proper time in the program?

Curriculum and the Overall Training Effort

The entire training effort and the curriculum should be evaluated at least once a year. Even the most carefully conceived, designed, and implemented program becomes stale because the needs of the bank, the requirements of the trainees, and the state of the art all change with time.

The evaluation process should incorporate a review of all relevant statistical information and any written evaluations prepared by instructors and trainees currently involved in the program. Furthermore, comments should be requested from individuals who now supervise former trainees and from "graduates" employed at the bank. Valuable ideas might also be received from trainees who did not complete the program. If a critical look is taken at the training effort, some degree of change, be it major or minor, will probably result.

Some questions that should be addressed during this evaluation include:

Is the number of trainees adequate for the bank's needs?

How much money was spent on training this year? What is the proposed budget for next year?

What do the comments from supervisors of former trainees tell us? Are we providing a curriculum that is relevant to the jobs actually being performed?

Where are our former trainees now? In the bank? In what departments? Are they performing satisfactorily?

Are we losing trainees to other banks? Why?

Do the instructors need to spend some time developing their teaching techniques? Are varied methods being used?

Do the results of the program justify its costs? Is it too soon to tell? Is there a difference between former trainees' career paths compared with those of employees who were not in the program?

Is the overall balance of the curriculum correct? For example, do we overemphasize statement spreading and neglect administrative skills?

Should our hiring practices be reviewed? Do we have the mix we need and want?

Are any favorable or unfavorable trends emerging? What is the percentage of trainees who leave the program?

Should we continue a training program at all? Can major elements of the curriculum be eliminated and taught elsewhere more efficiently?

Even if only a few trainees enter the program each year, it is important that banks take the time to review, evaluate, and, when indicated, modify the program to meet identified needs.

Summary

The credit department can play an invaluable role in training many individuals for successful careers in the bank's credit and lending functions. A systematic approach to the training function should be developed, and management support should be elicited. The ability to teach a specific concept or skill, not a person's position within a bank, should determine who actually does the training.

As the first step in formulating the curriculum, individuals responsible for the training function should identify those skills and concepts the trainees will need to perform specific duties within the bank. Inventories of resources that will assist in the learning process should also be compiled and maintained. Regardless of the structure of the program, it must retain a degree of flexibility and allow for the individual goals and needs of the trainees. Continual evaluation of the training effort should also be an important part of the program.

A well-planned training effort, regardless of the size of the bank or the numbers of trainees involved, will have a positive effect on all participants, and, in time, a positive effect upon the bank's performance as a whole.

A Case Study* — Sybaritic Industries

Instructor's Notes

Case studies should be part of a well-designed training program and can be used to instruct beginners and those experienced loan officers who need a refresher course. Basic case studies, such as this one, can be developed easily by a trainer or other personnel. Ideally, such problems should be based on actual situations. However, the imaginative instructor will probably choose to adjust or embellish the facts to enhance the presentation and accomplish specific teaching objectives. Different aspects of the same actual situation can be used to focus on such facets of the curriculum as accounting, lending decisions, loan documentation, workouts, and liquidations.

To the students, the primary value of any case problem is the challenge in attempting to solve it for themselves. As a result, cases are often assigned as homework and discussed later in the classroom or group atmosphere. If possible, the lenders who were involved with the actual loan situation should be the instructors for the problem. Role playing is usually quite effective in case presentations, because the students actively participate in the learning process.

The Sybaritic Industries Case has three primary objectives:

1. To acquaint the trainee with the components and development of the statement of changes in financial position and cash flow.
2. To interpret these statements from both the borrower's and lender's points of view.
3. To introduce the student to basic lending principles, including loan management.

Experience demonstrates that, despite the simplicity of this case, many participants need considerable time to prepare the financial statements and the letter of response. The classroom discussion of a basic case like Sybaritic Industries needs only about an hour and could easily lead into discussions of working capital components, secured lending techniques, loan documentation,

*This case study was prepared by Edgar M. Morsman, Jr., United States National Bank in Omaha, in connection with an advanced loan officer development seminar.

and other subjects. Of course, this and similar cases could be embellished with such additional facts as ages of the principals, the inclusion of a hypothetical D&B report, or observations on the condition of the plant. Whether or not the instructor chooses to add such background information, "Sybaritic" is a good example of a basic case problem.

Problem: Sybaritic Industries, Inc.

In order to cash in on the impressive growth in the leisure industries, a group of local investors contributed $210,000 to capitalize a new corporation which assembled electronic barbecue sets, bars, and general patio equipment. To balance the seasonal nature of the patio line somewhat, they carried similar equipment for recreation rooms. The company was established in early 19X8, and the stockholders were pleased with sales for the year of $100,000. Imagine their joy when 19X9 year-end figures disclosed sales of $300,000!

A substantial backlog of orders indicated continued phenomenal sales growth. But physical facilities were not sufficient to support present and anticipated volume, in addition to the attendant increase in inventories. As a result, John Felice, chairman of the company, acquired a new building in December 19X9 for $27,000 in cash and a 10-year $120,000 mortgage.

In view of the sales record, the favorable outlook, and the satisfactory net profit, bound to increase once start-up costs were eliminated, Felice was puzzled about Sybaritic's declining cash balances. The company was conservatively capitalized at inception, and cash had never been a problem. Felice went to his banker with the following financial statements to discuss a line of credit.

Balance sheet (000s omitted)

Assets	12/31/X8	12/31/X9
Current		
Cash	$ 60	$ 21
Accounts receivable	18	60
Inventory	42	120
Prepaid expenses	6	12
Total current assets	$126	$213
Fixed assets (net)	150	273
Total assets	$276	$486
Liabilities and net worth		
Current		
Accounts payable	$ 42	$117
Accrued taxes payable	3	9
Total current liabilities	$ 45	$126
Mortgage	—	120
Capital	210	210
Retained earnings	21	30
	$276	$486

Income statement and reconciliation of retained earnings for the year ended Dec. 31, 19X9 (000s omitted)

Sales		$300
Less cost of goods sold:		
Inventory 12/31/X8	$ 42	
Purchases	297	
	$339	
Inventory 12/31/X9	120	219
Gross profit		$ 81
Less other expenses:		
Operating expenses including depreciation of $24		57
Operating income		$ 24
Taxes		12
Net income		$ 12
Dividends		3
Net income for period retained		$ 9
Retained earnings 12/31/X8		21
Retained earnings 12/31/X9		$ 30

Student Assignment

Prepare the following:

1. A statement of changes in financial position.
2. A statement of cash flow (sometimes referred to as historical cash flow or statement of cash receipts and disbursements).
3. A letter to John Felice explaining why cash decreased while sales, net income, and working capital were rising. Point out the dangers the company is running, some of the danger signs, and some possible courses of action.

The Solution

1. Statement of changes in financial position for the year ended Dec. 31, 19X9 (000s omitted)

Source of funds:		
Funds provided by operations:		
Net income	$12	
Depreciation (an expense deducted from net income but which does not require the use of working capital)	24	
Mortgage	120	$156
Application of funds:		
Dividends	$ 3	
Purchase of fixed assets	147	150
Net increase in working capital		$ 6

2. Statement of cash flow for the year ended Dec. 31, 19X9 (000s omitted)

Cash balance 12/31/X8			$ 60
Receipts from operations:			
Collections from customers		$258	
Operating disbursements:			
Inventory	$222		
Operating & prepaid expenses	39		
Taxes	6	267	(9)
Cash available for use			$ 51
Disbursements:			
Dividends		$ 3	
Purchase of fixed assets	$147		
Less mortgage	120	27	30
Cash balance 12/31/X9			$ 21

3. Letter to John Felice, Chairman of Sybaritic Industries, Inc.

Dear John:

In asking for a line of credit you requested an explanation of Sybaritic Industries' increasing cash problems. Your situation is not unlike that of many newly formed companies with growing markets. As sales rise, you need higher levels of inventory to support them and a larger portfolio of receivables is generated. Unless your suppliers change their terms dramatically, the inventory and receivables will not turn fast enough to meet your payables as they become due. Sybaritic's illiquidity was increased by investing $27,000 in the new plant that was needed to sustain sales growth.

I am attaching two financial statements to illustrate the problem. The "statement of changes in financial position" explains how Sybaritic's working capital changed from $81,000 at the end of 19X8 to $87,000 at the end of 19X9. Although working capital increased by $156,000 through operations and long-term debt, working capital was depleted by $150,000 through the payment of dividends and the purchase of fixed assets. The net effect was an increase of only $6,000. Sales have tripled while your working capital has remained virtually the same. In examining the components of Sybaritic's working capital, the increase in inventory and receivables has been financed primarily through trade payables which are probably past due unless you have received extended terms.

Because of Sybaritic's rapid growth and investment in fixed assets, cash balances have declined by $39,000 even as working capital showed a slight increase. This is illustrated by the attached "statement of cash flow." Although you collected $258,000 in cash (the difference between $258,000 and sales of $300,000 is explained by the $42,000 increase in receivables), your disbursements, primarily for inventory, were $267,000. The large investment in inventory was necessary to support higher sales, but the net effect was that operations actually depleted cash rather than generated it.

Cash was further depleted through dividends and fixed asset purchases. Companies with less dramatic sales increases will normally generate cash from their operations, depending on their receivable and inventory position.

The danger in such a situation is that, despite the high profit potential, Sybaritic Industries may become insolvent or unable to meet its debts as they mature. The high level of payables is an indication of potential insolvency.

There are several courses of action which could be considered singly or in combination. These would include:

1. Increasing the turn of your receivables and inventory
2. Negotiating longer terms with your suppliers
3. Long-term working capital financing
4. Restricting dividends and officers' salaries
5. Increasing capital
6. Restricting sales

I would suggest that you prepare quarterly projections for several years to include balance sheets, income statements, and cash flow statements. These estimated budgets will require that you consider all phases of Sybaritic's operations including sales growth, personnel, plant capacity, financing, etc. Once you have prepared these statements, we should meet and discuss how we can assist your company's progress.

Sincerely,

Appendix A

Code of Ethics for the Exchange of Commercial Credit Information Between Banks

FOREWORD

The basic precepts of RMA's Code of Ethics have existed since 1916 and remain virtually unchanged. In 1976, RMA appointed a select committee to evaluate the Code of Ethics and its use in the current banking environment. This committee revised the Code by reducing the number of Articles, developing comments to explain each Article, and simplifying the language used. The group also approved a revised symbol (logo) for use by banks on their stationery to show they are RMA members and Code subscribers. A sample of the logo appears on the last page. Both the revised Code and the new logo were approved by RMA's Board of Directors in June 1976.

Over 150,000 copies of the revised Code have been distributed since 1976, evidencing its wide acceptance by the banking industry.

This April 1980 reprinting contains some minor modifications. First, the Preamble and Article 3, Comment 5 have been amplified in regard to the securities law. Second, the title now states that the Code applies to the exchange of commercial credit information between banks.

Those involved in the credit information exchange process should become familiar with two additional documents. Through the efforts of RMA and the National Association of Credit Management, a joint *Statement of Principles for the Exchange of Credit Information Between Banks and Business Credit Grantors* is available. RMA has also developed *Guidelines for the Exchange of Foreign Credit Information*.

RMA believes that one way to maintain professionalism in credit information exchange is for all banks to adhere to the Articles of the Code of Ethics which follow.

Preamble

Robert Morris Associates, recognizing the importance of the free and responsible exchange of information in the credit-based American economic system, originally adopted this Code of Ethics in 1916. Since then, the Code has become the ethical standard for conduct in the exchange of commercial credit information. Although intended to relate to information exchange between banks, the precepts of the Code have served as the foundation for all commercial credit information exchange.

Adherence to this Code of Ethics is essential. Upon joining RMA, members acknowledge and agree to abide by these principles, and they expect others with whom information is exchanged to respect them also.

This Code is designed for commercial transactions, and its use is subject to applicable federal and state laws. Such laws include securities statutes regulating disclosure of material inside information and other laws affecting the exchange of credit information. In particular circumstances, these could include the antitrust laws, credit reporting regulations, and limitations on the use of confidential records and customer information or computerized data.

Since under the securities laws, "material inside (nonpublic) information" may, in some cases, be neither disclosed nor withheld as to transactions in connection with the sale or purchase of a security, care should be exercised and the advice of counsel sought where any such inside information may be in the possession of the respondent.

Article 1

There are two cardinal principles in the exchange of credit information: confidentiality and accuracy of inquiries and replies. This includes the identity of inquirers and sources which cannot be disclosed without their permission. Adherence to these and the other principles embodied in this Code is essential, since offenders jeopardize their privilege to participate further in the exchange of credit information.

Comments:

Confidentiality, as it is used here, is based on the reliance placed upon the fidelity of another with whom information is being exchanged. A trust is placed in all parties involved that the information has been requested for a legitimate purpose and will not be used indiscriminately.

When conducting investigations, the identity of the inquirer should not be divulged without its authorization. Similarly, the identity of the source of the information should not be made known without its authorization.

The facts presented must be accurate because the bank reference is one of the most pertinent sources of credit information. When discussing data, favorable or unfavorable, the responding bank must give a reply that is restricted to or based on fact. If a discrepancy is discovered within a reasonable time after an inquiry has been answered, and is considered to be significant in relation to the purpose of the inquiry, it is prudent and ethical that the discrepancy be disclosed to the inquirer.

It is expected that, as a matter of professional courtesy, no liability will be attached to or result from the good faith exchange of information.

If the information is for a customer, it should be screened according to the customer's needs, credit sophistication, and ability to handle the information discreetly.

Adherence to these and the other principles embodied in this Code of Ethics is essential. Violations of the Code could damage the reputation of offending banks and individuals. If they demonstrate an inability and/or unwillingness to handle and exchange credit information responsibly, they risk losing the privilege.

In addition, violations of the Code by RMA member banks may lead to the termination of their membership in the association, in accordance with Section 2.07 of the RMA By-Laws.

Article 2

Each inquiry should specifically indicate its purpose and the amount involved.

Comments:

One of the most important elements of an inquiry is its purpose. The bank receiving the inquiry has a right to know why the information is needed. If no purpose is given, there is no obligation to respond. Knowing and understanding the purpose of an inquiry places the recipient in a better position to respond with the type and amount of information needed to satisfy the inquirer. When the purpose of the inquiry is solicitation, acquisition, merger, competition, or actual or contemplated legal action, reply is at the discretion of the bank of account.

The inquirer should state the initial steps taken, as well as the information on hand, in order to avoid duplication of effort.

The legitimate use of credit information is to assist an inquirer who expects to extend credit or otherwise rely on the subject of the inquiry in business dealings. An inquiry should not be answered without first determining its legitimacy and establishing the identity of the inquirer. For example, when receiving a telephone inquiry, information should not be disclosed on the first call unless the inquirer is known and identified. A return call will usually establish the identity of the inquirer.

In the majority of instances, a specific amount is involved in the transaction which generates an inquiry. When initial trade credit is involved and no amount is established, the inquiring party should be asked for the normal size of its transaction. A range of figures such as $500-$1,000 or $50,000-$60,000 is acceptable. It is unacceptable to use fictitious figures or to inflate the amount involved to induce the responding bank to provide details beyond what may be necessary to answer the inquiry suitably. If for some reason there is no amount involved, the inquirer should state this in a manner which would logically satisfy the respondent as to the overall purpose of the inquiry.

A proper inquiry should contain the following:

1. SUBJECT: The subject of the inquiry should be identified as completely as possible including full name, address, and names of the principals.
2. PURPOSE: The reason for the inquiry should be given in sufficient detail to allow the recipient to make an appropriate response.
3. EXPERIENCE: If the inquirer has had experience with the subject, a summary of that experience should be provided. Doing this creates a true *exchange* of information and helps to eliminate duplication of effort.
4. REQUIREMENTS: The inquirer should be specific about the information required to satisfy the needs of the inquiry, such as deposit relationships, loan experience, financial information, assessment of management, etc.
5. OTHER: Any other factors relevant to the inquiry should be disclosed.

Article 3

Responses should be prompt and disclose sufficient material facts commensurate with the purpose and amount of the inquiry. Specific questions should be given careful and frank replies.

Comments:

Prompt and accurate replies are signs of dependability and professionalism that help the users of the information conduct business on a timely basis. Although response time to inquiries will vary depending upon the amount of information needed, the following general guidelines are considered appropriate:

TYPE	RESPONSE TIME
Wire or cable inquiry	Within 24 hours of receipt
Telephone inquiry	Within 24 hours of receipt
Written inquiry	Within 4 days of receipt
Telephone investigation	Two working days
Written investigation	Six working days

If unusual delays are expected, the inquirer should be informed.

Once the legitimacy and the requirements of the inquiry are established, it is answered by providing a summary of the bank's experience and knowledge of the subject commensurate with the amount involved and the respondent's confidence in the inquirer.

A full response may include:

1. The opening date of the relationship
2. History of the subject
   - How long established
   - Legal form of organization

- Names of the principals as well as their background and experience
- Line of business

3. Demand deposit relationships
   - Opening date—if different from the opening date of the relationship
   - Average collected balances, for at least the past three months, in RMA General Figure Ranges*

   Several cautions in this area:

   A. General figure ranges are ordinarily not used in mutual revisions. Rather, industry practice is to describe balances simply as "compensating" (or "commensurate"), "less than compensating," etc. Or, if there is no compensating balance requirement, that fact may be revealed, followed by words such as "satisfactory," "less than satisfactory," etc.

   B. Do not use the term "substantial" to describe the balances in demand deposit accounts. Also avoid "satisfactory," except in the limited situation noted in (A.) above.

   C. It is not recommended that compensating balance *requirements* be disclosed if they exist. Exchanging information about compensating balance requirements does not, in itself, constitute an antitrust violation. However, if after such an exchange there is anything approximating parallel action manifested by similarity of terms, it could be claimed that the information exchanged was used illegally. This applies to the disclosure of interest rates charged on loans as well. Like compensating balances, the rates charged are arrived at by the lending bank and the borrower on particular transactions and cannot be used by others as a basis for similar arrangements.

   - Number and frequency of returns
   - Rating on the account—here, words like "satisfactory," "generally satisfactory," "unsatisfactory" are appropriate.

4. Summary of the borrowing relationship, if any
   - Types of loans. If a loan is secured, describe the collateral.
   - Aggregate high credit and outstanding balances in RMA General Figure Ranges.* These figures may be broken down further by specific loans if the situation warrants it.
   - Guarantees and endorsements, if any, should be made known.
   - Dates, length, and frequency of payouts.
   - Ratings—for example, "satisfactory," "unsatisfactory," etc.
   - Interest rates charged on loans should not be disclosed because of the possibility of antitrust violations. (See comments in (3C.) above regarding compensating balance requirements.)

5. Financial statement data. Where the subject is a publicly held company publishing current financial information, the release of financial statement data will normally be in compliance with the securities laws.** When financial statements of nonpublicly held companies are submitted to the bank, with no instructions to the contrary, a general summary of the data may usually be disclosed. This disclosure should be tempered by the re-

*See definition of RMA General Figure Ranges

**See comments in Preamble.

spondent's confidence in the inquirer and by the amount and nature of the inquiry. The summary may consist of:

- Dates of the statements and the period they cover
- Auditor's opinion
- A description of the financial condition and trends of the subject, which should include current assets, total assets, current liabilities, net worth, sales, and an indication of profitability. It is the option of the responding bank to disclose this data in actual figures or in RMA General Figure Ranges.* Even when financial statements are submitted in confidence, a brief general description of the company's strength, size, and trends may usually be disclosed.

If comments are made regarding the financial standing of the subject, they should be based on the bank's analysis of the company, pointing out to the inquirer that "our analysis shows" or using other such wording.

It remains at the discretion of the responding bank to provide the inquirer with recommendations and opinions. If a recommendation or opinion is asked for, the account officer should be consulted unless the person answering the inquiry is authorized to provide this information.

If a respondent cannot answer specific questions brought up in the inquiry, the inquirer should be told why.

Article 4

It is not permissible when soliciting an account to make an inquiry to a competitor without frankly disclosing that the subject of the inquiry is a prospect. Reply is at the discretion of the bank of account.

Comments:

The free exchange of information between banks depends to a large degree on the confidence that the inquiring bank will not use the credit information it receives to solicit the respondent's accounts. Providing credit information is a courtesy, and, in some instances, revealing information could jeopardize the account relationship between the responding bank and the subject.

Violations of this confidence are very serious. They not only damage the inquirer's relationship with the responding bank, but also create a guarded situation that can only impede the exchange of credit information. For this reason, when solicitation is the purpose of an inquiry, this fact must be clearly stated to the bank of account, which has the option to decline information on such inquiries.

If a bank is soliciting an account of a competitor and is asked by a customer to obtain credit information on that account, the soliciting bank should explain the ethical considerations involved and suggest that the inquiring customer contact the subject's bank directly.

All parties to credit inquiries that involve solicitation must be aware of the

*See definition of RMA General Figure Ranges

basic confidence inherent in the exchange of information and act in a responsible manner to preserve that confidence and trust.

Article 5

A request for information based on actual or contemplated litigation shall be clearly identified as such. Reply is at the discretion of the bank of account.

Comments:

When the purpose of a request for information is actual or contemplated legal action, full disclosure of this fact by the inquirer is necessary. It is clearly unethical to disguise the purpose of any inquiry. This could be detrimental to the parties involved, especially when legal action is associated with an inquiry. Under those circumstances, the potential for damages is such that all parties must exercise considerable judgment before conducting an investigation or answering an inquiry of this nature.

Whenever the bank of account is placed in a conflicting position of providing information and, at the same time, protecting its customers, the amount of information, if any, will be at the discretion of the responding bank.

Article 6

All credit correspondence, including form letters, should bear the manual signature of a responsible party.

Comments:

Manual signatures on all credit correspondence, both inquiries and replies, are essential. Good faith responsibility for the accuracy of the information contained in the correspondence is assumed by the signer. This is the case whether the signer gathers the information or not. The title, if any, and name of the authorized signer should also be typed or printed on the correspondence. Doing this will help to address responses correctly and to identify clearly the person to contact if questions arise regarding the inquiry or reply.

Article 7

The sharing of credit information on a mutual customer should not be more frequent than annually, unless a significant change in the relationship requires an earlier revision.

Comments:

Credit information on mutual customers is normally reviewed annually. It should not be necessary to inquire more frequently unless interim financial data, news items, agency information, or other sources point out an actual or potential problem. Information should not be requested when there is no real need.

The bank requesting the information should give a summary of its experience first. This sharing of information by both inquirer and respondent is stressed because it prevents duplication of effort and is consistent with the cooperative spirit inherent in the exchange of credit information. On mutual revisions in particular, care should be taken regarding discussion of interest rates charged and compensating balance requirements since revealing these data could have antitrust implications.

Article 8

When multiple inquiries are made simultaneously on the same subject, the inquirer should clearly state that information from the bank's own files is sufficient.

Comments:

There are basically two situations under which simultaneous inquiries are made to banks within the same city: where it is known that the subject has account relationships with more than one of them, or where the subject's bank(s) of account is not known (which gives rise to what is commonly known as a "fishing expedition").

In the first instance—more than one known bank of account—courtesy dictates that each responding bank be told that research beyond its own files will not be necessary.

The second situation—"fishing"—should be avoided whenever possible. The inquiring bank should make every effort to determine the subject's bank(s) of account before initiating any inquiry.

But if for some reason the name of the bank(s) of account cannot be determined, the inquiring bank then has two courses of action open to it. It could make multiple inquiries as described above, again indicating to each bank that research beyond its own records will not be necessary. Or, preferably, it can approach just *one* bank in the city in question and ask if it would either conduct the investigation or at least locate the name of the bank of account—which the inquiring bank, in turn, can then approach separately. All banks, particularly RMA member banks, are encouraged to assist one another in situations like this, as long as this courtesy is not abused.

RMA General Figure Ranges

To ensure accuracy and consistency when exchanging credit information, the RMA General Figure Ranges should be used. It may be necessary, at times, to clarify these terms so that the inquirer and respondent are "speaking the same language."

Low 4 figures = $1,000 to $1,999
Moderate 4 figures = $2,000 to $3,999
Medium 4 figures = $4,000 to $6,999
High 4 figures = $7,000 to $9,999

Ranges are adjustable to accommodate all amounts in the following manner:

"Nominal" = under $100
"3 figures" = from $100 to $999

"4 figures" = from \$1,000 to \$9,999
"5 figures" = from \$10,000 to \$99,999
"6 figures" = from \$100,000 to \$999,999 and so on.

RMA Code of Ethics Logo

Reproduced below is the revised symbol (logo) which identifies a bank as a member of Robert Morris Associates and a subscriber to its Code of Ethics.

We urge RMA members to imprint the logo on their credit information exchange stationery in order to facilitate communication among them.

Special reproduction copies of the logo are available free from the RMA National Office, 1616 Philadelphia National Bank Bldg., Philadelphia, PA 19107.

MEMBER
rma
SUBSCRIBER TO
CODE OF ETHICS

Appendix B

Statement of Principles for the Exchange of Credit Information Between Banks and Business Credit Grantors

FOREWORD

By developing the Statement of Principles, Robert Morris Associates (RMA) and the National Association of Credit Management (NACM) have recognized the need to foster and maintain a high level of professionalism in the exchange of business credit information between banks and business credit grantors. The Principles are designed to apply to both business credit grantors and banks.

Through the joint efforts of both Associations, the Statement of Principles was revised in 1978. The Associations' respective committees on cooperation with RMA and NACM modified the language of the original Statement to reflect current usage. They also developed explanatory comments for each of the seven Principles.

Both RMA and NACM encourage their members and others with whom credit information is exchanged to become familiar with and respect the Statement of Principles. In addition, each party to the exchange of business credit information must understand its obligation to its respective customers and the need for considerate, fair, accurate, and prompt replies in relation to the extension of business credit.

Preamble

Robert Morris Associates (RMA) and the National Association of Credit Management (NACM) originally adopted the Statement of Principles in 1955.

By doing so, RMA and NACM recognized the need for the free and responsible flow of credit information to support the credit-based American economic system.

Revised in 1978, the Statement provides guidelines for the mutual exchange of business credit information between banks and business credit grantors. Members of RMA and NACM are urged to adhere to the Statement of Principles. Others with whom information is exchanged are also encouraged to respect them.

The Statement of Principles is designed for commercial transactions, and its use is subject to applicable federal and state laws. Such laws include securities statutes, regulating disclosure of material inside information, and other laws affecting the exchange of credit information. In particular circumstances, these could include the antitrust laws, credit reporting regulations, and limitations on the use of confidential records and customer information or computerized data.

Principle 1

Confidentiality is the cardinal principle in the exchange of credit information. The identity of inquirers and sources should not be disclosed without their permission.

Comments:

A trust exists between the parties involved that the information is being requested for a legitimate purpose, and will be handled discreetly and confidentially.

It is important that information not be used indiscriminately, since the purpose of exchanging credit information is to assist the inquirer in making a business decision concerning the creditworthiness of the subject.

Principle 2

All parties involved in the exchange of credit information must base inquiries and replies on fact.

Comments:

Accuracy is fundamental to the proper exchange of credit information. If a respondent discovers within a reasonable time that a response given contained a significant error, it is desirable to notify the inquirer as soon as possible.

It is understood that, as a matter of professional courtesy, credit information should be exchanged in good faith.

Principle 3

The purpose of the inquiry and the amount involved should be clearly stated.

Comments:

Each inquiry should identify a clear need for the information. If no purpose is given, there is no obligation to respond. By knowing the purpose of an inquiry, the recipient is better able to respond with the type and extent of information needed.

The inquirer's experience should be provided to create a true exchange of credit information.

File revisions should be instituted only when a real need for the information exists.

Principle 4

If the purpose of an inquiry involves actual or contemplated litigation, the inquirer should clearly disclose this fact.

Comments:

The potential for damages in this situation is such that all parties must exercise judgment before conducting an investigation or answering an inquiry involving actual or contemplated litigation. The extent of information provided, if any, will be at the respondent's discretion.

Principle 5

The inquirer should make every effort to determine the subject's bank(s) of account before placing an inquiry, and indicate the extent of information already in file.

Comments:

When requesting a bank to obtain credit information from another bank, the complete name and address of the subject's bank(s) of account should be provided. This information should be obtained before an inquiry is initiated, and can be acquired through references or remittance data.

If multiple inquiries are made at the same time, each respondent should be informed that investigation beyond its own files will not be necessary.

By knowing what information the inquirer already has in file, duplication and inconvenience are avoided and time is saved.

Principle 6

Proper identification should be provided in all credit communications.

Comments:

Manual signatures are essential on all credit correspondence. However the information is gathered, it is prudent for the signer to use reasonable procedures to ensure its accuracy. The title, if any, and name of the authorized signer should also be typed or printed on the correspondence. This will help address responses correctly and clearly identify the person to contact if questions arise.

When an inquiry is made by telephone or in person, the inquirer should provide clear identification. If the recipient is unfamiliar with the inquirer, a return call will usually verify identity.

Principle 7

Replies should be prompt and contain sufficient facts commensurate with the purpose and amount of the inquiry. If specific questions cannot be answered, the reasons should be clearly stated.

Comments:

The purpose, amount, importance and specific questions posed by the inquirer will normally determine the amount of information to be provided. The inquirer may further emphasize the importance of the inquiry by providing information regarding the amount and its relationship to the size and financial position of the inquirer.

The response may include:

1. Opening date of the relationship.
2. Background of the subject and principals.
3. Bank Response
   a. Deposit relationships in RMA General Figure Ranges, and a rating of the account. Terms such as "satisfactory," "generally satisfactory," "unsatisfactory," are appropriate.
   b. A summary of the borrowing relationship, including: types of loans; repayment schedule; high credit; amount outstanding; amount past due; collateral and the existence of guarantees and endorsements, if any.
   c. Overall experience and other comments.
4. Trade Response
   a. A summary of the credit relationship, including: date of last sale; recent high credit; amount outstanding; amount past due (aged); terms of sale; collateral and the existence of guarantees and endorsements, if any.
   b. Overall experience and other comments, including manner of payment (discount, prompt, days slow).
5. Where the subject is a publicly-held company publishing current financial information, the release of financial statement data will normally be in compliance with the securities laws. In other cases, summaries of information from financial statements may usually be provided, based on the scope of the inquiry, knowledge of the inquirer, and policies affecting the respondent. The respondent may provide financial statement information in actual figures or RMA General Figure Ranges. Since under the securities laws, "material inside (non-public) information" may, in some cases, be neither disclosed nor withheld as to transactions in connection with the sale or purchase of a security, care should be exercised and the advice of counsel sought where any such inside information may be in the possession of the respondent.

Recommendations and opinions are given at the discretion of the respondent, and if given should be based on fact.

If the respondent cannot answer specific questions bought up in the inquiry, the inquirer should be told why.

If unusual delays are encountered in responding to an inquiry, the inquirer should be informed.

RMA General Figure Ranges

To ensure accuracy and consistency when exchanging credit information, the RMA General Figure Ranges should be used. It may be necessary, at times, to clarify these terms so that the inquirer and respondent are "speaking the same language."

Low 4 figures = $1,000 to $1,999
Moderate 4 figures = $2,000 to $3,999
Medium 4 figures = $4,000 to $6,999
High 4 figures = $7,000 to $9,999

Ranges are adjustable to accommodate all amounts in the following manner:

"Nominal" = under $100
"3 figures" = from $100 to $999
"4 figures" = from $1,000 to $9,999
"5 figures" = from $10,000 to $99,999
"6 figures" = from $100,000 to $999,999 and so on.

Prompt and accurate replies are signs of dependability and professionalism that help the users of the information conduct business on a timely basis. Although response time to inquiries will vary depending upon the amount of information needed, the following general guidelines are considered appropriate:

Type	**Response Time**
Wire or cable inquiry	Within 24 hours of receipt
Telephone inquiry	Within 24 hours of receipt
Written inquiry	Within 4 days of receipt
Telephone investigation	Two working days
Written investigation	Six working days

If unusual delays are expected, the inquirer should be informed.

Appendix C

Glossary Pertinent to the Exchange of Commercial Credit Information

Sixty terms that are frequently used in the exchange of credit information are included in this glossary. These basic definitions provide a concise, easily understood vocabulary guide that would assist a credit department trainee.

It should be noted that some of the terms presented are used more frequently in certain geographical areas than in others. *Furthermore, the definitions are not all-encompassing nor do they reflect legal interpretation.* They are provided only as a convenient reference source and to encourage uniformity in the exchange of credit information.

accommodation. Lending or extending credit to a borrower: a loan or a commitment to lend money.

accounts receivable financing. A form of secured lending in which borrowings are typically limited to a percentage of receivables pledged as collateral.

agent bank. A *formal* designation which applies to the bank that is responsible for negotiating, structuring, and overseeing a loan or commitment to a borrower in which more than one bank is involved. (See also **lead bank.**)

aggregate balances. The combined total of two or more demand deposit accounts.

allocation. A sublimit within a total accommodation which is to be used for a specific purpose.

amortization. The reduction of a loan by steady principal and interest payments.

average collected balances. The average dollar amount on deposit in a checking account during a given period of time calculated by totaling the daily ledger balances, deducting daily uncollected items, and dividing the remainder by the number of days in the time period. (See also **uncollected funds**.)

balloon payment. A final payment on a loan that is significantly larger than preceding payments.

banker's acceptance. A draft or order to pay a specified amount at a specified time, drawn on individuals, business firms, or financial institutions. The draft becomes an acceptance when a bank formally acknowledges its obligation to honor such a draft, usually by writing or stamping "Accepted" on the face of the instrument. When accepted in this manner, the draft becomes a liability of the bank. (See also **draft** and **time draft**.)

charge-off. The portion of a loan which a bank considers uncollectible. This amount may be partially or fully recovered in the future.

clean up. The period during which a particular loan or the entire borrowing has been paid off. The term is frequently used to describe the out-of-debt period required under a line of credit.

collateral. An asset pledged by a borrower in support of a loan. (See also **secured loan**.)

commensurate. A term generally used in mutual account revisions to convey that deposit balances are in acceptable proportion to the size of a loan or commitment.

commitment. An agreement between a bank and a borrower to make funds available under certain conditions for a specified period of time.

compensating balances. The amount of money a bank's customer may keep on deposit as part of the compensation for accommodations or other bank services.

contingent liability. A liability in which a person(s) or business(es) is indirectly (contingently) responsible for the obligations of a third party. Such indirect liability is usually established by guarantee or endorsement, and the lender may turn to the guarantors or endorsers for satisfaction of the debt. (See also **endorsement** and **guarantee**.)

dealer loan. See **floor planning**.

default. Failure to meet an obligation or terms of a loan agreement, such as payment of principal or interest on a debt.

demand deposit account (DDA). Funds on deposit in a checking account which are payable upon demand of the depositor. (See also **time deposits**.)

discount. (1) Interest deducted from the face amount of a note at the time a loan is made. (2) A trade term used for the reduction of the invoice amount when payment has been made within specified terms.

discounted note. (1) A borrowing arrangement where interest is deducted from the face amount of the note before the proceeds are advanced to the borrower. (See also **note**.) (2) A term used when a bank's customer endorses a note received from another party and presents it to a bank to obtain funds.

draft. A written order by one party (the drawer) directing a second party (the drawee) to pay a sum of money to a third party (the payee.) See also **banker's acceptance, letter of credit, sight draft,** and **time draft.**)

endorsement. The signature on the reverse of a note to another party (or parties) who accepts liability for payment of the obligation in the event of a default or subsequent inability to perform by the maker. (See also guarantee.)

escrow account. A deposit account to which access is restricted or limited by the terms of a written agreement entered into by three parties, including the bank.

evergreen revolving credit. A commitment to lend money that remains in effect unless the lender takes specific action to terminate the agreement. The agreement may provide that, in the event of termination, any outstanding amount will convert to a term loan.

file revision. The routine gathering of credit information by a business credit grantor to update its files.

floor planning. A loan made to a dealer for the purchase of inventory acquired for resale and secured by that inventory, such as automobiles or appliances.

generally satisfactory. Description of a bank's experience when a relationship has been handled essentially as agreed but with some irregularities.

guarantee. A separate agreement by which a party (or parties) other than the maker assumes responsibility for payment of an obligation if the principal debtor defaults or is subsequently unable to perform under the terms of that obligation. (See also **endorsement**.)

high credit. The largest amount of credit used by a borrower during a specified period of time.

indirect liability. A term used interchangeably with contingent liability. (See **contingent liability**.)

inquiry. A request for credit information on a bank's own customer.

insufficient funds. A term used interchangeably with **not sufficient funds**. (See **not sufficient funds**.)

investigation. The gathering of credit information on a party who is not a bank's own customer.

lead bank. An *informal* designation which normally applies to the bank that has the primary deposit or lending relationship in a multibank situation. (See also **agent bank**.)

letter of credit. A letter or document issued by a bank on behalf of a customer which is evidence of the financial backing of the bank and ensures that payment will be made when proper documents confirm completion of the related transaction. Such letters authorize the drawing of sight or time drafts when certain terms and conditions are fulfilled. (See also **banker's acceptance, draft, sight draft, standby letter of credit,** and **time draft.**)

lien. The legal right to hold or control property pledged as collateral until the debt which it secures is repaid or satisfied.

line of credit. An informal commitment by a bank to lend funds to a borrower up to a given amount over a specified future period. Lines of credit are normally reviewed annually and are usually withdrawable at the bank's option.

mutual account revision. A routine exchange of credit information between two or more banks that have extended credit to the subject of the inquiry.

note. An unconditional written promise by a maker (borrower) to pay a certain amount of money to a lender on demand or at a specified or determinable date. This instrument should meet all the requirements of laws pertaining to negotiable instruments. (See also **discounted note**.)

not sufficient funds (N.S.F.). A term used when collected demand deposit balances are less than the amount of a check being presented for payment and the check is returned. (See also **overdraft**.)

offering basis. A situation in which a customer's loan requests are considered individually on the merits of each proposal.

overdraft. A term used when collected demand deposit balances are less than the amount of a check being presented for payment and the check is paid. (See also **not sufficient funds**.)

participation. A purchase by one bank of a portion or all of a loan to a borrower originated by another bank. Such transactions normally occur when the originating bank is not large enough to lend the entire amount of the requested credit.

revolving credit. A commitment under which funds can be borrowed, repaid, and re-borrowed during the life of the credit. Such credits have a stated maturity date at which time the borrower may have the option to convert the outstanding balance into a term loan. (See also **evergreen revolving credit**.)

routine, nonborrowing account. A relationship where no extension of credit is involved.

satisfactory. Description of a bank's experience when the relationship has been handled as agreed.

secured loan. A loan supported by the borrower's pledge of an asset (collateral) such as marketable securities, accounts receivable, inventories, real estate, equipment, etc.

sight draft. A draft payable on demand when presented to the drawee. (See also **draft, letter of credit,** and **time draft.**)

standby letter of credit. A type of letter of credit issued by a bank which may only be drawn on by the payee if the party who makes the letter of credit (the drawer) defaults or does not perform according to the terms of a specific contract or agreement.(See also **letter of credit**.)

subject. The party on which credit information is requested.

time deposit. Interest-bearing funds deposited in a bank for a specified period of time such as certificates of deposit and savings accounts.

time draft. A draft payable on a fixed date or a certain number of days after sight or date of draft. (See also **banker's acceptance, draft, letter of credit,** and **sight draft**.)

trade payment record. A summary of the performance of a company in meeting the terms of its business credit obligations.

uncollected funds. Deposits not yet collected by the bank such as checks that have not yet cleared.

unsatisfactory. Description of a bank's experience when the relationship has not been handled as agreed.

unsecured loan. A loan made on the strength of the borrower's general financial condition. (See also **secured loan**.)

write-off. A term used interchangeably with charge-off. (See **charge-off.**)

zero balance account. A demand deposit account where the exact amount of checks paid during any given day is funded at the end of that day by transfers from a master account.

Bibliography

Accounting

Accounting: A Learning Experience. Englewood Cliffs, NJ: Prentice-Hall, 1973.

Accounting Principles and Applications, Parts I and II. 3rd ed. Washington, DC: American Bankers Association, 1974.

Anthony, Robert N. *Essentials of Accounting*. 2nd ed. Reading, MA: Addison-Wesley, 1977 (instructor's guide and tests available).

Buckley, John W., and Lightner, Kevin M. *Accounting: An Information Systems Approach*. Encino, CA: Dickenson, 1973 (work book available).

Carson, A.B., and Carlson, Arthur E. *Principles of Accounting*. 10th ed. Chicago: South-Western Publishing Company, 1977.

Davidson, Sidney and Weil, Roman. *Handbook of Modern Accounting*. 2nd ed. New York: McGraw-Hill Book Company, 1977.

Davidson, Sidney, et al. *Accounting: The Language of Business*. 3rd ed. Glen Ridge, NJ: Thomas Horton and Daughters, 1977.

Jaedicke, Robert K., and Sprouse, Robert T. *Accounting Flows: Income, Funds, and Cash*. Englewood Cliffs, NJ: Prentice-Hall, 1965.

Kelley, Thomas P. "Compilation and Review—A Revolution in Practice." *The CPA Journal*, April 1979, pp. 19-27.

Kohler, Eric L. *A Dictionary for Accountants*. 5th ed. Englewood Cliffs, NJ: Prentice-Hall, 1975.

Meigs, Walter B., and Mosich, A.N. *Financial Accounting*. 2nd ed. New York: McGraw-Hill, 1975 (worksheets and study guide available).

Nickerson, Clarence B. *Accounting Handbook for Nonaccountants*. Boston: Cahners Books International, 1975.

Objectives of Financial Statements. Vol. 2. New York: American Institute of Certified Public Accountants, 1974.

Winsten, Irwin. "New Language in the Accountant's Report." *Credit & Financial Management*, June 1979, p. 10.

Communication Skills

Brock, Luther A. *How to Build Goodwill through Credit Correspondence*. New York: National Association of Credit Management, 1976.

Koenig, Arthur W. "How to Go about Visiting your Customers." *Credit and Financial Management*, April 1977, p. 8.

Ley, Patricia S. "Style in Analytical Writing." *The Journal of Commercial Bank Lending*, April 1974, pp. 61-66.

Mitchell, Dan W. "Linguistic Overkill." *The Journal of Commercial Bank Lending*, June 1973, pp. 32-34.

Morris, John O., and Wilcox, Thomas R. "Well-Written Credit Reports: A Successful Program." *The Journal of Commercial Bank Lending*, July 1974, pp. 51-63.

Pace, Edmond E., and Simonson, Donald G. "The Initial Loan Interview (A Training Feature)." *The Journal of Commercial Bank Lending*, April 1977, pp. 17-23.

Pinalto, Gary L. "Improving Loan Officers' Communications in the Customer Interview." Thesis, Stonier Graduate School of Banking, 1969.

Royal Bank of Canada. "How to Write a Report." *Banking*, June 1976, p. 43.

Stapleton, Tom. "Ten Steps Toward Better Writing." *Banking*, March 1978, pp. 63-65.

Strunk, W., Jr., and White, E.B. *The Elements of Style*. 3rd ed. New York: MacMillan Publishing Company, 1972.

Compliance—General

Badders, Donald L. "The Privacy Issue and the Bank Industry." *The Journal of Commercial Bank Lending*, December 1975, pp. 48-56.

Comptroller's Handbook for Consumer Examinations. Washington, DC: Comptroller of the Currency, Administrator of National Banks, 1979 (supplements issued periodically).

Financial Privacy 1979. Washington Credit Letter Privacy Report. Washington, DC: Capitol Reports, 1979.

Hearn, William R. "Why Have a Compliance Officer?" *The Journal of Commercial Bank Lending*, August 1978, pp. 29-39.

McCord, Thom. "A Regulatory Perspective: Coping with Consumer Credit Regulations." *Issues in Bank Regulation*, Winter 1978, pp. 3-5.

McCord, Thom. "Unscrambling the Alphabet of Bank Regulations." *The NABW Journal*, Sept./Oct. 1977, pp. 19-21.

Palmer, Robert T., and Palmer, A.T. Darin. "Complying with the Right to Financial Privacy Act of 1978." *The Banking Law Journal*, March 1979, pp. 196-224.

Roderick, Jerome L. "Privacy—Not Just a Consumer Issue." *The Journal of Commercial Bank Lending*, September 1978, pp. 30-37.

Saxon, Joyce M. "Implementing a Program for Consumer Regulation Compliance." *The Magazine of Bank Administration*, November 1977, pp. 18-21.

Saxon, Joyce M. "Implementing a Program for Consumer Regulation Compliance, Part V." *The Magazine of Bank Administration*, March 1978, pp. 32-35.

Saxon, Joyce M. "Implementing a Program for Consumer Regulation Compliance, Part VI." *The Magazine of Bank Administration*, May 1978, pp. 32-36.

The Compliance Handbook. Washington, DC: Consumer Bankers Association, 1977.

The Compliance Handbook for Consumer Credit. Washington, DC: Capitol Reports, 1979.

Credit Department Management

A Biennial Survey of Bank Officer Salaries. Park Ridge, IL: Bank Administration Institute, 1977.

Brignet, John F. "A Centralized Credit Department in the Branch Banking System of a Medium-Sized Bank." Thesis, Southwestern Graduate School of Banking, 1966.

Cole, Robert H. *Consumer and Commercial Credit Management*. 5th ed. Homewood, IL: Dow Jones-Irwin, 1976.

Credit Research Foundation. *Credit Management Handbook*. Homewood, IL: Dow Jones-Irwin, 1965.

Job Descriptions for Bank Personnel: A Comprehensive Guide. Park Ridge, IL: Bank Administration Institute, 1975.

Kreps, Clifton H., Jr., et al. *Credit Administration*. 2nd ed. Washington, DC: American Institute of Banking; American Bankers Association, 1972.

Pipkin, John B., II. "The Role of the Credit Department in a Regional Bank." Thesis, Colgate Darden Graduate School of Business Administration, 1968.

Credit Information Exchange

Babb, Larry D. "Revision of RMA–NACM's Statement of Principles." *The Journal of Commercial Bank Lending*, November 1978, pp. 2-7.

Brannen, James S. "Trade Creditors and the Banks—Friends or Foes?" *The Journal of Commercial Bank Lending*, November 1975, pp. 26-32.

Code of Ethics for the Exchange of Commercial Credit Information Between Banks. Philadelphia: Robert Morris Associates, 1980.

Commercial Credit Information Exchange: A Two-Way Street. Philadelphia: Robert Morris Associates, 1979.

Dearhammer, William G. "Improving Credit Information Exchange Between Bankers and Trade Creditors." *The Journal of Commercial Bank Lending*, September 1977, pp. 53-60.

Directory of Credit Information Personnel: 1979. Philadelphia: Robert Morris Associates, 1979.

Eckstrom, C.L., Jr., and Snowdon, David T. "Shared Expectations of Bankers and Commercial Credit Managers." *The Journal of Commercial Bank Lending*, October 1975, pp. 10-20.

Guidelines for the Exchange of Foreign Credit Information. Philadelphia: Robert Morris Associates, 1978.

Johnson, Herman A. "Establishment of Credit Inquiry Costs and Prices." Thesis, Stonier Graduate School of Banking, 1969.

Jolly, Bruce O., Jr. "Furnishing Joint-Credit Account Information Under Reg. B: A Checklist." *The Independent Banker*, 1977, pp. 26-28.

Neff, Dennis C. "Credit Executives, Bankers and the Exchange of Credit Information." *Credit and Financial Management*, January 1973, pp. 35-37.

Pace, Edmond E. "Credit Investigation (A Training Feature)." *The Journal of Commercial Bank Lending*, May 1977, pp. 3-8.

"RMA Revises Code of Ethics for the Exchange of Credit Information." *The Journal of Commercial Bank Lending*, October 1976, pp. 2-13.

Redding, Harold T. "The Use of the Dun & Bradstreet Business Information Report by Commercial Banks." *The Journal of Commercial Bank Lending*, May 1978, pp. 44-48.

Scarfo, S. George. "What Has Happened to the Exchange of Credit Information?" *The Journal of Commercial Bank Lending*, October 1974, pp. 9-15.

Statement of Principles for the Exchange of Credit Information Between Banks and Business Credit Grantors. Rev. Philadelphia/New York: Robert Morris Associates/National Association of Credit Management, 1978.

White, Martin W., Jr. "Credit Inquiries and the Feasibility of Charging for Same." Thesis, Stonier Graduate School of Banking, 1969.

Wright, A.W. "Bankers' Credit Inquiries: A Comparison of British and American Practices." *The Journal of Commercial Bank Lending*, April 1978, pp. 40-48.

Fair Credit Reporting Act

Clontz, Ralph C., Jr. *Fair Credit Reporting Manual–Text, Forms & Procedures*. Boston: Warren, Gorham & Lamont, 1977 (1979 supplement).

Denney, Max A. "Federal Fair Credit Reporting Act." *The Banking Law Journal*, July 1971, pp. 579-590.

Financial Institutions and the Fair Credit Reporting Act. A pamphlet distributed jointly by the Federal Reserve Board, Office of the Comptroller of the Currency, Federal Deposit Insurance Corporation and Federal Home Loan Bank Board. May 1971.

Geltzer, Robert L. "Fair Credit Reporting Act: Survey and Checklist." *The Banking Law Journal*, March 1977, pp. 223-247.

Neff, Dennis C. "A Recent Development Concerning the Fair Credit Reporting Act." *The Journal of Commercial Bank Lending*, September 1971, pp. 32-33.

Nelson, Lester. "Fair Credit Reporting Act: Questions and Answers on Business Credit." *Credit and Financial Management*, March 1974, p. 16.

Redding, Harold T. "The Fair Credit Reporting Act and Non-Consumer Credit Information." *The Journal of Commercial Bank Lending*, September 1971, pp. 24-31.

"The Fair Credit Reporting Act: What Bankers Are Puzzling Over." *The Journal of Commercial Bank Lending*, March 1971, pp. 2-8.

Files

Bank Secrecy Act and Retention of Bank Records. Park Ridge, IL: Bank Administration Institute, 1974.

Basic Microfilm Standards. Silver Spring, MD: National Micrographics Association, 1977.

Bates, Charles F., Jr. *Central Information File–Conversion and Implementation* (Bank Study Series). Boston: Bankers Publishing Company, 1976.

Emergency Preparedness and Security Measures: Guidelines, Policies, and Procedures for Financial Institutions. Park Ridge, IL: Bank Administration Institute, 1978.

Gottheimer, Debra. "For Micrographics the Next Five Years Are Crucial." *Administrative Management*, May 1978, pp. 36-48.

Guide for Developing Simplified Credit Files. New York: Bank Management Committee, American Bankers Association, 1970.

Guide to Record Retention Requirements. Washington, DC: S/N-022-003-00985-0 U.S. Government Printing Office, 1979.

Heinemeyer, Glenn R. "Credit Data, Its Retention and Retrieval." Thesis, Stonier Graduate School of Banking, 1974.

Introduction to Micrographics. Silver Spring, MD: National Micrographics Association, 1973.

Kish, Joseph L., Jr. *Microfilm in Business*. New York: John Wiley & Sons, 1969.

Kish, Joselph L., Jr. *Micrographics: A User's Manual*. New York: John Wiley & Sons, 1979.

The Retention and Destruction of Bank Records. 2nd ed. Washington, DC: American Bankers Association, 1969.

Financial Statement Analysis

Analyzing Financial Statements. 5th ed. Washington, DC: American Bankers Association, 1978 (workbook available).

Anderlik, John A. "How Bankers Make Their Credit Decisions." *Credit and Financial Management*, August 1974, p. 14.

Anderson, Gary G. "The Role of Economic Information in Commercial Lending Analysis." *The Journal of Commercial Bank Lending*, December 1977, pp. 30-46.

Asson, Thomas H., and Jones, Seymour. *The Banker's Guide to Audit Reports and Financial Statements*. Boston: Warren, Gorham & Lamont, 1979.

Backer, Morton, and Gosman, Martin L. "The Predictive Value of Financial Ratios in Bank Term Loan Decisions." *The Journal of Commercial Bank Lending*, March 1979, pp. 53-67.

Banker's Guide to Commercial Loan Analysis. Washington, DC: American Bankers Association, 1978.

Banker's Guide to Small Business Loans. Washington, DC: American Bankers Association, 1978.

Bernstein, Leopold A. *Financial Statement Analysis: Theory, Application, and Interpretation*. Rev. ed. Homewood, IL: Richard D. Irwin, 1978.

Bogen, Jules I., ed. *Financial Handbook*. 4th ed. New York: Ronald Press Company, 1968.

Bowles, Howard Clay. "Beyond Financial Analysis." *The Bankers Magazine*, Spring 1972, pp. 52-58.

Chazen, Charles. "Unaudited Financial Statements—Beware of Hidden Dangers." *The Journal of Commercial Bank Lending*, July 1975, pp. 51-59.

Crigger, Jack R. "An Ocean of C's." *The Journal of Commercial Bank Lending*, December 1975, pp. 2-8.

Draughon, Clyde O., Jr. "Three Basic Credit Questions." *The Journal of Commercial Bank Lending*, October 1975, pp. 21-27.

Davis, James R., et al. "Financial Statements and the Concept of Fairness." *The Journal of Commercial Bank Lending*, March 1976, pp. 53-60.

Desmond, Glenn M., and Kelley, Richard E. *Business Valuation Handbook*. Llano, CA: Valuation Press, 1977.

Financial Statements for Bank Credit Purposes. Philadelphia: Robert Morris Associates, 1970.

Foulke, R. *Practical Financial Statement Analysis*. 6th ed. Accounting Series. New York: McGraw-Hill Book Company, 1968.

Fox, Harold W. "A Dynamic Perspective for Credit Analysis." *Credit and Financial Management*, January 1977, p. 30.

Funds Statement and Funds Flow Analysis. Washington, DC: American Bankers Association, 1970 (includes supervisor's manual and tests).

Helfert, Erich A. *Techniques of Financial Analysis*. Rev. ed. Homewood, IL: Dow Jones-Irwin, 1977.

Houget, George R. "Techniques of Term Loan Analysis." *The Journal of Commercial Bank Lending*, March 1975, pp. 30-36.

How to Read a Financial Report. Rev. ed. Bala Cynwyd, PA: Merrill Lynch, Pierce, Fenner & Smith, 1975.

Kennedy, Ralph D., and McMullen, Stewart Y. *Financial Statements: Form, Analysis and Interpretation*. 6th ed. Homewood, IL: Richard D. Irwin, 1973.

Krasnoff, Mitchell. "How to Read a Financial Statement." *L & H Perspective*, Spring/Summer 1977, pp. 25-27.

Kreps, Clifton H., Jr., and Wacht, Richard F. *Analyzing Financial Statements*. 5th ed. American Institute of Banking, 1978.

Levess, Herbert H., and Winsten, Irwin. "How Credible Is That Financial Statement?" *Credit and Financial Management*, August 1977, p. 14.

Levine, Sumner N., ed. *Financial Analyst's Handbook*. Vols. 1&2. Homewood, IL: Dow Jones-Irwin, 1975.

O'Malia, Thomas J. *Banker's Guide to Financial Statements*. Boston: Bankers Publishing Company, 1976.

O'Malley, Charles A., III. "Financial Forecasting and the Credit Decision." *The Journal of Commercial Bank Lending*, November 1977, pp. 42-48.

Pace, Edmond E., and Simonson, Donald G. "Guidelines for Small Borrower Financial Statements." *The Journal of Commercial Bank Lending*, October 1977, pp. 10-17.

Ratio Analysis for Small Businesses. 4th ed. (Series #20) Washington, DC: Small Business Administration, 1977.

Sangster, Bruce F., and Raguso, Jr., Sam. "An Implementation of Computerized Credit Analysis." *The Journal of Commercial Bank Lending*, March 1973, pp. 55-63.

Smith, Victor D. "A Reflective Primer on Lending." *The Journal of Commercial Bank Lending*, April 1974, pp. 49-60.

Sorenson, Kenneth A. "Changing Credit Evaluation Techniques as Seen by a CPA." *The Journal of Commercial Bank Lending*, August 1978, pp. 40-45.

Sorenson, Kenneth A. "Your Customers' Financial Statements and How the Lender Should View Them." *The Journal of Commercial Bank Lending*, November 1975, pp. 33-38.

Statement Analysis Series. Washington, DC: American Bankers Association, 1968 (four-part program with supervisor's manual).

Tischler, Peter J. "Evaluating a Firm's Liquidity and the Bank Credit Risk." *The Journal of Commercial Bank Lending*, October 1974, pp. 24-26.

Williams, Jan Robert, and Davis, James R. "Implications of the Audit Report for Financial Statement Users." *The Journal of Commercial Bank Lending*, February 1975, pp. 9-18.

General Reference

Bankers Schools Directory, 1979-80. Washington, DC: American Bankers Association, 1978.

Baughn, William H. and Walker, Charls E. eds. *The Bankers' Handbook*. Homewood, IL: Dow Jones-Irwin, 1977.

Cumulative Catalog of Theses. The Stonier Graduate School of Banking. Vol. I: 1937-61. Vol. II: 1962-75. Vol. III: 1976-77. Washington, DC: American Bankers Association, 1976.

Financial Terminology. Dayton: National Cash Register Company, 1973.

Garcia, F.L. *Glenn G. Munn's Encyclopedia of Banking and Finance*. 7th ed. Boston: Bankers Publishing Company, 1973.

Johnson, H. Webster. *How to Use the Business Library*. 4th ed. Cincinnati: South-Western Publishing Company, 1972.

McCaffrey, Bill, et al. *The Language of Business*. Cambridge, MA: Cambridge Business Research, 1975.

Redding, Harold T., and Knight, III, Guyon H. *The Dun & Bradstreet Handbook of Credits and Collection*. New York: Thomas Y. Crowell Company, 1974.

Reed, Edward W., et al. *Commercial Banking*. Englewood Cliffs, NJ: Prentice-Hall, 1976.

Selective Bibliography on Commercial Lending. Washington, DC: American Bankers Association, 1978.

Wood, Oliver G., Jr. *Commercial Banking: Practice and Policy*. New York: D. Van Nostrand Company, 1978.

Legal Considerations and Documentation

Banking Law Journal Digest. 2 vols., 6th ed. Boston: Warren, Gorham & Lamont, 1962 (1979 cumulative supplement available).

Beutel, Frederick K. *Bank Officer's Handbook of Commercial Banking Law*. 4th ed. Boston: Warren, Gorham & Lamont, 1974 (1977 supplement available).

Commercial Law League of America. *Bankruptcy Reform Act Manual*. New York: National Association of Credit Management, 1979.

Credit Manual of Commercial Laws. New York: National Association of Credit Management, 1979 (published annually).

Gilkey, Duane C., et al. "Some Legal Considerations for the Commercial Loan Officer (A Training Feature)." *The Journal of Commercial Bank Lending*, August 1977, pp. 12-22.

Law and Banking. Washington, DC: American Bankers Association, 1971.

Loan and Discount Book 1–the Promissory Note. Washington, DC: American Bankers Association, 1967.

Loan and Discount Book 2–Examining the Promissory Note and Supporting Documents. Washington, DC: American Bankers Association, 1968.

Loan and Discount Book 3–Examining Notes Secured by Stocks, Bonds, and Savings Account Passbooks, and Supporting Documents. Washington, DC: American Bankers Association, 1970.

Pace, Edmond E., and Simonson, Donald G. "Loan Documentation Guidelines (A Training Feature)." *The Journal of Commercial Bank Lending*, July 1977, pp. 14-23.

Quinn, Thomas M.; Quinn, Robert J.; and Pilgrim, Lily, eds. *Modern Banking Forms*. 2 vols. Rev. ed. Boston: Warren, Gorham & Lamont, 1974 (cumulative supplements available).

Quinn, Thomas M. *Uniform Commercial Code Commentary and Law Digest*. Boston: Warren, Gorham & Lamont, 1978.

Rome, Donald Lee. "The New Bankruptcy Act and the Commercial Lender." *Banking Law Journal*, May 1979, pp. 389-417.

Schimberg, A. Bruce. "Legislative and Judicial Developments Affecting Commercial Lending, 1977-78." *The Journal of Commercial Bank Lending*, January 1979, pp. 55-73.

Shane, Alan R. "Legal Compliance in Bank Loan Documentation." *The Bankers Magazine*, Jan.-Feb. 1978, pp. 65-68.

Small, A. Thomas. "The Bankruptcy Code from the Viewpoint of the Secured Commercial Lender." *The Journal of Commercial Bank Lending*, May 1979, pp. 2-14.

Uniform Commercial Code and Related Procedures Guide. 5th ed. Minneapolis: Registre' 1979.

Van Cise, Jerrold G. *Understanding the Antitrust Laws*. 7th ed. New York: Practicing Law Institute, 1976.

White, James J., and Summers, Robert S. *Handbook of the Law under the Uniform Commercial Code*. St. Paul: West Publishing Company, 1972.

Loan and Credit Policies

Developing a Written Loan Policy. Philadelphia: Robert Morris Associates, 1976 (two one-hour cassettes).

Fundamental Principles of Sound Bank Credit. Say Yes or Say Why! Washington, DC: American Bankers Association, 1976.

Gillis, John R., Jr. "Developing a Written Loan Policy for the Small Bank." Thesis, Southwestern Graduate School of Banking, 1968.

Guide to Developing a Written Lending Policy. Washington, DC: American Bankers Association, 1977.

Hendrick, Charles W., Jr. "Loan and Credit Administration Policies for a Medium-Sized Commercial Bank with Extensive Branch System." Thesis, Stonier Graduate School of Banking, 1973.

MacFarland, David S. "The Creation of a Written Lending Policy in a Small Commercial Bank." Thesis, Stonier Graduate School of Banking, 1974.

Maloane, Robert B. "Written Loan Policies." *The Journal of Commercial Bank Lending*, June 1976, pp. 18-24.

Mott, Hubert C. "Establishing Criteria and Concepts for a Written Credit Policy." *The Journal of Commercial Bank Lending*, April 1977, pp. 2-16.

Pace, Edmond E., and Simonson, Donald G. "The Elements of Loan Policy (A Training Feature)." *The Journal of Commercial Bank Lending*, June 1977, pp. 11-19.

Loan Profitability/Loan Pricing

Back, Edward W., Jr. and Hough, III, C. Royce. "Commercial Account Profitability Analysis: Some Considerations in Developing a System." *The Journal of Commercial Bank Lending*, December 1972, pp. 51-68.

Buck, Walter H. "A Risk Management Approach to Pricing Loans and Leases." *The Journal of Commercial Bank Lending*, April 1979, pp. 2-15.

Flynn, Thomas M. "Loan Profitability—A Method to the Madness?" *The Journal of Commercial Bank Lending*, March 1978, pp. 3-11.

Hoeven, James A., and Oldham, Jerome S. "Commercial Loan Profitability—Pricing Analysis." *The Journal of Commercial Bank Lending*, June 1976, pp. 44-57.

Jeppson, Samuel P., and Parkinson, Richard A. "A Simplified Account Analysis to Assist in Loan Pricing." *The Journal of Commercial Bank Lending*, May 1976, pp. 39-44.

Jilk, Lawrence T., Jr. "The Art of Interest Rate Negotiating." *The Journal of Commercial Bank Lending*, July 1978, pp. 28-34.

Reich, Kenneth E., and Neff, Dennis C. *Customer Profitability Analysis: A Tool for Improving Bank Profits*. Park Ridge, IL: Bank Administration Institute. Philadelphia: Robert Morris Associates, 1972.

Shanahan, Thomas J. "*A Policy for Pricing Business Loans at Major Commercial Banks*." Lake Success, NY: Credit Research Foundation, 1976.

Simonson, Donald G., and Pace, Edmond E. "Loan Pricing (A Training Feature)." *The Journal of Commercial Bank Lending*, September 1977, pp. 13-22.

Smith, Charles A. "Customer Profitability for Banks." Thesis, Southwestern Graduate School of Banking, 1973.

Watson, William D. "Profitability Analysis and Loan Pricing in Smaller Banks." Thesis, Stonier Graduate School of Banking, 1974.

Loan Review

Allen, William T. "Commercial Loan Quality Control, Phase 2. (An Analysis of Loan Review Programs in Five California Large Branch Banks)." Thesis, Pacific Coast Banking School, 1972.

Burt, William S., et al. "Loan Quality Control Techniques for Banks in the Over $200 Million Size Category." *The Journal of Commercial Bank Lending*, January 1978, pp. 40-53.

Clew, Harry T., Jr. "Monitoring the Quality of a Loan Portfolio." *The Journal of Commercial Bank Lending*, February 1977, pp. 2-9.

Conlin, P. Graham. *Commercial Loan Review Procedures*. Philadelphia: Robert Morris Associates, 1978.

Davis, Robert E. "Don't Miss Those Natural Loan Review Opportunities!" *The Journal of Commercial Bank Lending*, April 1979, pp. 16-26.

Ellis, Cato. "Loan Review: An Organizational Dilemma." *The Journal of Commercial Bank Lending*, October 1975, pp. 28-42.

Kamowski, Chester F., Jr. "Effective Loan Administration Can Prevent Excessive Losses." Thesis, Stonier Graduate School of Banking, 1975.

Loan Review: A Guide. Park Ridge, IL: Bank Administration Institute, 1978.

Maloan, W. Thomas. "Loan Review: A Possible Alternative Method." *The Journal of Commercial Bank Lending*, September 1978, pp. 22-29.

McMillan, David. "Loan Review and Data Processing, a Practical Program for a Medium-Sized Bank." Thesis, Stonier Graduate School of Banking, 1967.

Penick, Edward M., Jr. "Loan Review—A Positive Approach." *The Journal of Commercial Bank Lending*, September 1976, pp. 44-51.

Sax, Samuel Wm. "Loan Review—Bank Quality Control and R & D." *The Bankers Magazine*, Spring 1973, pp. 72-76.

Weaver, Robert W. "Computer Programs for Credit Review." Thesis, Stonier Graduate School of Banking, 1969.

Management Skills

Caruth, Donald L. *Work Measurement for Commercial Banks*. Boston: Bankers Publishing Company, 1971.

Crosse, Howard D. and Hempel, George H. *Management Policies for Commercial Banks*. 2nd ed. Englewood Cliffs, NJ: Prentice-Hall, 1973.

Gellerman, Saul W. *Management of Human Resources*. New York: Holt, Rinehart and Winston, 1976.

Kolesnik, Walter B. *Motivation: Understanding and Influencing Human Behavior*. Boston: Allyn and Bacon, 1978.

Mahler, Walter R. *How Effective Executives Interview*. Homewood, IL: Dow Jones-Irwin, 1976.

Mali, Paul. *How to Manage by Objectives: A Short Course for Managers*. Somerset, NJ: John Wiley & Sons, 1975.

Matthews, Lawrence M. *Practical Operating Budgeting*. New York: McGraw-Hill Book Company, 1977.

Problem Loans

Behrens, Robert H. *Commercial Problem Loans: How to Identify, Supervise, and Collect the Problem Loan*. Boston: Bankers Publishing Company, 1974.

Behrens, Robert H. "Handling Commercial Problem Loans in a Medium-Sized Bank." Thesis, Pacific Coast Banking School, 1973.

Corn, Merton. "On Being Handed a Work-Out Portfolio." *The Journal of Commercial Bank Lending*, September 1974, pp. 51-55.

Holman, John F., et al. "Problem Loans: Centralized vs. Decentralized Approaches." *The Journal of Commercial Bank Lending*, June 1975, pp. 11-28.

Hunn, Paul H. "Big Trouble—Managing Major Problem Loans." *The Bankers Magazine*, Autumn 1978, pp. 22-32.

Hunn, Paul H., and Schwartz, Robert. "Problem Loans in Perspective." *The Bankers Magazine*, Summer 1973, pp. 42-50.

MacDonald, D.J. "Problem Loans: Their Prevention, Handling, and Cures." *The Journal of Commercial Bank Lending*, December 1977, pp. 54-64.

Martin, K.D. "Problem Loan Signals and Follow-up." *The Journal of Commercial Bank Lending*, September 1973, pp. 38-45.

Pace, Edmond E., and Simonson, Donald G. "Solving Problem Loans (A Training Feature)." *The Journal of Commercial Bank Lending*, July 1977, pp. 24-31.

Sinclair, Alford C. "Problem Loans—At the Eyeball-to-Eyeball Level." *The Journal of Commercial Bank Lending*, June 1975, pp. 29-39.

Yellon, Donald J. "Problem Loans in the '70's: Some Legal Pitfalls in Drafting and Collection." *The Journal of Commercial Bank Lending*, April 1975, pp. 6-13.

Regulation B—Equal Credit Opportunity Act

"A Banker's Primer on Credit Discrimination." *The Bankers Magazine*, Summer 1977, pp. 63-64.

Butera, James J. "Regulation B Revisited." *The Banking Law Journal*, May 1977, pp. 388-423.

Butler, Nathaniel E., et al. "Equal Credit Opportunity Act." *The Business Lawyer*, February 1978, special issue, pp. 1073-1093.

Clontz, Ralph C., Jr. *Equal Credit Opportunity Manual*. Rev. ed. Boston: Warren, Gorham & Lamont, 1977 (1978 supplement).

Comprehensive Compliance Manual, Regulation B of the Equal Credit Opportunity Act. Washington, DC: American Bankers Association, 1977.

Equal Credit Opportunity. Washington, DC: Federal Reserve Bulletin, February 1977.

Geary, Anne, J. "Equal Credit Opportunity—An Analysis of Regulation B." *The Business Lawyer*, April 1976, pp. 1641-1658.

O'Connor, William J., Jr. "The Equal Credit Opportunity Act and Business Credit—Some Problems Considered." *The Journal of Commercial Bank Lending*, January 1979, pp. 20-36.

Saxon, Joyce M. "Regulation B: Achieving Compliance Through Internal Controls, Part III." *The Magazine of Bank Administration*, January 1978, pp. 26-31.

What Creditors Should Know About Revised Regulation B–A Guide to Compliance. St. Louis: International Consumer Credit Association, 1977.

Sources of Information

Companies, Industries, and Composite Financial Data

Annual Statement Studies. Philadelphia: Robert Morris Associates, 1979 (published annually).

Colgate, Craig, Jr., ed. *National Trade and Professional Associations of the United States and Canada and Labor Unions*. 14th annual ed. Washington, DC: Columbia Books, 1979.

Cost of Doing Business—Corporations. New York: Dun & Bradstreet, 1978.

Cost of Doing Business—Proprietorships & Partnerships. New York: Dun & Bradstreet, 1978.

Dun & Bradstreet Middle Market Directory, 1979. New York: Dun & Bradstreet, 1978 (published annually).

Dun & Bradstreet Million Dollar Directory, 1979. New York: Dun & Bradstreet, 1978 (published annually).

Dun & Bradstreet Reference Book of Corporate Managements, 1978-80. New York: Dun & Bradstreet, 1979 (published annually).

Hampton, Robert J. "Analysis of 1977 Composite Ratios of Installment Sales Finance and Consumer Finance (Direct Cash Lending) Companies." *The Journal of Commercial Bank Lending*, August 1978, pp. 16-23.

Jablonski, Donna M., ed. *How to Find Information About Companies*. Washington, DC: Washington Researchers, 1979.

Key Business Ratios—Wholesaling, Retailing, Manufacturing & Construction. New York: Dun & Bradstreet, 1978.

Levine, Sumner N., ed. *The Dow Jones-Irwin Business Almanac, 1979*. Homewood, IL: Dow Jones-Irwin, 1979.

1979 U.S. Industrial Outlook with Projections to 1983 for 200 Industries. Washington, DC: U.S. Department of Commerce/Industry and Trade Administration, Government Printing Office, January 1979.

1977 Business Statistics. 21st Biennial Edition. Washington, DC: U.S. Department of Commerce, Bureau of Economic Analysis, May 1978.

Sources of Composite Financial Data—A Bibliography. (Supplement from the *Annual Statement Studies*.) Philadelphia: Robert Morris Associates, 1979.

Standard & Poor's Register of Corporations, Directors and Executives. Vol. I and II. New York: Standard & Poor's 1979 (published annually).

Subject Bibliography Index. Washington, DC: U.S. Government Printing Office, 1978.

Troy, Leo. *Almanac of Business and Industrial Financial Ratios*. 1978 ed. Englewood Cliffs, NJ: Prentice-Hall, 1978.

Wasserman, Paul, ed. *Encyclopedia of Business Information Sources*. 3rd ed. Detroit: Gale Research Company, 1977.

Training

Adamson, Bruce. "Training Commercial Lending Officers." *The Journal of Commercial Bank Lending*, June 1977, pp. 41-47.

Brown, James W., et al. *AV Instruction: Technology, Media, and Methods*. 5th ed. New York: McGraw-Hill Book Company, 1977.

Clark, George L., et al. "Developing a One-Year Basic Loan Training Program." *The Journal of Commercial Bank Lending*, March 1977, pp. 2-9.

Commercial Loans to Business. Philadelphia: Robert Morris Associates/Omega, 1979.

Craig, Robert C. *The Psychology of Learning in the Classroom*. New York: The MacMillan Company, 1966.

Credit Skills Development System. Philadelphia: Robert Morris Associates, 1979.

CSDS Recommended Reading. Philadelphia: Robert Morris Associates, 1979.

Dickerson, Charles S. *The Credit Department: Its Role in Training*. Philadelphia: Robert Morris Associates, 1975.

Dyer, Frank R., Jr. "The Hurry Up But Take Your Time World of Loan Training." *The Journal of Commercial Bank Lending*, October 1973, pp. 2-8.

Field, George F., Jr. *Loan Officer Development Seminar*. Washington, DC: American Bankers Association. Philadelphia: Robert Morris Associates, 1973 (trainer's kit available).

Field, George F., Jr. "Training Tomorrow's Loan Officers." Thesis, Stonier Graduate School of Banking, 1964.

Handbook for Credit Training. Rev. ed. Washington, DC: American Bankers Association, 1978.

Hannah, J.L. "The Training of Commercial Lending Officers: One Problem Area in the Organizational Development Dilemma of Large Branch Banking Systems." Thesis, Pacific Coast Banking School, 1973.

Lineberger, Donald R. "Training Programs for Commercial Lending Officers." *The Journal of Commercial Bank Lending*, August 1975, pp. 49-57.

Morsman, Edgar M., Jr. "Development of the Commercial Loan Officer in a Medium-Size Bank." Thesis, Stonier Graduate School of Banking, 1974.

Myers, Bob L. "Meld Computer Skills and Credit Training and You Get—A Commercial Loan Operations Officer." *The Journal of Commercial Bank Lending*, March 1975, pp. 56-60.

Otto, C.P., and Glaser, R.O. *The Management of Training: A Handbook for Training Directors*. Reading, MA: Addison-Wesley, 1970.

Pace, Edmond E., and Simonson, Donald G. *Developing a Basic Loan Training Program*. Philadelphia: Robert Morris Associates, 1978.

Supervisory Development Guidebook for the Training Officer. Washington, DC: American Bankers Association, 1971.

Wells, John W. "Credit Training—A Systematic Approach." *The Journal of Commercial Bank Lending*, February 1976, pp. 18-29.

Index